WHAT IS HUMANISM, AND WHY DOES IT MATTER?

STUDIES IN HUMANIST THOUGHT AND PRAXIS

Series Editor   Anthony B. Pinn
            Institute of Humanist Studies, Washington, DC

At this point in the twenty-first century, humanism encounters a unique historical moment, one full of creative possibilities to bring the benefits of humanist thinking and practice to bear on the challenges facing humanity. The *Studies in Humanist Thought and Praxis* series explores the pressing sociopolitical, economic and cultural issues we face.

WHAT IS HUMANISM, AND WHY DOES IT MATTER?

Edited by Anthony B. Pinn

ACUMEN

Dedicated to Larry Jones

Editorial matter and selection © Anthony B. Pinn 2013.
Individual contributions © contributors.

First published in 2013 by Acumen

Acumen Publishing Limited

4 Saddler Street
Durham
DH1 3NP, UK

ISD, 70 Enterprise Drive
Bristol
CT 06010, USA

www.acumenpublishing.com

ISBN: 978-1-84465-659-2 (hardcover)
ISBN: 978-1-84465-660-8 (paperback)

British Library Cataloguing-in-Publication Data
A catalogue record for this book is available from the British Library.

Printed in the UK by the MPG Books Group.

CONTENTS

PREFACE

In significant ways Europe has provided a model of public humanism; many people in other areas of the world mark the humanism of places like the Netherlands as a highpoint of possibility for a rational and logic-driven world. This is not to say that all nations within Europe have the same relationship toward humanism; however, it appears that humanism is more integrated into the fabric of public and private life in Europe than it is in other locations such as the United States, if for no other reason than a somewhat different perception of and reception of secularization. My point in making these comments, however, is not to debate the secular nature of European societies, but instead simply to point to the manner in which the simple perception of a more humanism-friendly environment in Europe has motivated certain developments elsewhere in the world. For instance, things are changing in the United States, despite its public discourse saturated with religious vocabulary and grammar. Within the context of the United States, a push for humanist sensibilities within the public arena of debate over political policy, socioeconomic arrangements, and cultural worldviews is gaining energy. In fact, current political and cultural developments have resulted in new opportunities for and altered attitudes towards humanists and humanism-based enterprises. A clear symbol of this shift is captured by the inclusion of non-theistic orientations in President Obama's inaugural speech. Through his brief but positive comment concerning "non-belief" new openness to a fuller scope of thought and practice in the United States became a subject of public conversation and debate in ways extending beyond the typical discourse of stigmatized difference. Some years after this initial moment of inclusion, the aim for humanists (of all types) is now to foster open and honest reflection on and attention to the nature and meaning of humanism. By so doing, humanism is brought more fully into the public arena and better known for its ability to provide significant insight and strategies for transformation that is much needed at this point in human history.[1]

There are still misperceptions and uninformed questions concerning humanism—is it anti-American to the extent it is anti-God? Is it possible to be moral and ethical *and* humanist?—that prevent its full participation in the life and workings of the United States within the context of the global community. Nonetheless, at this point in the twenty-first century, humanists encounter a unique historical moment, one full of creative possibilities to address this problem of perception and to bring the benefits of humanist thinking and practice to bear on the challenges facing humanity.

ORGANIZING THOUGHT ABOUT HUMANISM

With sensitivity to the manner in which European humanism and secularization have served as a heuristic of sorts in the United States, this volume notes that, while humanism's presence in the United States is as old as the country itself, it is only within the past several decades that the posture and tone of humanist thought and praxis have marked out robust defiance in a consistent, popular imagination-grabbing, and democratic manner. By the term "democratic" I am not referencing anything more than a general process by which large-scale and informed participation determines and maps out the logic and approach of various humanist organizations to the life challenges facing a diversity of communities. There have always been larger-than-life figures representing the aims of humanisms, and such figures continue. Nonetheless, there is something about recent developments—including the impressive growth in the population of "Nones" (people who claim to have no religion)—that points to a more egalitarian turn. In a word, the contemporary "Humanist Movement" is not simply a matter of a few elite players determining the guiding rationale and direction of humanism. To the contrary, the structure is more mosaic in form because within this movement is an array of individuals and complex organizations committed to working through agendas with awareness of and sensitivity to diversity, political shifts, alterations to the economic landscape, philosophical turns, cultural battles, and so on. One such organization—the Institute for Humanist Studies—is behind the work this particular book seeks to encourage. More to the point, the Institute provides the contextual framework and overarching set of considerations shaping this book.[2] *What is Humanism, and Why Does it Matter?* has grown out of the Institute's agenda. In fact, most of the chapters were initially presented at a conference (April 2011) sponsored by the Institute and intended to bring together a group of scholars and activists to generate creative and imaginative thought regarding how humanists might think about, discuss, and "do" humanism.

THIS BOOK

The Institute is not alone in its concern to advance humanist thought and practice. It is also not the first—nor only—organization committed to the production of thought-provoking materials related to this concern. Many volumes—a good number of them referenced in this book—have been produced over the course of the past several decades, addressing various aspects of humanist thought and praxis. These include volumes providing apologetics for humanist orientation(s) as well as others offering a glimpse into the ethics of humanism. Each work has made important contributions to discourse regarding the value of humanism. Yet, meriting more attention is a basic set of questions: What is humanism? Why does it matter? And what do we do with humanism? Other volumes allude to such questions, but vital at this stage of humanism's growth and public appeal is focused attention on these questions through synergy between more academic responses and "on the ground" activist responses—as well as some combination of these positions.

This book, beginning with its title, is an effort to fill this gap by offering pieces by well-regarded figures that take seriously the need for humanists to respond in thoughtful ways to these basic questions. It is not the aim of this book to provide *a* way of defining humanism; nor is it the goal to limit the range of approaches to activism deemed suitable. To the contrary, this volume offers a variety of perspectives and opinions on the meaning and function(s) of humanism. What holds the book together, then, is not consensus on the definition and application of humanism. Rather, the contributors share recognition of the importance of humanism as well as a need to give serious and thoughtful consideration to the workings of humanism—and to do this from a variety of sociocultural angles and sociopolitical perspectives.

The contributors represent the diversity of humanism with respect to gender, race, national origin, and so on. They also constitute a variety of perspectives on humanism—from atheism to religious humanism—and take as a starting point a variety of locations for humanist thought and practice: from academia, to national organizations, to local initiatives. And these differences in orientation are acknowledged through the particular style of presentation offered by the various contributors. For example, attention is given in some cases to the weaving of personal narrative together with larger and more "objective" frameworks, and some authors work with a much more journalistic style than others as their way of suggesting a need for recognition of humanism as more than an academic exercise. These differences, however, do not constitute a problem; they do not point to inconsistencies and unevenness. No, these differences are intentional and are meant to give some representation to the diversity of presentation that marks humanism writ large. The idea is to present the texture and tone of humanism in the very presentation of humanist thought and practice, and to do so in a way that builds, as each section is connected in a general sense to the previous one. In this way, the layered and complex nature of humanism as lived and thought takes on important and graphic detail.

The volume is divided into three parts, the first of which takes on the question "What is humanism?" It is composed of three chapters offering overlapping but distinct opinions on the definition(s) of humanism. In Chapter 1, Howard B. Radest traces various philosophical perspectives and opinions on the question before settling on a sense of humanism as "a puzzle," difficult to capture in significant ways in isolation from "reflection and organization." While Radest's take on the question is heavily philosophical in nature and draws from the wealth of insight and influence represented by the Enlightenment, Anthony B. Pinn responds in Chapter 2 in a manner guided by cultural studies and religious studies. Pinn suggests that humanism is a method for the making of meaning—a means by which to wrestle with the large and pressing existential and ontological questions of human existence. He argues for a need to recognize the manner in which the racial discourse of difference has impacted—for good or ill—the growth and naming of humanism. Enlarging the scope of concern to an international context, Peter Derkx recognizes similar challenges to those presented by Radest and Pinn, but he concludes in Chapter 3 that humanism is a "meaning frame," with deep implications for human health and aging. Taken as a whole, the three chapters in the first part of the book suggest that the most useful thinking about the nature and meaning of humanism involves recognition that it is a system—however difficult to capture fully—for fostering the shape and content of human life. It is not a fixed or reified conceptual framework, but rather it is an organic and evolving response to human questions and concerns. With this in mind, the chapters in this section hint at the reasonable nature of much of the debate over what humanism is or isn't, but instead of simply languishing in the quagmire of incomplete definitions, the authors suggest an ongoing need to connect any definition of humanism with practice. That is to say, humanism is best understood in connection to the naming available through the process of "doing."

The second part of the book moves beyond the question of humanism's nature and meaning, and addresses the next logical question: "Why does humanism matter?" In response, Sharon D. Welch (Chapter 4) argues that humanism offers a mode of social ethics equipped to address pressing sociopolitical issues on the national level and the global level through thoughtful public policy and a discourse that values the integrity of life and privileges the positive impact of creativity on our circumstances. Monica R. Miller's response in Chapter 5 uses hip hop and youth culture as a way of siphoning out the importance of humanism as a means by which to address the absurdities of human relationships and encounters in their most graphic form. Through this investigation, Miller suggests the importance of scoping out the ways in which humanism grows organically in unlikely places, and the creative means by which diversity of expression might serve to provide the intellectual and cultural tools required to transform social arrangements. In both cases, humanism matters not simply because it provides an alternative way of naming experience and, as a result, provides new ways of thinking about human life. No, both Miller and Welch connect the importance of humanism to its ability to "do work." Yet, as with the chapters on defining humanism, room is left for creativity and expansion of humanism. All the chapters in the first two parts appreciate the plasticity of humanism and acknowledge the manner in which fluidity and flexibility with respect to the nature and meaning of humanism afford greater opportunity for it to make a difference in the world.

Having given attention to both the meaning of humanism and why it matters, the final part of the book provides attention to concrete moments of application in line with a third question: "What do we do with humanism?" It begins with Sikivu Hutchinson's call in Chapter 6 for the use of culturally sensitive humanism as a way to address gender discrimination, racism, and classism embedded in the culture of the United States in general and the infrastructure of the humanist movement in particular. In this way, Hutchinson encourages humanists to embrace both an internal and external critique as a way of promoting healthier life options for all. By making this argument, Hutchinson calls for recognition of both humanism's promise and its problems as the best way of advancing a transformative humanist agenda. Chapter 7 follows, with attention to the application of humanism on the level of individual relationships and encounters with the world. In this case, for Dale McGowan, humanism affords a means by which to tackle the trauma and reality of life in the form of death. The last chapter of the book, written by Maggie Ardiente and Roy Speckhardt, gives clear attention to the means by which humanism serves as tool for policy development and for restructuring negative opinions concerning humanists. In this way, they promote three steps or approaches for advancing a humanist agenda as a means by which to transform societies consistent with humanism's historical *and* secular framing.

As these chapters show, over the course of time, some have worked to articulate individual and collective visions of thought and practice based on humanist posture(s) toward the world. Often prompted by large shifts in the sociopolitical and economic conditions of life in the United States and the larger global community, these vision statements have typically taken the form of manifestos meant to capture the potential of humanist thinking for individual and collective human existence. Because these manifestos provide useful context for the perspectives on humanism provided in this volume, several have been included in an appendix for consideration. These are Humanist Manifestos I–III, and a more recent pronouncement offered by Paul Kurtz. These materials range historically from the fourth decade of the twentieth century to the first decade of the twenty-first century, and respond to a range of world conditions as well as alterations within the humanist community.

Anthony B. Pinn

ACKNOWLEDGMENTS

This book has been a few years in the making and, while there have been rough patches, the Institute for Humanist Studies Board has been a consistent source of support and encouragement. As editor of the volume, I would like to express my gratitude to the members of the Board: Warren Wolf, Carol Wintermute, Jim Craig, Roy Speckhardt, Louis Altman, Amanda Knief, Jennifer Kalmanson, and the founder of the Institute for Humanist Studies, Larry Jones. I would also like to express my appreciation to the contributors who took time away from other projects to participate in this volume. In addition, the Institute for Humanist Studies has a host of supporters and well wishers, and I take this opportunity to thank them for their efforts on behalf of the organization. Furthermore, and of great importance, Janet Joyce's enthusiasm for and willingness to publish this series and this volume are greatly appreciated. In addition, I am grateful for the support and the ongoing encouragement offered by Tristan Palmer.

Finally, I must also express gratitude to the American Humanist Association and to Paul Kurtz for permission to reprint the materials found in the appendix: Humanist Manifestos I–III (American Humanist Association website: www.americanhumanist.org), reprinted by permission of the American Humanist Association; "Neo-Humanist Statement of Secular Principles and Values: Personal, Progressive, and Planetary" (http://paulkurtz.net), reprinted by permission of Paul Kurtz.

PART I. WHAT IS HUMANISM?

1. HUMANISM AS EXPERIENCE

Howard B. Radest

Of all things the measure is man, of the things that are, that [or "how"]
they are, and of things that are not, that [or "how"] they are not. —Protagoras

I am a man, nothing human is alien to me. —Terence

WHAT IS HUMANISM?

When visiting with humanists in their varied habitats,[1] I often hear arguments about world-shaking ideas. I see little of the acts that ought to follow
from them in personal and social life. Perhaps all this talk is a search for
stability in a chaotic world; perhaps it is inevitable, given our roots in the
academy and the pulpit. But still I am haunted by these repetitions of "metaphysical" arguments like the being or non-being of the deity, or institutional
arguments like whether humanism is secular or religious. There is, too, a
less than critical liberal politics most of us share that at times borders on
self-righteousness.

I know that reason easily turns into rationalism and that acts are more
elusive than words. Nor is humanism immune to the Platonic temptation,
the escape to the "heaven beyond the heavens." Of course, I take pleasure
in words and word-games—I am a philosopher by training after all! At the
same time, I am a pragmatist. So I ask: What difference to the world we live
in does our talk make? What practical consequences does it have for me and
for others? Soon enough, my humanism becomes uncomfortable.

To be sure, there is something about us that enjoys the *word.* The Tal-
mudist and the Scholastic among our more traditional brothers and sis-
ters testify to this. We humanists are not alone. Nevertheless, our frequent
inattention to justification by results prevails despite the fact that modern
humanism takes its being from participatory democracy and from the sciences. Thus:

> The basic idea is presented ... scientific theories are *instruments* or
> *tools* for coping with reality ... What is essential is that theories pay
> their way in the long run—that they can be relied upon time and
> again to solve pressing problems and to clear up significant difficul-
> ties confronting inquirers ... though we must always allow for the

possibility that it will eventually have to be replaced by some theory that works even better.[2]

Words can be powerful, stirring passions like those that played no minor part in the American and French revolutions. They were inspired by the Enlightenment with its salons and pamphlets, its arts and literature, and not least of all its *philosophes* and Diderot's *Encyclopedia*. In the nineteenth century, although he denied the humanist label, Felix Adler established Ethical Culture, a non-creedal reformist religious movement that surely deserves the adjective, *humanist*. A charismatic speaker, Adler condemned the self-satisfied churches and temples of his day and called instead for a religion of the "deed." Thus, in resigning the presidency of the Free Religious Association in 1882, he said

> What has Boston done for the honor of our principles? What great charitable Movement has found its source here among those who maintain the principle of the freedom of religion? What living thing for the good of mankind, for the perfecting of morality among yourselves and others emanated within the last twenty years from the Free Religious circles of this city? I say to you friends ... these annual meetings will not answer.[3]

Adler and the Ethical Culture societies followed with a dramatic record of achievements in education, housing, law, business, politics, health care, settlement houses, and so on. He and his colleagues created a legacy of the act that still motivates his successors nearly 150 years later.

Adler had company. Unitarian radicals in the first half of the twentieth century, ministers like Curtis Reese, formerly a Southern Baptist preacher, John Dietrich, formerly a minister in the Reformed Church, and Charles Potter, formerly a Baptist minister, led the way to institutional and organizational change. The move—and not just among Unitarians—toward ethical and naturalist religion gained momentum here and abroad. With that move, the market place and the laboratory joined the academy and the pulpit as the scene of religious reform. From that move in religion and philosophy emerged consequences for person and society, and, indeed, for inquiry itself. For example, Dietrich wrote:

> There are two theories of the world—the theistic view, which holds that the world is under the control of a supernatural being ... and that without his will nothing can be done. The other is the Humanistic view, which teaches that everything that is done in this world is done by man in accordance with the laws of nature

3

... it depends upon man what the world shall be like. The adherents of this view hold that if man wants more water, he must build reservoirs and lay pipelines; if he wants freedom from pestilence, he must develop medical science; if he wants food, he must cultivate the soil; if he fears natural forces, like fire and water, he must devise his own protection, build dikes and form fire companies; if he would eliminate his woes, he must do it himself ... Man in his own strength must grapple with the forces of nature. Man in his own strength must face and solve his problems. Man in his own strength must work out his own salvation ... the good fairies are gone forever.[4]

Humanism thus received its inspiration and its agenda; people less enamored of the traditions found in ethical and liberal religion a new home.

Not too long after these pioneering moments, the humanist habit of issuing manifestos (1933, 1973, 2003) emerged, joined also by less formal statements such as "A Secular Humanist Declaration"[5] or, more recently, "Neo-Humanist Statement of Secular Principles and Values: Personal, Progressive, and Planetary."[6] These tried in vain to offer in humanist guise an equivalent to Martin Luther's *95 Theses* nailed to the church door. Nor was the word "manifesto" accidental. It was intended to offer an alternative to Marx's *Communist Manifesto*. Rooted in the urban and intellectual middle class, however, modern humanism failed to gain a popular following in either religion or politics.

Following on the first manifesto, humanists, led by Ed Wilson, organized the American Humanist Association (AHA) in 1941. Then and now, however, there have been many more humanists than are counted in the membership of humanist organizations. Over and over again, here and abroad, I have met women and men who claim they are "humanists." When asked, they answer with language and feeling that looks very much like faith, all the while denying that they are religious. They cite or paraphrase the statements cited above. All of them refer to the "dignity and worth" of the human being. They affirm with the intensity of belief that reason, science, and free inquiry are the only reliable methods of knowing, and that participatory democracy is the only morally acceptable form of political and social institution. To be sure, the substance of their passions may be differently nuanced and may include all or only some of the following: free thought, atheism, naturalism, secularism, ethical religion, or even a romantic or esoteric revision of the deity or deities.

Humanism at times calls itself a "movement." In reality, it is an agglomeration of individuals and a plurality of small organizations. Modern humanism, like its Enlightenment predecessor, affirms democratic values like autonomy and moral competence of the person. But it lacks the coherence of a movement and the instruments for continuing research into the epistemic and metaphysical status of the ideas it uses or their import for personal and social conduct. Typically, it relies on a literature that more often than not fails to identify itself as humanist. Absent disciplined inquiry, the language of humanism becomes commonplace, trite.

Humanists do not exhibit strong commitment to humanism's organizations. They are for the most part "non-joiners."[7] A relatively well-off urban middle class, they are "non-givers" too. So humanist organizations struggle to survive. As it were, humanists long ago discovered the non-responsible notion that they could be humanist without associating formally or otherwise with other humanists, a phenomenon now visible among more traditional faiths, too, where we find people, particularly the young, claiming to be "spiritual" without being "religious." On the whole then, most humanists are what I may call *humanists by themselves.* A pervasive and erosive individualism, perhaps another instance of Dewey's "ragged individualism,"[8] subverts modern humanism.

The Enlightenment was an incarnation in naturalistic and democratic terms of the Classical, Catholic, and Renaissance humanisms that preceded it in the West. Like them, it celebrated the richness of the world and the powers of the person. Unlike them, it turned to a nature that was being illuminated by the sciences and to a human being able to play a responsible role in the arts, sciences, politics, and cultures. Denied were the kings, princes, and priests of history who had once provided humanism's resources and who received the status of cultural leadership as the reward for their generosity, such as many of Catholicism's high churchmen. With the Enlightenment, the demands of science, technology, and democracy, a new politics and a new knowledge, reshaped institutions and gave birth to less romantic bourgeois governments and pseudo-governmental organizations, such as the corporation, today's not-for-profits. These organizations grew with their rules, technologies, and bureaucracies. By the twentieth century, they had evolved in a counter-humanist direction, that is, toward depersonalization and blandness, a verification of the alienation that Marx and the left-Hegelians had predicted.[9] Humanism has yet to figure out how to challenge the modern corporate organization with an effective alternative. Instead, while critical of corporate behavior, it uncritically accepts the mechanistic and imitative structure of organization typical in the for-profit and not-for-profit world, that is, the illusion that an organizational form can simply be transported from one kind of institution to another.

The first Humanist Manifesto illustrated humanism's failure as well as its success. It called for a new religion but relied on existing organizations, such as liberal, and not-so-liberal, churches, to carry its banner. Except for a nod toward a "socialized and cooperative economic order" in the fourteenth of its fifteen affirmations, it did not call for establishing the organizations or the leadership and the authority needed to do the work. While it was a creature of some of the better-known intellects of the period, they had other organizational locations, such as a church, a university, and so on. The Manifesto had its lead figures but no single charismatic figure as its publicly identifiable author. Its mode of creation forecast the committee as its style. Thus, thirty-four men signed it (women and people of color had yet to be discovered by humanism). About a third were academics and the rest were liberal ministers. Manifestos II and III and the efforts that followed its inspiration grew in verbiage and complexity. Lacking the elite impulse of the original document, the numbers of their signers (I was among them) grew as well. These successor statements reflected the emerging world of mass populations, of problematic moral and political situations, and of a pace of change unknown to human history.

The humanist message, unconnected to place and party, was all too easily lost in a world of ever-expanding and by now nearly anarchic communication. It is alien to the minimalist speech popular in today's culture. To be sure, the hero or saint with his or her rallying cry is still sought in the larger society and many have borne humanist values if not humanist identities. Save the rare political or religious genius—a Gandhi, a Martin Luther King, a Nelson Mandela, an Eleanor Roosevelt—the search is unsuccessful, and probably inevitably so in our times. To be sure, the demagogues of left or right, the madmen and madwomen of politics and religion, are quite visible these days. But while humanism enjoys and sometimes punishes its current-day founders, for example Ed Wilson, Paul Kurtz, and Sherwin Wine, it lives in a world of collective structures, team leaderships, and rationalized methods. The processes of participatory democracy to which humanism is committed are slow and cumbersome, often trapped in conflicting interests, and resistant to the rallying cries that excite populist movements.

As world and society grow more complex and unmanageable, simplification becomes a defense against chaos and unmanageability. Thus, we witness the rise of orthodoxy in religion, ideology, and politics. Committed to taking the democratic world seriously, humanism cannot desert the values of equality and freedom. Nor can it surrender intellect and the processes of reason. But loyalty to scientific methods and values becomes a frustrating struggle for time and resource, under contemporary conditions. The rich textures of eighteenth-century Enlightenment, nineteenth-century idealism and transcendentalism, and early twentieth-century humanism ask for their successor. Yet, the size and speed of things these days make replies to that plea a mystery. Perhaps, then, reliance on the *word* may serve as a placeholder for something not yet available, a next humanism, a humanism for the post-contemporary world that we cannot yet know.

In this setting, the question "What Is humanism?" is problematic. A superficial illustration: A Google search for definitions of humanism—and what contemporary research can exist without a Google search?—results in over one million entries, many of them, to be sure, repetitions. A search of humanism *per se* results in nearly seven million entries. These numbers are symptoms of the irrationality of the world we live in, for only Google has the capacity to sort, review, and evaluate the information Google provides; truly a vicious circle. A "quick and dirty look" at just a few of the entries shows that humanism is variously defined as religious and secular and sometimes both, is modern and classical and sometimes both, Renaissance and Enlightenment and sometimes both, existential and Marxist and sometimes both, modern and post-modern and sometimes both, Buddhist and Confucian and sometimes both, and so on. Humanism, with its outspoken atheists, is variously an enemy of traditional Western religions and found within those same traditions, as in Christian and Jewish humanism. Humanism appears as an ideology, a theology, an anthropology, a philosophy, a psychology, a politics ... a noun, an adjective, a verb. In short, it is many things and no single thing. There seems no definitive reply to the question: What is humanism?

The effort to cut the Gordian Knot of linguistic plenitude is often made by simply adding together a limited number of relevant but unspecified descriptors. One example can stand for many:

> Humanism is a progressive philosophy of life that, without supernaturalism, affirms our ability and responsibility to lead ethical lives of personal fulfillment that aspire to the greater good of humanity. The life-stance of Humanism—guided by reason, inspired by compassion, and informed by experience—encourages us to live life well and fully. It evolved through the ages and continues to develop through the efforts of thoughtful people who recognize that values and ideals, however carefully wrought, are subject to change as our knowledge and understandings advance. This document is part of an ongoing effort to manifest in clear and positive terms the conceptual boundaries of Humanism, not what we must believe but a consensus of what we do believe.[10]

Meant to be inclusive, terms like "ethical lives of personal fulfillment" and the "greater good of humanity" could as easily be adopted by any number of religious and secular ideologies. "Progressive philosophy of life, without supernaturalism" could be an affirmation of Stalinist, Maoist, or fascist ideologies.

Defining modern humanism remains a puzzle!

SIGNALS AND SYMBOLS

From fifth-century Athens to revolutionary Paris, humanism proclaimed a view of the human being as a creative and morally responsible creature. That history went back to the Greek city-state, to the Roman Empire and the Ciceronian ideal of citizenship; to Catholic humanism with its criticisms of scholasticism—for example Dante, Petrarch, Erasmus—of the fourteenth to sixteenth centuries.[11] Their successors were the Renaissance and the Enlightenment. With these came novel adventures in the arts and sciences, rebellion in politics and social custom, innovation in religion, and opportunity in personal life.

To be sure, these humanisms, and those of the East as well, differed in their metaphors and myths, in their inclusions and exclusions, above all in the substance they gave to what it meant to be human. In Western history, the *imago humani* was set against the orthodox *imago dei*. Humanists responded critically to the worlds in which they found themselves: Greek polity, Roman Empire, Christian scholasticism, aesthetic realism, and naturalism.[12] They suffered the limitations of their moments in history, for example ethnic supremacy as in classical Greece, imperialist politics as in Rome, theological rationalism as in the Medieval Church, aesthetic elitism as in the Renaissance, and so on. Our humanism inherits that pattern of celebration, response, criticism, and limitation. Embedded as we are in our own culture, however, it will be for our successors to tell of our limitations—and they surely will as they depart our insights for their own.

Perhaps the most exciting fact of modern humanism is that its world is becoming genuinely global and that it is viscerally and ideologically prepared for that fact.[13] Humanist universalism is matched for the first time in history by geo-political and cultural realities. Earlier humanisms spoke of "persons" in a more narrowed fashion. There were persons and non-persons: "Greeks and barbarians," "saved and damned," Roman citizens and alien others. Jefferson's "all men are created equal" or the French "Rights of Man" marked our difference from the past. Yet, these announced their limitations too: their record on slavery, and on gender and class blindness, for example. Made aware of these inadequacies by abolitionists, feminists, and the civil rights movement, modern humanism is amending its exclusion of women and people of color, and its ignorance of places in the world that have been long neglected. Today's humanism seeks to be species-wide in fact and not just in aspiration.

Increasingly visible are the likely challenges to human exceptionalism. Intelligence and moral sensitivity, even altruism, the use languages of sign and symbol, are beginning to be found in other primates and no doubt will be found in other species too as research advances and new habits of perception replace our parochialism. A recent report illustrates the point:

At a session on the ethical and policy implications of dolphin intel-ligence ... today at the annual meeting of the American Association For The Advancement Of Science ... according to panelist Lori Marino, an expert on cetacean neuro-anatomy at Emory University in Atlanta, they may be earth's second smartest creature ... Marino bases her argument on studies of the dolphin brain. Bottlenose dol-phins have bigger brains than humans (1600 grams versus 1300 grams), and they have a brain-to-body-weight ratio greater than great apes do (but lower than humans) ... dolphins also have a very complex neo-cortex, the part of the brain responsible for problem-solving, self-awareness, and variety of other traits we associate with human intelligence ... researchers have found ... neurons which in humans and apes have been linked to emotions, social cognition ... the ability to sense what others are thinking ... cognitive psycholo-gist Diana Reiss of Hunter College of the City University of New York brought the audience up to speed on the latest on dolphin behavior ... their social intelligence rivals that of the great apes. They can recognize themselves in a mirror (a feat most animals fail at—and a sign of self awareness). They can understand complex gesture "sentences" from humans. And they can learn to poke an underwater keyboard to request toys to play with. "Much of their learning is similar to what we see with young children," says Reiss.[14]

Our environment forecasts the road for us, a redefinition of humanism that was barely begun in the eighteenth and nineteenth centuries by forerunners like deism, rationalism, and transcendentalism. The dynamics of our envi-ronment—technical and cultural innovation we can hardly keep up with—forecasts a radically changed sense of ourselves sooner or later by an as yet unknowable humanism.

All too often, definition is only an exchange of words for words, such as in a dictionary or thesaurus. However, words may be used as signals to memory, as commands and rules, mathematical tables, and so on. Nuance, however, is sacrificed for brevity as in "texting" and "tweeting." Politics becomes a battle of slogans and scare-words. Little wonder that a divided polity is the outcome and that the public, made politically illiterate, blindly chooses sides.

Signals invite boundaried realities. Words thus can become instruments of our alienation from each other, of my kind and the other's kind, as in the "know-nothings" of yesterday or the "tea-party movement" of today. Self-righteousness and dogmatism result on left, right, and center. Words like "atheist" or "gay" on one side or "bigot or "right-winger" on the other estab-lish walls and stir deeply felt resentment and anger. Many of us come to believe that we live surrounded by enemies. In "polite" society, we agree not to talk about religion or politics or anything else of substance, thus reinforcing alienation and assuring the superficiality of discourse. Slogans like "government is the enemy" become surrogates for intelligence in public life. All of this reminds me of nothing so much as the totem animals, body tattoos, and drum beats of the tribalism of earlier cultures. Ironically, our technological society echoes this primitivism, only now it has a sophisticated armory that it uses but does not understand. Society does not understand itself.

Fortunately, words need not be as sterile and as destructive as they have become. Dictionary and thesaurus can illuminate reality, as when alternative ways of speaking, synonyms and antonyms, for example, open visions and revisions of what is and what is not meant. The other side of signals, a move away from the primitive, allows the abbreviation of actions and reactions in a multi-dimensioned world, thus, the benefit, even the necessity, of "habit," as both William James and John Dewey described it.[15]

Overcoming the passivity of its user, signal can be a tool of the imagination. Thus, it need not be entirely reactive as in Pavlovian stimulus and response. Language, after all, is a living thing and signals, too, can evolve in their complexity, for example "best practices" in organizations or "standard of care" in clinical medicine. Definitions thus transform and grow. At the same time, in the presence of novelty—the pace, size, and variety of things in our world—signals fail us all too often. We are forced by its limitation to deadly repetition, or to remain silent, or to turn to the riches of symbol and so to release the energies of signals again. Symbol offers unboundaried meanings, hints, suggestions, and realizations. Poetry surely announces the richness of words, music the richness of sound and tonality. Visioning invites activity as in the experimentalism of today's arts. The aesthetic environment, that is, the symbolic environment, becomes experimental, radically diverse, almost anarchic. New signals, indeed new languages, are also invented.

The needs of the sciences call for new language as in Newton's calculus. Geometric alternatives opened up Euclid's axioms and assumptions and suggested new ones. Algebra became activity, mathematics, a type of doing. Probability and its arithmetic allowed for parsing the possible, no longer caught in the metaphysical dilemma of either/or, of is and is not.[16] Topology—so-called "rubber sheet geometry," another eighteenth-century legacy—reached a climactic moment with Einstein's notion that gravity was a property of space–time geometry. Today, as a consequence of quantum physics, cosmologists speculate about the existence of an indefinite number of parallel universes, much as the Pythagorians speculated 2,500 years ago about the harmonic structure of the universe.[17] Sadly, when we teach mathematics and logic these days, this world-creating and world-revealing power of symbols is scarcely mentioned.

To be sure, such imagined worlds have no necessary connection to what is. But it is the genius of modern science that they can be used to shed light on the world that is or hypothesize the worlds that might be. An elaborated empiricism finds its partner in symbols. Ideas and things come alive. The sciences that humanism claims among its parents provide an entry to its definition far more challenging and various than in the eighteenth century. For example, a brief and non-technical description of Einstein's general relativity when compared to Newton's classical laws of motion offers the following: "In this new picture, there is no gravitational force that masses exert on other masses. Instead, there are space–time distortions. Space–time in the presence of a mass is curved."

In flat, empty space–time, small test particles follow straight lines. However, just as there are no straight lines on the surface of a sphere, the closest we can come to the notion of a straight line in a curved space–time is what mathematicians call a geodesic (a space–time line that is *as straight as possible*). Small particles in the vicinity of a massive sphere follow space–time geodesics, which send them plunging toward the mass, or into an orbit around it. Gravity doesn't deflect these particles from their straight lines. It redefines what it means to move in the straightest possible way.

As a consequence, Einstein's universe performs an ongoing cosmic dance in which matter and space–time interact. A given configuration of matter distorts space–time geometry (not only because of mass, but also with its energy, inner tensions or pressure) and this distorted geometry makes matter move in certain ways. This movement, in turn, changes the matter configuration, and space–time geometry changes correspondingly. Now that space–time geometry is a bit different, it also acts on matter in a different way, matter moves, geometry changes, and so on in an endless dance.[18]

Of course the imaginings of the world are not confined to cosmology and arithmetic. Philosophy, the arts, literature, theology[19]—the latter probably anathema to most humanists—each exhibits the power of symbols. The world of fact and event is mirrored inventively, as in the philosophic idealism of Plato in one way and the Neo-Kantian idealism of Felix Adler in another.[20] Or that world may be dismissed as illusory, as in the Nirvana of the Hindu or the enlightenment of the Buddhist. History may become the "eternal return" of the Egyptians or Stoics of antiquity or of the philosophy of Nietzsche or Schopenhauer in nineteenth-century Germany. The world of fact and event may be illuminated by novel or drama, by portrait or still life, by dance or song. Aesthetic possibility in other words—world-creating symbol, imagination, and interpretation—joins the genius of the sciences in all their diversity and complexity. Metaphor and imagery are no strangers to either, nor are the arts and sciences.

As with the sciences, aesthetic illumination will in turn have consequences for critical thought and for human conduct. I may echo Emerson that beauty

HOWARD B. RADEST

is "its own excuse for being."[21] But I also know that beauty is a powerful stimulus to thought and action. The novel creates alternative worlds, and both author and reader are asked to reconceive their world over and over again. The poet, the playwright, the composer—I think of Whitman or Frost, of Aeschylus or Shakespeare or O'Neill, of Mozart or Beethoven—reshape perception with metaphor and tonality. I return a different person from their ministry to me. In a similar mode, Aristotle wrote of tragedy:

> A perfect tragedy should ... imitate actions which excite pity and fear ... It follows plainly ... that the change of fortune presented must not be the spectacle of a virtuous man brought from prosperity to adversity: for this moves neither pity nor fear; it merely shocks us. Nor, again, that of a bad man passing from adversity to prosperity: for ... it neither satisfies the moral sense nor calls forth pity or fear. Nor, again, should the downfall of the utter villain be exhibited. A plot of this kind would, doubtless, satisfy the moral sense, but it would inspire neither pity nor fear; for pity is aroused by unmerited misfortune, fear by the misfortune of a man like ourselves ... There remains, then, the character between these two extremes— that of a man who is not eminently good and just, yet whose misfortune is brought about not by vice or depravity, but by some error or frailty. He must be one who is highly renowned and prosperous—a personage like Oedipus, Thyestes, or other illustrious men of such families.[22]

Then too, symbol calls for caution. Given its power to generate worlds, it is likely to entomb our prejudices. We are even more likely to turn what is a speculative idea into the rigidities of dogma when those around us—a group, a congregation, a community, a movement, for instance—agree with us. Humanism is not immune. Its organizations can become a type of pseudo-verification. Humanist language becomes a credo even while the presence of creed is vehemently denied. The need is for the challenge of diversity, a particular problem of relatively small institutions where defensiveness reinforces blindness marked by parochial arguments of aye and nay. But humanism claims allegiance to free inquiry and to reason and intelligence. It follows that it needs to address these powers to itself, that is, create a discipline that does for it what theological study and university religion departments do for religions.[23]

WHAT IS TO BE DONE?

In what follows, I have deliberately not dealt with social action. My silence, however, should not be read as indifference. Humanist circles, whatever their differences in origin, style, or self-image, pay attention to matters like church/state separation, ecology, human rights, economic justice, and so on.[24] But our actions, all too often, remind me of Adler's caution, the risk of "this reform or that," that is, a menu of good deeds with little strategic connection. Typically, they echo a liberal agenda and rarely demonstrate derivation from an articulated humanist philosophy. On the other hand, although issues like those noted above are surely worthy of our efforts, they are not unique to humanism. They are shared concerns of the wider democratic community. By way of summing up the point, I turn to Adler's demand for "common ground."[25] It appeared in his inaugural comments but lacked the depth of what he came to identify as "an ethical philosophy of life." On this point, permit me to note my comments upon receiving the Felix Adler Award (June 2011, at the annual meeting of the American Ethical Union, the national organization of Ethical Culture societies):

> *In the beginning*—1876—it was the moral agenda: the horrors of slavery and reconstruction, the corruptions of politics, the exploitation of labor, of children, of women. But it was also a time of hope—emancipation, a labor movement being born, public schooling taking shape, a fruitful marriage of science and technology, a promise of undreamed of wealth. Felix Adler recognized the moment and its possibilities. Ethical Culture was his response; it became our response too and still should be.
>
> *Today*—2011—the agenda continues—The gap between rich and poor grows; terror is likely anywhere and everywhere; we choke on our own wastes; dogmatism and superstition delude a desperate people. But, ours is also a time of hope. Silent for all these ages, people everywhere demand their right to be heard and they *are* heard today in the Middle East, in Africa, in Latin America, yes and here at home in our cities and towns too. It's messy and unpredictable but it's constructive too. We create wealth where none existed before but it is, sadly, a wasteful wealth that needs its critics and its corrections. We have skills never before dreamed of but they are used to trivialize and demean rather than to enrich and celebrate. We reach across the chasms of culture and geography in a world grown more various and connected than ever before in human history. And that world is echoed daily in the places we live, the communities we have. So, a movement dedicated to the

"knowledge, love, and practice of the right" still has work to do. We have a chance to give life to it in the Societies and Fellowships we create, no matter where we are and no matter how large or small they may be.

But reform ought to be a commitment to reconstruction and replies to the question: What needs to be made or remade in our society so that the problems of action in the present do not recur over and over again? For example, Adler's pioneering schools were models of democratic and moral education, forerunners of John Dewey's progressive education movement.[26] Stanton Coit and John Elliott, Leaders in the Ethical Culture Society, founded settlement houses as institutions for democratic reconstruction. In particular they aimed to empower the new immigrants coming to the US or the new citizens moving into a rapidly emerging urban society. Their ventures were models of what Jane Addams in Chicago was developing as a national settlement house movement. Algernon Black, also an Ethical Culture Leader, founded The Encampment For Citizenship after World War II in order to educate young people in democratic values and as an ongoing defense against the temptations of authoritarian government. Each of these, and there were others, instanced the view that reform is strategic, not tactical.[27] Parenthetically, this theme deserves an essay in its own right, but that is for another time. Meanwhile, I address several other items for a humanist agenda.

GRANDCHILDREN OF THE ENLIGHTENMENT

The history of humanism can be understood as a series of *paradigm shifts*.[28] While Thomas Kuhn developed this notion in his groundbreaking history of the sciences, it is a useful way of exploring changes in what and how a theory, a movement, or an ideology is enacted and perceived, for example Classical, Christian, Renaissance, and Enlightenment humanisms. Core continuities are reaffirmed so as to make the name "humanism" recognizable under new conditions in ideas and world. With that affirmation, we unwittingly reinforce what may be called the "normal" humanism that is already passing away. A tendency to humanist conservatism follows, reflected in routine language and reference, the appearance of a humanist common sense as it were. This makes for a comfortable humanism; a humanism where the humanist can say "I know where I am."

The humanism of the present seems to settle for repetition and formula. Thus, I suggest, a partial reason for the humanism of the *word* with which I began. It may help us find our location in modern humanism's trajectory.

14

At the same time, the shift from one humanism to another entails a radical reformulation of many things and not least of all, of *imago humani*, for example the moves from Christian to mankind, from mankind to humankind, and so on. Consequently, each humanism is, sooner or later, in conflict with itself. Its known past, its lived present, and its hidden future confront each other. The conflicts linger. However, at a dramatic moment of discovery—the "Eureka" of Archimedes—a "shift" is in place and a new cycle of comfort and discomfort begins. We experience this moment without realizing that its ancestor, present humanism, is already in the past. It announces a next occasion for humanism. But there is also a meanwhile. We live on the shaky ground between today and tomorrow, and that is disorienting and even painful. This is where we are in our time but we cannot know the meanings of that experience until the bridge is finally crossed.

Nothing is ever entirely new. However radical the shift, threads of the past are woven into both present and future. Thus, a look at humanism's history reveals an evolving *imago humani* that serves as an index of change. It tells us that we stumble, move forth and back, but that ultimately the change has direction: emerging inclusions in a present react to deliberate exclusions in a past; for example, in our time, the civil rights movement and women's liberation reacted to the presumed "inferiority" of "colored peoples," of "women," and of "lesser races." These clearly redefined the person and were not simply changes of social practice or statute. They change the substance of society and culture and of modern humanism as well. Often these changes uproot a society. They may involve violence, as with the American and French revolutions, the American Civil War, urban rioting in the 1960s, or the current populist uprisings in the Middle East. These changes may be forecast by the *word* but are not trapped by it, for example the salons of the French Revolution, the "broadsides" of the American Revolution. Individual and social expectations are redefined, from hierarchy to equality, from patronage to participation, from heaven and hell to the natural world, and so on. Talents and responsibilities are refocused, such as in the reconception of work-life in the modern era. The humanisms of the past are not forgotten. History plays a generic role in all of them. So the past becomes part of the present. Thus, "reconstruction" is the favored humanist term. Humanism's new home echoes its old one(s). At the same time, comfortable humanism, the humanism of the "old-timers" turned conservative and not yet vanished, is fixated in repetitions. Thus, it mirrors the pattern of orthodoxy found in traditional ideologies and faiths. For all their complexity and messiness, these moves may appropriately be called progress.

We can speculate about the next road humanism may take while being aware that we are unable to foresee it with any certainty. As already noted, research into the lives and abilities of higher apes and other mammals suggests a move away from what is called by its critics "speciesism."[29] Human beings may lose the superior status they have enjoyed in both the Hebrew Scripture[30] and the humanist story. *Imago humani* may become an expansion of location, a reference to abilities, and a move to *primus inter pares* in a world of diverse companions who may also be described as "rational beings." Ecology, the interdependence of all that is, has this and other surprises awaiting us and our descendants. The technological transformation of human being itself is foreseen by what is called *transhumanism*.[31] Seeking inclusiveness in a global world without the ideological rigidities of today's Western bias is the *Neo-Humanism* of one of humanism's contemporary prophets, Paul Kurtz.[32] It may even be that humanism will recur to Nietzsche's *overman*,[33] recapturing the *imago humani* with a Darwinian perception now fleshed out by modern micro-biology and free of twentieth-century distortions like the "master race," the Aryan nation of Nazism. Thus, as a student wrote:

> Nietzsche's *Thus Spoke Zarathustra* offers a potent figuration of this affirmative stance toward existence. Through the character of Zarathustra, a parodic prophet, Nietzsche explores the possibility of Humanism's self-overcoming. Surpassing and transmuting the world-denying values by which it has constituted itself and its image of the world, the human becomes something other-than or more-than human: the overman.[34]

Whatever may be its future and whenever it appears, I suspect that the next humanist moment will be a surprise and, not least of all, to humanists themselves.

Thus far in considering the humanist agenda, I have been looking at humanism as a line of development in the larger culture, from above as it were. But every humanism has its interiority, its tensions, differences, arguments, players, heroes and villains, and so on. Platonic idealism and Aristotelian empiricism confronted each other, Cicero's *"Civis Romanus sum"* challenged imperial authority, scholastics battled the hierarchy of the Church. Leading figures, cultures, emerging national powers and a new economics shaped the arts of the Renaissance and the democracies of the Enlightenment and inevitably the humanist moment of our time.

Today's humanism, like its ancestors, is by no means a single entity. At its core, we find common descriptions: the human being is a bio-social animal; the human being is an autonomous being; the human being is a "moral animal"; the human being is able to assess and advocate his/her interests, to choose his/her leaders and policies, with a consequent democratic politics; the human being has the ability to create and use tools to shape both environment and self. Taken together and whether in secular or religious form, these characteristics mark a departure from fatalist notions like "original sin" on the religious side and "economic determinism" on the secular side. Neither god nor history sets boundaries to human potentiality. When joined with the idea of progress, another enlightenment theme, there is an optimism inherent in modern humanism. Humanism becomes an ideology of hope.

Imago humani remains at the center of these biological, moral, political, psychological, literary, and anthropological realities, but its substance is altered by experience. These terms—biological, moral, political, psychological, literary, and anthropological—are not self-defining. Indeed they become an agenda for humanist study and debate, such as disputes about choices between freedom and equality. They are subject to alternative emphases, such as individualism, communalism, and so on. The encounter between this variety and that, however, reveals that humanist pluralism in the US is more illusory than real, more verbal than actual. European humanists, among others in the international humanist world, make no claim of ideological pluralism. Indeed, when I have met with leaders and members of other humanist organizations around the world, they say they are puzzled by the way that Americans divide up into groups that are hardly distinguishable from each other. In fact, when we look at the actual discourses, practices, and personalities of American humanism we must wonder at the anger that fragments it. In short, the contemporary portrait of *imago humani* is recognizable whether we are in the presence of Unitarian liberal religion or Free Thought atheism and everything in between, for example commitments to human autonomy, moral agency, democratic polity, and so on.

For modern humanism, freedom and equality are core values. It exhibits these by breaking the barriers of class and gender that were still present in Enlightenment's eighteenth-century incarnation, that were being seriously challenged in the nineteenth century, and that in the twentieth century were relocating personal and gender responsibilities in the family, at work, and in the state.[35] By now, these have become features of humanism's common sense in the West. By contrast, protest movements in the Middle East and in the "Third World" contain a latent humanism that does not yet have a "common sense," although equality and freedom are their rallying cries. Whether or not the outcomes will build on this Western inspiration remains to be seen given different religious, social, and cultural traditions. It is probable that new forms of democratic polity will appear. In India, for example, Justice V. M. Tarkunde[36] advocated a non-party democracy, given India's size and complexity and following the inspiration of M. N. Roy's "radical humanism."[37] In China, we find an interesting mixture of Maoist communism, Confucian hierarchy, and market economics. But it is not yet clear how Confucian and Buddhist humanisms have been affected by these. Nor can we forecast what

17

humanism with Islam or sub-Saharan Africa as their cultural environments will ultimately look like. What seems clear is that the humanism that will emerge globally will be culturally diverse to a degree not known in the West.

Humanism in the US seems to have lost much of its élan. Its organizational disputations do not augur well. Its Enlightenment inheritance is hardly visible; for example most humanists make pious reference to the sciences but are less than literate about their contemporary development. The tedious interest-group politics of today's democracies compare unfavorably with the energies, enthusiasms, and passions of the eighteenth and nineteenth centuries. Public institutions have surrendered to sterile partisanship and the increasing power of economic and social elites. Yet democratic reconstruction hardly plays a role in humanist discourse. In short, given an inescapable global setting, humanism exists on the edge between yesterday's common sense—a universalism in principle that is hardly universal in practice. At the same time, we witness a struggle in more and more parts of the world for humanism not yet formulated and located in spaces esoteric to the West. Lurking in the background is an as yet non-visible radical creativity, a shift, whose humanist form and time of arrival is unpredictable.

Modern humanism seems to be caught between the influence and power of the West's ideological and colonial history on one side and the unresolved tensions between tribalism and nationalism on the other, for example Christianity and Islam, Confucius and Mao, Gandhi and M. N. Roy, and so on. To be sure, some of us speak of humanist "community" but this is mere sentimentality and is as misleading as the CIA's talk of the "intelligence community." Alternatively, and following Wittgenstein on language,[38] we might reconceive modern humanism with homelier metaphors, that is, as a *neighborhood* with an indefinite number of residents, or as a *family* with an indefinite number of members. These metaphors, with their familiar imagery and empirical models, suggest an approach to connections across diversities, a possible next future for today's humanism. There is a certain realism to both images. Family suggests a connection to Confucianism—another bridge to be crossed—and neighborhood suggests the village culture of much of Asia and Africa. At the boundaries there are, of course, idiosyncratic residents of the neighborhood or members of the family. Both metaphors ground a challenge to those who look upon themselves as sole possessors of humanist truth: "sects" as the religious call them. They also suggest that technocratic and bureaucratic organization need not be our only models.

Modern humanism is several centuries away from its original moment so perhaps fatigue is not surprising. Borrowing from Gilbert Murray on the deterioration of Greek culture in the third century BCE, it may be that modern humanism is experiencing its "failure of nerve."[39] Diversity, and even more so global diversity, can be felt as a threat to the comforts of commonsense humanism, with its roots in Western culture and practice. Differences in behaviors and relationships introduced by a global environment can stir feelings such as betrayal, frustration, and annoyance. For the Western humanist who claims ownership of it, humanism can become a burden and not an opportunity.

I suggest homely metaphors like "neighborhood" or "family" intentionally. They remind us that the human species is not a single thing, nor does it speak with a single voice. They also direct us to relational terms like loyalty, friendliness, warmth, acceptance, and so on. Further, rationality may be a major characteristic of humanism, but it is surely not the only one. As William James taught us, we are more often than not creatures of temperament, a less than conscious determinant of our passions that is far more influential than reason.[40] Class and culture, the hidden curricula of human experience, are far more powerful than rationality. If this is so, and if today's diversity is problematic, then a "psychoanalysis" of modern humanism would be useful, something the above comments are intended to stimulate. Our alleged pluralism, in short, may be less a matter of ideological difference than of the accidents of history, of styles of thought and feeling, and of the biographies of founders and followers. Without abandoning our commitment to rationality, this would suggest a more careful look at its complement, the humanist psyche, its emotional construction, its motivations, and so on, and the consequences of these for the humanist's passion or lack of it.

MYTHOS AND TRADITION

We are storytellers. From the earliest cave pictures found variously from southern Europe to the Australian Outback and from tribal song and dance to the mysteries of Joyce's *Ulysses*,[41] human beings have created and enjoyed stories. We tell them around the dinner table, when having a drink with friends, when sharing an anecdote at work or play. Encountering a stranger, we find ourselves, sooner or later, telling stories to each other, often biographical, stories of boast or complaint that we would scarcely tell someone we lived with, knew, and cared for. Stories invite us to experience the experiences of the other, thus celebrating the empathetic animal in each of us. We laugh or cry. We enter into the realities that stories create, some familiar, others weird and wonderful. We label them "fiction," or "poetry," or "history," or "biography," or "fantasy." But story is richer than words. We not only read and listen but see and hear, touch and smell. There is story in gesture, painting, and sculpture. Whatever their category, stories connect us to each other. Literature owns stories grandly told: epic tales like Homer's *Iliad*; Rabelais' *Gargantua*; comedies, histories, and tragedies like those of

Shakespeare; more personal seeming, yet carrying worlds into our consciousness, are poems like those of Whitman or Frost; science fiction like that of Isaac Asimov[42] or Gene Rodenberry.[43] Parthenon and Pentagon tell stories too. Portrait and still life tell stories. Movements as in dance or pantomime or gesture tell stories. Stories speak to us in the first person singular. The "I and Thou" of Martin Buber captures the relationship between self and story.[44] Stories remind us of the other: of family, tribe, or clan; of companions facing life or death in warfare or from disease; of success or failure at work; of friends and enemies, of big things and little things in our lives.

Stories are never passive. A third year medical student captures their activity as she writes:

> [W]hen ... I started my third year of medical school ... soon I came across an elderly woman with hyponatremia, a sodium deficiency ... In pediatrics, my team discovered long, thin scratches on a child's back—made by metal clothes hangers that someone had dug into her skin ... In physical medicine and rehabilitation, we supervised occupational therapy for a 10-year-old who'd shot himself in the head ... In neurology, a stroke patient went off life support on his daughter's birthday ... In internal medicine, I cared for a woman who had been so badly beaten by her late husband that her eyes pointed in different directions ... In surgery, a handsome young man was being eaten alive by cancer ... In psychiatry, a waifish princess look-alike ... was committed to our ward for hearing voices not of this world ... How do you process the pain of your patients? I found my way back to stories. The Grimm fairy tales once seemed as if they took place in lands far, far away, but I see them now in my everyday hospital rotations ... fairy tales and medical charts chronicle the bizarre, the unfair, the tragic. And the terrifying things that go bump in the night are what doctors treat at 3 a.m. in emergency rooms. So I now find comfort in fairy tales. They remind me that happy endings are possible ... They also remind me that what I'm seeing now has come before ... "Cinderella" originally ended with a blinding, and Death, in his tattered shroud, waits at the end of many journeys ... Healing, I'm learning, begins with kindness, and most fairy tales teach us to show kindness wherever we can.[45]

Of course, humanism has its stories, or could have: for example the death of Socrates, the encounter of Galileo and the Inquisition, the tale of Newton and the falling apple.[46] But these are typically told apart from the "real" business of humanism, the debates and differences, the expositions and analyses and meetings of its organizations. It is only before or after, as it were, that they appear. We take a walk, visit a building, share a memory. The struggles for freedom and integrity are surely worthy of story and ought not be resigned to manifesto or resolution or statement of principle. For all that these capture the logic of thought, they fail to capture us.

The story does. There is no lack of humanist themes for stories yet to be told. *Discovery* is a persistent theme of humanism; *resistance* is another. Both are crucial to humanism's story and both invite us to picture heroes, heroines, and villains, prophets and founders, and the rest of us too. At times, as with the existential writings of Sartre or the absurdist writings of Camus, stories may incarnate a philosophy explicitly. Philosophy and belief are latent in the style and personality of text or object. Whatever the creative voice chosen, stories picture the struggle of human being to find or create humanism. Thus, Camus ends *The Myth of Sisyphus* with the following:

> I leave Sisyphus at the foot of the mountain! One always finds one's burden again. But Sisyphus teaches the higher fidelity that negates the gods and raises rocks. He too concludes that all is well. This universe henceforth without a master seems to him neither sterile nor futile. Each atom of that stone, each mineral flake of that night filled mountain, in itself forms a world. The struggle itself toward the heights is enough to fill a man's heart. One must imagine Sisyphus happy.[47]

In short, stories reach us in ways that exposition and argument and slogan do not. Stories would seem an inevitable mode of humanist expression, but they are not.

Stories, whatever their mode, can provide depth to the humanist experience as they have to other worldviews and movements. Secular and humanist, we sing the songs of the traditions like carols at Christmas time. We enjoy the celebrations like the Passover Seder of neighbor and friend. We admire the grandeur of temple and cathedral although we may complain of their cost in the presence of poverty. We can look for insight in our experiences of the other who is, despite difference, also a fellow human being. At risk of heresy, we might even model a humanist aesthetic after the "bibles" of the world. Humanism ought to understand and appreciate them as human creations. For thousands of years and in cultures everywhere on the globe, these have spoken to and for human being, his/her needs and dreams, hopes and fears. Bibles, hymns, and chants are evidence of human inventiveness. To be sure, bibles may be read theologically. For some, they are the source of absolute morality and unchallengeable truth, as with the "creationism" of literalist Christians who turn the Genesis of Hebrew Scripture into a science textbook. But bibles are more subtle than their dogmatists. Many of those for whom a bible is sacred read it critically as we do, and at times, even skeptically. For example, Andrew Greeley, a brilliant commentator and Catholic priest, writes:

> Catholicism has great stories because at the center of its heritage is "sacramentalism," the conviction that God discloses Himself in the objects and events and persons of ordinary life ... It may seem that I am reducing religion to childishness—to stories and images and rituals and communities. In fact, it is in the poetic, the metaphorical, the experiential dimension of the personality that religion finds both its origins and raw power. Because we are reflective creatures we must also reflect on our religious experiences and stories; it is in the (lifelong) interlude of reflection that propositional religion and religious authority become important, indeed indispensable. But then, the religiously mature person returns to the imagery, having criticized it, analyzed it, questioned it, to commit the self once more in sophisticated and reflective maturity to the story.[48]

Ironically, for all its aesthetic neglect, humanism is more fortunate, potentially at least, than its believing neighbors. Its sanction is the "nothing human" of Terence, the "man the measure" of Protagoras. Thus, the doors are open wide in ways not true of our neighbors. For humanism, faith and its expressions are open too, are human; "all too human," Nietzsche might add. For the humanist, the world and all that is in it is accessible and none of it is taboo. Its variety is an occasion for appreciation as much as negation.

Gathered together, stories might serve as building blocks of humanism's *mythos*, freeing the celebration of its values from reliance only on the abstractions of rationalism, the charisma of this or that personality, or the inanity of the *word*. *Mythos* is not inevitably revelation of another world or miracle in this one, or a god's delivery from on high, or the secret writings of a mystery cult. Nor does *mythos* replace reason with dogma or creed. *Mythos*, the Greek word for story, legend, or plot, conveys meanings not readily reached by means of exposition or analysis. Thus, Plato, for all his idealism, resorts to *mythos* where argument fails and to story where dialogue fails, as in the "myth of the cave."[49] *Mythos* allows a wider participation for all of us in the truths and realities of humanism without sacrificing its rationality and purpose.

Not least of all, *mythos* is the seed and nourishment of tradition, connecting humanist stories across time and paradigm and connecting humanists to each other over time and space. Tradition can, of course, be a burden, even a prison. But it can also add dimensionality and depth to experience. With it, humanism reacquires a past seldom remembered and a complement to its more typical futurism. The present as lived is thereby opened to time. Of course, tradition has its risk as it does its promise. It can lead to blind loyalties, authoritarian powers, and alienation from those with other stories and connections, with other traditions. It can become the mere appearance of accessibility without its reality, setting humanism on a sectarian course while dogmatically announcing itself as anti-dogma, for example. Without tradition and without *mythos*, however, humanism is fated to convey a shallow and narrow reality, one that does not effectively house the passions and emotions of the persons who live in it. Tradition reminds us that others came before, without which criticism and analysis lose their depth and deteriorate into the humanism of the *word*.

INSTITUTION AND ORGANIZATION

I turn, finally, to what seems a more prosaic theme. The words "institution" and "organization" are often used interchangeably. However, they point us to the different dimensions of social structure. Organizations are tools. They specify the goals that implement the mission identified by the institution, and have members who provide the funds and other supports, such as leadership and volunteers, that are necessary for achieving these goals. Organizations derive their legitimacy from the institutions they serve. Of course, rogue organizations can develop, such as false prophets, multiple claimants to the papacy, *coups d'état*, and so on. The outcome is, more often than not, exploitation and anarchy. Authority is exercised in different ways depending on the institution that establishes it, such as divine grace, secular appointment, revolutionary elites, democratic election or what have you. Organizations have explicit rules and formal processes. They exist against a background of underlying meanings and values. Institutions have practices and customs that become part of our consciousness over time. Organizations respond to felt needs at their founding; the excitement of creation attends them. But needs change and time passes. Since institutions cannot help but evolve, organizations must evolve along with them. Otherwise, they become inappropriate to the tasks for which they were brought into being. At times, they may even become stumbling blocks to an institution's values. Similarly, institutions may atrophy. At that point, revolution, heresy, and desertion replace evolution.

Founders, if still present, understandably resist change. Female or male, they use the language of birth to describe their experience. Staff and members, on the other hand, develop interests in perpetuating the organization *per se*. They come to see themselves as owners but are in fact beneficiaries of place and status. Institutions, by contrast, have informal but powerful

23

leaderships who see themselves as servants, disciples, bearers of a cause or tradition. Institutions are naturally long-lived and subtle. An ownership claim, a "patent" if you will, simply makes no sense. As it were, the culture owns its children. Institutions are existential, almost organic entities. They emerge, as we have seen, as the cultural shifts of Western humanism from Greece and Rome to the modern world and the evolving content of their respective *imago humani*. In turn, these generate organizations to serve them politically, socially, pedagogically: among others, the Platonic Academy, the Aristotelian Lyceum, the Roman Senate, the Renaissance Church.

Institutions can be understood as the cultural reality of a movement, an ideology, or a faith, as the values and traditions that shape those who live in and by them, as the passions that motivate their inhabitants, and as the identities that are a significant part of who they are as persons. Institutions objectify that culture by having and celebrating traditions. Organizations are more likely to have formal records and histories. Institutions shape the "habits" that are taken as axiomatic by adherents or, put more emotionally, as "the way things are" by their followers, for example the unquestioned assertion that a country like the United States or a region like western Europe is Christian despite the facts of their histories or populations. Institutions sanction an organization's existence, nurture its development, and justify its replacement. Organizations, in turn, make possible the realization of the missions and values of institutions. Institutions thus provide the substance of and ends for which an organization is created.[50]

Given this distinction, the "non-joiner" mentioned earlier may rightly claim to be a humanist. But without organizational affiliation and consequent action, that claim is radically limited, as in the humanism of the *word*. An institution without organization(s) may have being, for instance in the consciousness and customs of those who identify themselves thereby, perhaps even in the ways they conduct their personal lives. But, transcending the subjectivity of an individual or set of individuals, institution evolves slowly, more often invisibly. It bears little fruit except in the enrichment of personal or communal life or when a public individual attaches a generic adjective to his/her activities, such as Christian, humanist, socialist, atheist, and so on.

Organizations provide entry to the world of give and get. In turn, they depend on the ends they serve for their meaning and, in principle, have no life of their own. Of course, organizations may try to perpetuate themselves, by gathering together a set of bureaucratic functions that serve this or that ad hoc purpose, or no purpose at all except to satisfy the interests of its functionaries, keeping them busy and paid. Hence the much misused and maligned "bureaucrat," the servant who functions without an underlying and evolving culture, that is, without institution. In today's world we mechanize the bureaucrat, imagining that he/she can transfer freely between this or that organization.

"Job skills" are conceived as objective and neutral functions seeming to have no institutional specificity. A similar illusion applies to organizational development, that is, the making of tools that have no underlying culture. Institutions and organizations, however, need each other, shape and reshape each other. Neither evolves successfully when apart. Their boundaries may not be clearly marked but their distinctive roles are clear enough.

Applying this distinction to modern humanism suggests a source of today's discontent. The original Humanist Manifesto (published in 1933) was the symbolic event of humanism nearly a century ago. It was inspired by Enlightenment, transcendentalism, Ethical Culture, Unitarian reform, and Free Thought. It owed its ideas to the emergence of naturalism and pragmatism. It celebrated the break with the theistic and supernatural past by calling for their replacement by a democratic religious future. The year 1933, in other words, signaled a prophetic alternative. Not least of all, it sought to offer an alternative to proletarian revolution, to set democratic community against the bloodiness of class warfare, that is, the call of the Communist Manifesto.

A look at the descendants of the original Humanist Manifesto, however, reveals a humanist institution—humanism's culture—that has hardly succeeded in connecting its values and mission to action in a world of global dimension and mass populations. Its organizations, originally seen as ways of reconstructing traditional but liberal religious church and temple, are relatively small and weak, and too often given to parochial quarrels. By way of grasping modern humanism's situation, imagine an Enlightenment that had stopped at the point of elaborating its salons and pamphlets, producing only a literature. Imagine an Enlightenment that had not overthrown kings and princes or that had not established organizations that struggled for equality and freedom, that failed to organize states and parties, schools and societies, to give life to its culture. Or imagine a Renaissance without its arts and sciences, its teachers, its critics and its organizations, the university, the studio, and so on.

Humanism's non-joiners inhabit a culture without teeth, so to speak. By their absence, they condemn other humanists to the same fate. Most humanists fail to grasp a rather simple notion: "to will the end is to will the means." Without effective organizations, the culture that invests them with reality will no doubt still persist, but quietly. Humanism in the modern and post-modern world will not disappear. But it will remain a small voice growing smaller and scarcely heard in a populous and complex environment, in a national and global environment.

To be sure, humanism has been fortunate in its pioneers and this has sometimes masked the inadequacies of its instruments. These pioneers lived the institution, created its organizations often in their own image, and inspired the first and even second generations of their followers. The remnants of their efforts, perhaps only a "saving remnant" to cite Hebrew

Scripture, do not disappear. The inheritors of an original inspiration, how-ever, grow fewer and fewer, and memory grows dimmer and dimmer. Still, institution will continue to be a humanist presence in the world. But human-ism as cultural innovator and cultural critic cannot rely on the accidents of biography. Without giving birth to organization, institution remains latent, a promise awaiting its fulfillment.

"Institution" and "organization" are useful analytic concepts. They tempt us, however, to separate ends and means. So, I turn to praxis, a term bor-rowed from Aristotle's description of the activities appropriate to free human beings. A dialectical process, it captures the flow, back and forth, between concept, reflection, action, assessment, and reconstruction, and thus the persistent tension between achievement and challenge. As it were, praxis cures the faults of the means/ends dichotomy. In ethics, for example, that dichotomy permits righteousness "in principle" and indifference "in prac-tice." But means and ends are never really severable. That is an illusion, a device that often masks what is actually going on. It can result in organiza-tion with a hidden agenda, a Machiavellian ploy, on one side and the institu-tion without power on the other.

Praxis helps us understand the vitality of classical Greece, of Augustinian Christianity, and of Marxist revolution. As institution falters—the found-ing genius is abandoned—organization becomes an end-in-itself. This is, perhaps, a more intelligible device than Gilbert Murray's metaphor, "loss of nerve." Actual models existed or still exist. Thus, in the late twentieth cen-tury, the democratic socialism of the Yugoslav thinkers Mihaelo Markovic and Svetozar Stojanovic and their colleagues was a self-conscious adop-tion of praxis in place of the class division and class warfare of Leninism.[51] The "praxis movement," as it was called, served as a defense of freedom for research, teaching, and learning against Tito's efforts to control the univer-sity and the media, and to silence or imprison those who opposed him. Sadly, this experiment in humanist socialism vanished when Yugoslavia broke apart. Despite the obituary of socialism that is broadcast, democratic social-ism in Europe's north countries—Norway, Denmark, Sweden, and until recently the Netherlands—is yet another instance of the flow between social democratic ideology and social practice. And the obituary may indeed be premature.[52] Elsewhere, socialism deteriorated into Stalinism and Maoism, that is, statism and opportunism. The result is signaled by oxymoron, market socialism. But socialism is not the only instance of deterioration. The so-called pragmatism of interest group politics in the US threatens the demo-cratic state's descent into anarchic opportunism.

Praxis is a more complicated rendering of the deed/creed dualism that summed up Felix Adler's initial inspiration. He revealed his dissatisfaction with this two-word summary of Ethical Culture by his reformulations, over and over again, for example from "the deed" to "creed and deed" to "deed before creed," and so on. Ultimately, he embedded both deed and creed in his Neo-Kantianism idealism and the ongoing process of reconstruction.[53] On that ground, he criticized, rightly or wrongly, the typical social reformer of his day as satisfied with "this reform or that," a beneficent moral opportunism. In the same voice, he criticized liberal Unitarianism. For example, when asked by John Herman Randall, its associate minister, and John Haynes Holmes, its minister, to preach the dedicatory sermon at the new building of New York's Community Church, Adler refused, saying:

> The Community Church, your church, has no definite attitude toward life. It cultivates no philosophy, no basic set of ideas. It is all things to all men. Which means that nobody and everybody … can join your church and participate in its work. This means a hodge-podge of reality, an ultimate betrayal of truth.[54]

Felix Adler's background source was Immanuel Kant; John Dewey's was Friedrich Hegel. Both members of Columbia's Philosophy Department, Adler and Dewey insisted on their philosophic differences. But they were by no means as radically different as they or those who observed them thought.[55] Both were reformers and both framed their reforms with the idea of "reconstruction." Both were progressives. Like Adler, Dewey saw the dangers of a separation of ends and means in ethics, in politics, and in education. For Dewey, bridging that separation was the key to progressive education, widely misunderstood as "learning by doing." Dewey's images of the school as laboratory, as community, as democracy, and so on reveal a far more complex tapestry.

"Doing good," praxis teaches, is not good enough any more than "believing right" is. A dichotomous view of means and ends, sometimes misnamed pragmatism, is an error in theory, strategy, and tactic. The outcomes of action reflect back on the concept, forcing reconsideration, amendment, critique. Humanism's problem, in other words, is disclosed by praxis. It requires a challenge to the self-deluding individualism of the non-joiner as to the parochialism of its organizations. Humanism must fail when concept is isolated from reflection and organization. This becomes even more obvious as idea and reality change more and more rapidly and comprehensively than ever before. Paraphrasing Kant,[56] action without intelligence is blind; intelligence without action is helpless. A humanism that fails to grasp that fact can only wait for its replacement. But modern humanism, becoming aware of itself in a confusing yet fascinating and variegated world, can prepare the way for its successor. That is its future in the post-modern world.

2. HUMANISM AS GUIDE TO LIFE MEANING
Anthony B. Pinn

In my office, above the desk is a small, framed piece of paper. It is a rough rubbing of the tombstone for Richard Wright, a humanist writer who left the United States and lived in Paris, brought back for me by one of my former students at Macalester College. I imagine that I mentioned Wright so often during classes and casual conversations that this student couldn't resist making the pilgrimage to his burial site during his study abroad in Paris. I remain grateful for this act of kindness because I have always found the writings of Richard Wright compelling. My frequent appeal to him in my writings on humanism should demonstrate his powerful prose and sharp and vivid imagery. However, it was only with time that my appreciation of his many books moved from simple agreement with the absurdity of the world couched in his vocabulary and grammar of life to interest in his soft, but at times very vibrant, commitment to a humanist agenda. And with this recognition grew my interest in understanding and assessing humanism in light of the framing of life offered by Wright and thinkers like him.

In recent years I have been asked on numerous occasions to write down my thoughts on the nature and meaning of humanism for African Americans. In part this stems from a growing awareness of an embarrassing need for greater awareness of and attention to diversity within the humanist movement. When asked, I typically find myself providing differing snapshots of particular figures, ideas, themes, and institutions prominent in the landscape of African American non-theistic thought and ethics. The idea behind this approach is to offer a sense of how humanism develops within African American communities in response to particular class, gender, and race-based concerns and insights. This chapter is one of those opportunities. Mindful of this, and in light of Richard Wright and kindred "spirits" of sorts, much of what I offer here involves a reimagining and restating of my perspective on humanism, developed over the course of numerous years and presented in various lectures and publications. The difference here is the framing and intent of this discussion in response to an obvious but vital question, one that I have not been asked before in this particular way: What is humanism and why does it matter?[1]

FRAMING THE QUESTION

In an unapologetic manner, Wright's insights are premised on the complexities and tensions inherent in our material (embodied) existence. What he determines regarding this situation is challenging but, in an odd way, also comforting. Often using churches and Christianity as a foil against which his protagonists mark out an alternative form of life meaning, Wright, as some writers within the African American modern realism movement are wont to do, centers on a robust depiction of humans—as bodies occupying time and space—with all the difficulties of their tangled and mundane relationships. More to the point, his characters lament the dulling effect of theism and project, although never fully formed, a humanistic alternative. Take, for example, the words of Fred Daniels, a man forced into the sewer in an effort to evade the police who want him imprisoned for a crime he didn't commit. At this point in the story Daniels has left the sewer for a brief time and is in the darkness of a movie theater reflecting on what he observes:

> He stood in a box in the reserved section of a movie house and the impulse he had had to tell people in the church to stop their singing seized him. These people were laughing at their lives, he thought with amazement. They were shouting and yelling at the animated shadows of themselves. His compassion fired his imagination and he stepped out of the box, walked out upon thin air, walked on down to the audience; and, hovering in the air just above them, he stretched out his hand to touch them ... His tension snapped and he found himself back in the box, looking down into the sea of faces. No; it could not be done; he could not awaken them. He sighed. Yes, these people were children, sleeping in their living, awake in their dying.[2]

"Sleeping in their living," is Daniel's pronouncement, and readers know that Wright echoes this declaration with a hearty "amen!"

But what are the other options? If what can be understood as transhistorical assumptions and desires are illogical, what is the alternative for people trying to make their way through the world?

For Wright, life involves racialized absurdity enhanced and deepened by the workings of theistic belief. His sense of the dynamics and mechanisms of life defined by so-called democracy entailed a process of dehumanization and reification that could not be broken without the surrendering of old totems of life meaning.[3] In this instance, theistic belief, primarily in the form of Christianity, had to be exposed and challenged. Instead of reliance on divine beings and cosmic promises, Wright pushed for an embrace of human potential maximized and human accountability presented with all its promise and pitfalls. After all, as Wright notes in *The Outsider*, the human is a promise we must never break.[4]

WHAT IS HUMANISM?

The promise and pitfalls of a new democracy naturally generated a concern for human life—the felt and historically arranged nature of human needs and relationships. This was based on the manner in which blood, sweat, and toil generated the fundamental questions of life's meaning and purpose. The Revolutionary War, Civil War, Reconstruction, and so on, especially required the creation of a worldview that made sense of human promise and misery in the modern era. The result was the emergence of humanist-inspired thought and organizations.

Non-theistic humanism was under siege during the Great Awakening revivals between the mid-1700s and the early 1800s, when the misery of life led some to the assumption that better connection to God through personal salvation would alter the condition of their land. The harshness of existential conditions was met during the Great Awakenings with a turn to revelation as the basis for a sustainable sense of humanity's place in the world. In short, conditions within the context of history could not be the final word on human life and the meaning of human life. However, despite fiery sermons and emotional claims of regeneration, questioning of God and the countervailing idea of the centrality of humanity were never completely wiped out. Humanist sentiments continued to grow as a visible response to deep questions of life meaning.[5] Moving through the nineteenth century, into the twentieth century and now the twenty-first century, the impact of non-theistic thinking and practice is undeniable.

Although lagging behind the reception of secularization in many European countries, it still remains the case that according to recent studies, the 1990s marked a watershed period for the growth in non-theistic sensibilities in the United States, with an increase of more than one million adults each year until 2001. However, even after this period of significant increase subsided, the percentage of the US population categorized as "Nones" has remained significant, creeping up on 20 percent.[6] Put another way, one in six Americans is presently of "No Religion", while in terms of "Belief and Behavior" the ratio is higher, at around one in four. And what is more, for 68 percent of "Nones" surveyed, this position involves a movement away from earlier belief patterns in that only 32 percent indicate being "non-religious" as a pre-teen, and class as well as racial background are playing a declining factor in the "look" of this category of American.[7]

It remains the case that this group—"Nones" —is difficult to classify accurately. It is not a movement, not a group easily defined by atheism. While it is not fully accurate to label all "Nones" humanists (7% are atheists and 35% are "hard/soft" agnostics), the significance of this category of Americans does lay in the inability to understand them in terms of traditional theistic belief structures and patterns.[8] Furthermore, according to a recent study, "Nones, in general, are substantially more likely to self-identify as atheist or agnostic than are adults in the U.S. population generally."[9]

My argument regarding the "what" of humanism up to this point is vague and rather limited, but this doesn't damage my objective to simply suggest the long historical trajectory of humanism. Do not think of humanism as something new, the mind games of baby boomers. It does not take much to recognize at this point that a great deal of what I have said thus far is dependent on somewhat clear statements concerning the thought of particular figures, with more vague mention of humanism as a general ethos. And, although typically discussed with respect to leading intellectuals of the ages, humanism is, according to philosopher Corliss Lamont, a basic philosophy of life available to any and all. It provides a non-supernatural means by which to assess life options and perspectives on proper actions and thought.[10] Lamont, who offered me one of my first examples of a systematic effort to define humanism, is concerned to outline basic components of humanism and, in this way, remove some of the ambiguity surrounding the term and the way of life it entails. Whether one further distinguishes humanism as scientific, secular naturalistic, democratic, and so on, the following characteristics are present and are of fundamental significance. He argues that humanism is grounded in the aesthetically rich natural world, its evolving nature and observable laws. Furthermore, humanity is understood as an inseparable component of nature, one ending its existence with death; and although human life is fraught with hardships, humanity is capable of addressing its problems with appeal to reason and the scientific method.[11] In this way, humans create and fulfill their own personal *and* collective well-being without the intervention of divine forces. Humanism, then, is committed to the development, through continual self-reflection and critique, of a healthy world based upon democratic principles. Humanism, in keeping with Lamont's insightful perceptions, does not allow for (or at least is opposed to) the good of the individual at the expense of the collective community. Although humanism, like any other way of life, at times falls short of its objectives—for example racism, classism, and gender-bias within humanist movements—it nonetheless pushes toward the welfare of others as paramount.[12] Arguments concerning what it means to be a humanist are persistent.[13] There is a web of meanings and definitions for humanism, and this is even more telling in the context of current developments, marked by a growing body of non-theists who are searching for a way to define their thinking and label their practices.

Lamont's defining of humanism continues to intrigue me: its relative clarity and expansive nature are hard to resist in that it affords a centering of one's thinking and carves out a "place" for humanism, but I also find fascinating the manner in which his work suggests gaps to fill and interesting questions to address. That is to say, although his work is a comprehensive treatment, it points to the difficulties associated with defining the term "humanism" in a way that can remain stable despite socioeconomic, political, and cultural shifts over time and that can account for diversity within the groupings of citizens who claim (or reject) the "label." His is a defining of humanism in light of mid-twentieth-century concerns such as World War II and the accompanying angst over the nature and meaning of human advances in the sciences over against the preservation of life's integrity. It is a definition tied to a particular sociopolitical ethos. In addition to Lamont's work, various incarnations of a humanist manifesto have been tied to similar assumptions concerning the nature of the nation/state as a basic framing of human interactions and "belonging"—a backdrop of sorts for the structuring of humanism as life philosophy.[14] This all generates a range of questions, including this: Is the term "humanism" plastic enough to cover the meaning of life and thought within a quickly changing world?

The situation is messy, but efforts to define evolving realities always are. There are just too many "moving parts," too many nuances and ideological shifts for the situation to be otherwise. For example, many who would embrace the principles Lamont outlines (Who would reject an interest in harmony and world health?) are opposed to the label of humanism; and others are opposed to any label at all out of principle. This term, "humanism," as is the case for any conceptual paradigm or explanatory category, has been stereotyped and stretched, and those who embrace it have experienced many difficulties based on the shifting nature of its meaning. Others who claim the label of humanist are opposed to any hint that humanism is a religious orientation as opposed to a philosophical stance or "secular" worldview. Some of those in this latter grouping are opposed to religious labels because of what they consider the failure and harm done by organized religion. The world's most graphic tragedies stem from the workings and teachings of religion, and theology encourages a rejection of reason and logic—replacing both with faith and metaphor, the argument goes. Yet others are careful to consider humanism a religious orientation, not as a reaction to Christians' fears and not as an appeasement to the loud and aggressive religious right, and so on, but because of the way humanism provides, to borrow from theologian Paul Tillich, a synergy between one's ultimate orientation and ultimate concern.[15]

I find this latter possibility—humanism as ultimate orientation or, in my thinking, a fundamental and ongoing quest for complex subjectivity[16]—intriguing, and I would like to explore it briefly in what remains of this section on the definition of humanism.

My use of this framing—perhaps more familiar to theists than to many non-theists—is not simply a way of collapsing important distinctions. My intent is not to kowtow to irrational critiques based on stereotypical depictions of humanism. In that regard I am not offering a compromised sense of humanism meant simply to appease its most vocal opponents and thereby to safeguard "space"—as compromised and cramped as it might be—for humanism within a decidedly theistic society. I want more than that for humanism. Put another way, my aim is not simply to value humanism to the extent it mirrors organized religious traditions. I only aim to point out the manner in which humanism, like religious traditions through their own means, seeks to provide a way of thinking about and behaving. It, like those things we recognize easily as religious traditions, seeks to provide a systemic approach to life. Or, more to the point, it replaces god-based ways of making (life) meaning. Thereby it allows its adherents to wrestle with the looming questions of our humanity: the "who, what, why, when, and where we are" questions.

Call humanism "religion/religious" or not, there are ways in which it works to make sense of human existence—to wrestle with the nature and meaning of life in an absurd world laced with sociopolitical and economic difficulties; and it does so in a way that provides the potential for resolutions and at least a little hope.

Out of a commitment to humanism in general and non-theistic humanism in particular as a vital and vibrant way to address the challenges facing our collective life, my aim is to show the deep significance of humanism as a life orientation that addresses *both* the objective and subjective dimensions of our individual and group existence. To the point, I remain convinced that a non-theistic stance within the world is our best hope of producing clear thinking and robust action which might serve to transform in positive ways the range of life options currently available, particularly to those who suffer most in our current world community. And the growth of public advocacy for humanism in the United States and beyond points to an expanding recognition and embrace of this very commitment to non-theistic postures toward the world.

By saying that humanism entails a life orientation, attention to which maps out an ultimate orientation for life, I intend to say that humanism frames a quest for life full and healthy, the making of meaning in such a way as to capture perspective on and attention to the looming questions of our very complex and layered existence. To be sure, these fundamental questions of existence are wrestled with *firmly inside* human history, without appeal to trans-historical assistance and cosmic powers waging war on our behalf. Our movement through the world sets out the geography and context for this wrestling and the answers (to the extent we develop them) rest within the context of human ingenuity and creativity: nothing more, and nothing less. Humanism in this context involves an arrangement and interpretation of life with a grammar drawn from and reflective of the "stuff" of our historically situated lives. It offers a perspective on the challenges that humans face that grounds on earth our best chances to thrive. No heaven to comfort the weary. No god(s) to side with the disadvantaged. No sacred texts promising formulas and strategies to enhance life. It simply offers strategies for clear, secular, and grounded efforts to own our problems and demand of ourselves creative means by which to address them. Or, as the poet Henley claims:

> It matters not how strait the gate,
> How charged with punishments the scroll.
> I am the master of my fate:
> I am the captain of my soul.[17]

There is something mysterious about the human story—the nature and meaning of human life—but this does not entail the footprint of a divine something. Rather, this "mystery" is a marker of what is yet unknown to us but pursued through scientific investigation as well as the approaches to unpack human meaning found in the social sciences and humanities. It is true that humanism confines its conversation to what is scientifically verifiable and marked by materiality, but less clear is a sense of the nature and meaning of the human. In a word, *human*ism is about human thought and action; but what is the human? What is the nature and meaning of the human?[18]

Theistic life orientations typically posit the human as some type of being forged in the image of divine forces—*imago dei*. Instead of this, humanism—as is probably little surprise, based on the public visibility of the "New Atheism"—understands the human as strictly a biological reality, a product of evolutionary formation and development. The human is an embodied and aware self with deep flaws and great potential for imagination and creativity—a material being that is born, grows, lives, and dies, with an existence beyond this only in the memories of those who loved (or hated) him or her. The human so understood is of and in the world—all the while operating based on a rich set of interests, concerns, motivations, sensibilities, and capacities to wrestle with the deep questions humans confront as a result of our very existence. There is no need to talk about a soul or spirit as the animating dimension, and most important dimension, of the human. For humanism as I am presenting it, such ideas have no real importance. Talk of souls and spirits as anything more than a paradigm for human ingenuity and achievement is fantasy. Rather, we are fragile beings, aware of our fragility, and marked by movement in a variety of social locations simultaneously: for example one can be female, middle class, Latina, residing in the northern United States, and committed to a particular political party.

Humanism at its best promotes modesty regarding the nature and meaning of the human—recognition of human capacity but also shortcomings. In this way hyper-optimism related to human potential (and the tragedies such arrogance can produce) is tempered through recognition of the deep impact of racism, sexism, and so on on humans and their bodies and psychological development. We do our best work when we recognize that we are capable but deeply flawed creatures. All in all, the nature and meaning of the human for humanism as I understand it highlights the material nature of existence but, with modesty, a sense of hopefulness. To be human, it appears to me, involves an unavoidable recognition of and response to this drive and the resulting stories of our existence drawn from our working through this drive. This unfolding of human life is captured in what we say as well as what we do, and is lodged in the cultural worlds we construct, but without the nebulous framework of the sacred marking theistically contrived notions of the human animal. (Even science, though we often fail to acknowledge as much, takes place from within the frameworks of cultural worlds. It is incumbent on social scientists and humanists to provide persistent reminders of this.)

While this story of human meaning is important and we chronicle it as best we can, there is nothing sacred for humanism. Instead, there is great appreciation for cultural production—the worlds of meaning we create through words and other forms of artistic expression. There is admiration for the ways in which humans have discussed and explored our world and our place in it; but there is no sense of divine revelation, no salvific story granted humans by a transcendent force. And although much over the past few decades has involved a defining of non-theistic orientations through negation—strong rejection of theistic religious traditions and what they are said to encompass and promote—less, but no less significant attention has been given to the ways in which humanism affords more than anti-Christian or anti-Islam rhetoric.

HOW DOES HUMANISM WORK?

I can hear the question now; it is one humanists hear on more occasions that we care to acknowledge: If humanists do not believe in God, what keeps life from being a free-for-all? What keeps humanists in check? This question

35

has impact because it points to *the* common denominator, the primary category of meaning—the litmus test of moral belonging. God demands action in the world, and this provides a blueprint for human activity. Other elements of belief can be altered, shifted, or ignored to some extent without tremendous difficulty, as long as the person questioned maintains a basic belief in God as the organizing principle and shaper of life. The extension of this question revolves around the ethical connotations of belief. What keeps you focused in acceptable and productive ways?[19] For some humanists there is a form of radical individualism at work in how humanists move through the world in relationship to others. But what I propose involves the individual within the context of something more substantive. Humanism, as I have described it, recognizes the manner in which the notion of God or gods has promoted an unreasonable (and what is more, a fictitious) restraint on human accountability and responsibility by harnessing ultimately the workings of human history to the will of some greater force. Although theistic formulations of the world are limiting, humanism does recognize the sense that individual behavior needs parameters, or guiding structures, allowing for the promotion of a good greater than that of any particular individual's will or desire.[20]

Humanism values gatherings of the like-minded. There are too many humanist organizations, and organizations with annual meetings and shared communications between these formal meetings, for this to be the case. These organizations and gatherings are of vital importance. Hence, the need for connective tissue—relationships based on common understanding—is a persistent topic of conversation, particularly with respect to issues of diversity and human difference. Yet, this sense of the collective is insufficient as an organizing "something" that both humbles and motivates humanist thought and action. Humanism needs and has as its centering ideal something that includes sociopolitical, economic, and cultural concerns of the like-minded; but this centering ideal also points out the deeper dimensions and motivations behind these concerns. It is because of this deeper dimension—a dimension of existence still grounded in the human in human history—that humanism has something to say to the debates and passions marking human life.

Humanism involves a rather complex and compelling arrangement of thought and practice that helps a noteworthy percentage of the population move through the world. What I propose as undergirding humanism with respect to this organizing principle is a sense of community. By this I mean more than a collective of like-minded individuals motivated to shape life circumstances and options in a particular way. Whereas there are shared ideologies, values, and virtues within humanism as associated with this sense of community, it extends beyond traditional forms of the collective by omission. Some humanists understand themselves to be part of a collective under siege, a group rallied against by the theistic majority. And, while there is some truth to this concern, community as I intend it here is not simply the collective agreement on humanists as scapegoat. Community here means an organizing framework, a sought-after synergy or symmetry of life that guides and modifies the thought and actions of humanists. Community so conceived points out the promise of humanism but also entails firm recognition of absence, of incompleteness not as a problem but as the nature of human *be*-ing and living. It is the agreed upon posture toward the world, the accepted sense of obligation that defines and shapes humanists' thought and practice. It is the "more" of and out of life we seek but also the absence of this "more," which is just as real and compelling. This sense of community points to the beauty lodged in the tangled markers of our lives as well as highlighting the significance of the uncertainties confronted and confounding us. Unlike theists, who might initially think this sense of community involves agreement with their perspective on the divine, I would note that community here defined still privileges time and space—the parameters of human history—as the only "real" context for our interactions.[21]

Whereas theism might lean toward the fantastic as the way to harness and understand the human in relationship to metaphysical claims, community for the humanist appreciates the thick and unfolding nature of biology and connects this to a deep and fundamental awareness of and awe regarding life. Community, therefore, involves comfort with the uncertainty or blind spots of our existence, without attempting to fill them with gods and other supernatural things. I think this is something of what novelist Richard Wright had in mind when creating Cross Damon, the protagonist of *The Outsider*. Dying on the floor, Damon reflects on the life he lived, the attempt to be completely free from others, and recognizes that the search for meaning cannot be done in isolation. Rather, "never alone ... Alone a man is nothing ... Man is a promise that he must never break."[22] What Wright presents through this character is acceptance of life lived for self within the context of others as the last best option. The markers of meaningful existence are only measurable within the context of something larger than the self. Wright offers a trajectory of living, pointing out both the flaws and potential of humanity, and guarding against both insufficient hopefulness and unreasonable despair. Cross Damon realizes this before dying. Such is how one might interpret Damon's words: "I wish I had some way to give the meaning of my life to others," he says, "to make a bridge from man to man. Tell them not to come down this road ... Men hate themselves and it makes them hate others. We must find some way to being good to ourselves ... Man is all we've got."[23] Humanity is all we have. And with this brief statement Wright does structural damage to the framework of metaphysics undergirding so many theistic assumptions. One cannot gain perspective by looking beyond human history, beyond the stories of human movement and meaning. There are no hidden codes left behind for us by something greater than us.

There is no cosmic salvation for the humanist, no escape button that allows distance from the trauma of human existence. Yes, humanists seek a better world; but that is not a different state or *form* of life. Rather, humanism promotes a desire for wholeness or fullness of life made possible through the limited resources of human ingenuity, commitment, and creativity. This humanism pushes for a type of balance to life, again allowing for recognition of human potential within the context of human limitations. This not only entails the push toward fulfillment of material potential but also involves effort to understand and recognize fundamental structures of life, and the deep consistencies that mark these structures. In short, the outcome of life at its best—the life humanism seeks to promote—involves the enhancement of human engagement with self, others, and the larger world; and promotes the beauty of existence over against its trauma and absurdity. That is to say, to achieve life at its best, the aim is to make life dynamic and as saturated with meaning as possible.[24]

WHY DOES IT MATTER?

Why does humanism matter? I want to approach this question by simply and briefly highlighting some of the creative ways in which humanism advances efforts to live life meaningfully and within the context of nurturing relationships. Without engaging in a crude and unnecessary effort to close churches and destroy "organized" religions such as Christianity and Islam, one can reasonably claim humanism as having great potential to meet the needs of a growing population of "Nones" and others who find theistic orientations less than satisfying.

First a point of clarification: for some atheists and humanists, attention needs to be given to arguing against religion as a way of converting and bringing some out of the damaging environments called churches. While some might find these arguments convincing enough to leave their churches, mosques, and synagogues—there are anecdotal claims to this effect—I would argue that theism's deep reliance on faith claims does not in general fall prey to rational argumentation. Theistic doctrines, creeds, and theology exist precisely where human reason seems most inadequate. These three are the theist's effort to fill gaps: to make sense of the world and our place in it without reliance on strict human capacity to figure things out. Theology resolves the "I don't know" moments and topics with metaphysical claims and pronouncements, and theists position these in such a way as to short-circuit critique as a marker of disbelief and a general weak connection to

God. For many theists the attack by atheists only affirms their commitment to the faith. It wouldn't be uncommon for their reasoning to be this: "I must really be serving God, because the devil is out to get me."

There is something in the significant growth of non-denominational churches and a prosperity ministry that flies in the face of claims that one can argue theists out of churches. Some may leave, but those might be the very theists who were simply hiding out in those churches for non-theological reasons. Sure, there are some of those, and aggressive atheism and humanism might get them. But is that enough? Really? And what about all those who are non-believers looking for a place to land? They have already rejected what we argue against, but we haven't provided them with a positive message regarding the significance and impact of humanist thought and action. Why not concentrate on that growing percentage of the population? In a more focused response to this approach, one might also wonder how many Latinos/Latinas and African Americans—who represent a growing percentage of US "Nones"—have left churches because of aggressive atheism? There are those who will disagree (and have disagreed) with me on this point. So be it. There is space for all, and there is a need for multiple approaches (as well as civil conversation concerning differences in strategy). However, with respect to why humanism matters, I tend to privilege its ability to address the needs and wants of a growing number of non-believers. Let the hardcore theists (and atheists) stay where they are.

While some humanists hide out in churches, mosques, and so on for a variety of pragmatic reasons, there are numerous others actively seeking an alternative. The growing number of US citizens who do not claim a traditional and theistic religious tradition need a way of focusing their questions and interests, a way of naming and shaping their life practices and perspectives. Humanism can meet this need in that it promotes a posture toward the world and a way of acting in the world that holds the safeguarding of life over against ethical action based on personal reward and personal aggrandizement as being of primary importance. That is to say, humanism positions us in the world in ways that help us seek (as a fundamental responsibility and as a clear marker of our best selves) full confrontation with the pressing issues of our time—sexism, homophobia, class warfare, and so on. Humanism helps those who embrace it make the promotion of healthy existence of all life their starting point and end point, their *raison d'être*. And, I argue, they do so with attention to at least these underlying claims, which I believe are applicable across life geographies of all sorts:

1. Humanity is fully and solely accountable and responsible for the human condition and the correction of humanity's plight;
2. Rejection of traditional theism and an embrace of reason and the materiality of life;

3. There is a commitment to individual and societal transformation;
4. There is a controlled optimism that recognizes both human potential and human destructive activities.[25]

Humanism in this way entails a stance of mindfulness and recognition of the weight of our existence, noting our promise and our problems, our abilities and our shortcomings. Humanism notes the fragility and tender nature of life, celebrates it, and seeks to work toward its integrity.

There are ways in which theistic approaches to life overlook the everyday or mundane dimensions of our existence because they are preoccupied with the greater significance of transcendent concerns. There is something of substantive value in the manner in which humanism holds humans accountable and responsible for proper thought and action.[26]

Mindful of the above, *humanism matters because it provides a life orientation that takes seriously everyday occurrences, the ways in which the mundane nature of our existence houses something profound.* It gives us reasonable insights into the world, and perspective on how to move through the world. And it does so without the pitfalls associated with theistic orientations. Drawing from Henry David Thoreau, I argue that humanism teaches the importance of living life deliberating and fostering good people who exercise their capacity to do good things.[27] This is to see the value, the importance, of every dimension of individual and collective lives in ways that promote a deep sensitivity and commitment to the betterment of every area of life within the context of our material world. What one gathers from Thoreau, then, is sensitivity to the weight and seriousness of both individual awareness and social engagement. Each is more than superficial encounter without effect. Both involve uneasy confrontations and delicate balance between different impressions of the world.

We are "moved" to behave in certain ways, to value certain interactions, and to disregard others through the power of our creativity and our ability to make a difference. The outcome of this process is not necessarily fantastic nor extraordinary—perhaps a simple changing of a mind on an issue, a greater sensitivity to the nature of one's relationship to self, others, and the world.[28] A similar approach to the world, one that is earthy and deeply entrenched in human accountability and responsibility, is also echoed in the lessons offered by figures such as novelist Alice Walker, who many humanists claim as one of their own.[29] She, like Thoreau before her, calls for deliberate living: moving through the world in relationship to others and entrenched in the world in ways that recognize our interconnectedness, and hence deep responsibility to ourselves and to others. Such a perspective easily lends itself to sociopolitical activism as well as ethical conduct on the various levels of life. This perspective is also held by many people who are not well known. My grandmother, for example, phrased ethical living in a way that might appeal to a variety of humanists, beyond this writer. "Move through the world," she told me on many occasions, "knowing your footsteps matter." Such rhetoric might come across as too sermonic in tone, too subjective and laced with emotion for some. Yet, there remains in these words a basic and important stance, one that has come over the years to support my sense of humanism. It, humanism, pushes deep and multi-directional accountability, and provides a way of celebrating and encouraging human initiated actions meant to enhance healthy life options within the context of improving social-political, economic, and cultural relationships.

Humanism has always played a significant role in the celebration and utilization of human ingenuity and creativity. The difficulty or, better yet, challenge, however, has revolved around ways of promoting or making more visible and public the benefits of humanism-based thought and action. As I have noted elsewhere, a starting point for doing this might include at least the following:

1. Partnerships with national and international organizations (including religious organizations) that are committed to socio-political and economic advancement based on a progressive vision;
2. Aggressive branding (to be sure, a dirty word for many) strategies. Some may find this troubling, but the future success and recognition of humanism must involve concerted effort to establish its "brand" potential—to establish its uniqueness and importance;
3. Development of continually clear and concise presentations of humanism that provide a positive and proactive stance.[30]

Recent advertising campaigns to promote humanism and the like have generated much-needed attention. But what remains to be done is the further development and demonstration of humanism as a unique way to address the pressing problems of the day, problems that extend beyond the damage done to human life through the "un-reasonable" reliance on theistically contrived traditions of meaning-making. Humanism matters, but the ongoing challenges are concrete and "felt" demonstrations of this statement.

3. HUMANISM AS A MEANING FRAME

Peter Derkx

WHAT KIND OF THING IS HUMANISM?

Humanism is an important phenomenon in modern society, but what kind of thing is it exactly? Very often it is regarded as an alternative to the Christian (or another) religion, and thus functionally it is said to be a "religion." Many humanists, however, do not like this at all. They do not want to see humanism as a religion. So they look for another, more general word to capture the function of both humanism and religion. "Philosophy of life" and "world-view" have been used in this way. In the Netherlands *levensbeschouwing* (life-view) has acquired currency, even in the constitution and national laws. In the International Humanist and Ethical Union (IHEU) the phrase "life stance," originally proposed by the British humanist Harry Stopes-Roe, has been accepted. Furthermore, investigating the modernization of society and the concomitant trends of individualization and secularization, some social scientists have proposed the term "meaning system."[1] Yet, I would suggest that "meaning system" sounds too systematic and complete to refer to the mostly implicit "meaning frames" people use in the daily practice of their lives. Instead, I would argue for "meaning frame" as a way of capturing what is meant by the function of humanism. In what remains of this chapter, I explain what a meaning frame is and what humanism as a meaning frame might be.

RESEARCH ON A MEANINGFUL LIFE

To understand what a "meaning frame" is, it is essential to know what a "meaningful life" is. Some research has been done on this, but comparatively little. The following table gives the number of articles that have been published on "meaningful life" and some other related terms. As Table 3.1 demonstrates, there is a lot more research on well-being, quality of life, and happiness than on meaningfulness.

Table 3.1 Scientific research on "meaningful life" and some other related words and phrases (Dec. 8, 2010).

Search term	Articles in Google Scholar*	Articles in Scopus*
Well-being	2,520,000	17,593
Quality of life	1,760,000	16,015
Happiness	1,020,000	4,865
Psychological well-being	285,000	2,746
Subjective well-being	51,500	1,476
Meaning in life	21,100	231
Meaningful life	20,500	72

* Google Scholar references articles on the internet and Scopus is an important database of peer-reviewed articles from the social sciences and humanities.

WHEN IS A LIFE MEANINGFUL? SEVEN NEEDS FOR MEANING

According to the Dutch Humanist J. P. van Praag and the American social psychologist Roy Baumeister, "the essence of meaning is connection."[2] In a meaningful life one's experiences—one's whole life—have a place within a wider network of connected meanings. In his book *Meanings of Life*, Baumeister argues that this larger network involves four kinds of meaning, or four different *needs for meaning*: (1) one experiences one's life as having *purpose*; (2) one experiences life as having *moral worth* (i.e., it can be morally justified); (3) one has *self-worth* and is in control; (4) one has *competence*, influence, or as Baumeister calls it, efficacy.[3]

To further explicate these four, one might think of *purpose* as connecting your life and activities in the present with something of positive value in the future. It can be something outside of oneself. It can be a *goal*, for instance, a certain job, or an important award for pianists. But it can also be an inner *fulfillment*—the positive state of mind that accompanies reaching a goal or developing a personal talent.[4] In addition, this can involve a single thing, but at the same time it can involve many possibilities simultaneously.[5] The need for *moral worth*—for moral justification—refers to the human desire to know, in a moral sense, their acts and way of living (including the purposes they strive for) as right, good, legitimate, and having positive value. It should be noted that this desire is also present when the real or primary motives for actions and decisions are not of a moral kind. *Self-worth* entails positively valuing oneself. Typically this means one finds one or more aspect of one's life in which one is better than others, and is recognized and respected by others. It involves both the value of who one is and what one does. Regarding self-worth, cultural tradition and social hierarchy are of great importance.[6] Humans often compare themselves individually with others within their group or environment, but it is also possible to acquire a sense of self-worth through membership in a collective (a nation, a religion, an employment, a lifestyle, a fan club). With respect to the second option, individuals compare their group with another, less-valued group. As a point of clarification, it should be noted that self-worth is not the same as the more specific experience of moral worth, a morally justified walk of life. Regarding this distinction, Baumeister gives the example of couples that divorce, referencing research conducted by Diane Vaughan.[7] Based on her research, rejections by a partner resulted in a heavy blow to self-worth. However, the person who ends the relationship fares better because he/she is an active decision-maker and initiator. The same person, nonetheless, often feels guilty and has a problem with moral worth as a result. The need for a sense of *competence*, control or efficacy, speaks to the human need to know life as based on their decisions and choices, rather than seeing life as random and happening to them. Control can take two forms: (1) one adjusts the environment and makes it fit with what one wants, or (2) one adapts oneself to the environment. A form of the second is called "interpretive control," by which understanding why something happens produces an experience of competence, even if one cannot change what in fact happens. For Baumeister, more important than the mapping out of four needs for meaning is the total conceptual space they cover.[8] To some extent they show overlap and one need often contributes to the satisfaction of another. One might reduce the list to two or three, or one might make finer distinctions and expand the list to six or seven needs. I opt for the last possibility. I extend the list with three—at times overlapping with those presented by Baumeister—needs for meaning, and in this way I offer a means by which to get a sharper image of what a meaningful life entails.

In a 1998 article, my colleague Jan Hein Mooren added a need for *comprehensibility* (intelligibility) to Baumeister's needs for meaning, and did so partly on the basis of Aaron Antonovsky's theory regarding the human need for a sense of coherence.[9] Humans want to understand the world they live in and explain the events that happen to them: why or by what means do they occur? This speaks to a fundamental desire to replace chaos with order. In this way, creating a coherent story of one's life against a wider backdrop makes life comprehensible and manageable, and provides identity and continuity.[10] In other words, "meaning can be regarded as one of humanity's tools for imposing stability on life."[11] The need for comprehensibility fits nicely with the importance Baumeister attaches to interpretive control and thus overlaps with the need for competence. Moreover, comprehensibility fits very well with Baumeister's basic idea of meaning as connection in that comprehensibility refers to the ability to situate something in and connect it with what one knows already, and in this way to produce coherence. Thus, the need for comprehensibility can be seen as a further explication of the conceptual space covered by humans' need for meaning. The same might be said for the need to experience *connectedness*, added by my colleagues Adri Smaling and Hans Alma to the list of needs for meaning. They describe this as a need for contact, union, and abandon. Here the emphasis lies on attention to the other and not on control, dominance, and self-interest. Connectedness involves simply letting things happen, union, and care.[12] In presenting this additional need, Smaling and Alma refer to psychologist Hubert J. M. Hermans' theory in which human beings have two basic motives "assumed to give rise to two recurrent developmental tasks: the realization of an autonomous self and the establishment of contact and union with the other."[13] Smaling and Alma stress that the experience of connectedness requires that the other is felt to be other. That is, "the experiences of love for, friendship with and abandonment to another and recognition by another imply that that other really is an other for you and not an extension piece of yourself."[14] The need for connectedness might show some overlap with the need for moral justification in Baumeister's theory.

One might ask why Baumeister does not mention the need for connectedness as a need for meaning. He himself has done research on the "need to belong" and by that he means the need to create and maintain long-lasting interpersonal ties with a limited number of people—ties that are characterized by frequent and pleasant interactions in the context of a long-term relationship of care for and care about each other's well-being. He is of the opinion that it is an important human need, almost as strong as the need for food.[15] But evidently he does not view it as a need for meaning. However, if meaning *is* connection then it would be natural to present the need for connectedness, or the need to belong, as a central need for meaning, would it not? In a recent article Baumeister reports on research among American students that shows that a close and supportive relationship with family is a most important source of meaning for them. Baumeister suggests family is such an important source of meaning because family and relatives offer a unique possibility to satisfy belongingness needs. That is to say, the need to belong might provide the mechanism for the correlation between family and experience of meaning. In that Baumeister distinguishes between needs for meaning and sources of meaning, he must have decided to view positive personal relationships or interpersonal attachments—such as in love and family—as the most important source of meaning and not to add the need for them to his list of needs for meaning. Yet, this is all speculation in that he does not give an argument for his decision.[16]

It is noteworthy that Smaling and Alma interpret the need for connectedness in a wider sense than the need for frequent and caring interaction with a number of intimate friends and relatives. Connectedness can also be expressed in citizenship, work toward a more humane society, or work toward a better world. They also speak about connectedness with the impersonal other. I suspect that for connectedness to be meaningful it is important that the person or object to which one is connected be evaluated positively. I also suspect that the contribution of positive aesthetic experiences to meaningfulness is related to connectedness.

Smaling and Alma also propose the desire for *transcendence* as a need for meaning. They describe transcendence as "going beyond what is regular, expected, well-known and safe, exploring and reaching for what is new, different, unknown."[17] They also refer to Viktor Frankl, who writes that the meaning of life can only be complete if one transcends one's private interest by embracing moral values.[18] Thus, the need for transcendence overlaps the need for moral justification. Besides Alma and Smaling, many researchers mention transcendence as a defining characteristic of the experience of meaning or as characteristic of its deepest or highest variants. Gary Reker and Frits de Lange and Alfons Marcoen, for instance, do so.[19] However, if we look at their descriptions of transcendence, a problem arises. Robert Atchley writes, "when an individual makes a shift from experiencing personal existence as a solitary being to experiencing existence as part of a larger being or web of being, then transcendence can be said to have occurred."[20] And, de Lange writes:

> only if one is capable of relating oneself to a bigger, transcending structure in which one's individual life is embedded, is a life good. This structure can be the cosmos, religiously interpreted, but also a historical or a philosophical movement, a generation, a family. Without some embeddedness, an individual life is meaningless, because it does not participate in a larger structure of meaning. Individual life has a beginning and a destination that transcend it.[21]

Connectedness here seems to be an aspect of transcendence (or the other way round).[22] And connectedness, moral justification, and transcendence are linked in some way, but how?

Connectedness with the impersonal other and social connectedness with one or more other persons transcends what is mine and what is familiar to me. Consequently, let us regard this connectedness as an aspect of transcendence. The need for transcendence also includes a second aspect—the need for ethical values that go beyond limited self-interest and create limits for it. This offers normative but not absolute orientation for living. Hans Alma, however, emphasizes a third aspect of transcendence, referred to as wonder and curiosity. People want their lives to be interesting and exciting.

And if connectedness includes security and feeling at home, the connectedness aspect of transcendence is not only different from but can even conflict with wonder and curiosity.[23] Curiosity about the strange and unknown is not always innocent and can threaten security and connectedness. In short, it is not clear how exactly transcendence and connectedness relate to each other. Nor is it clear whether it is useful to view the need for connectedness and transcendence as two different needs for meaning. I do think, however, that adding transcendence and/or connectedness to the dimensions of meaning as elaborated by Baumeister is an improvement. The theory of a meaningful life would otherwise be too directed towards the self and control. It would contain too much *agency* and too little *communion*.[24] Dependency, attachment, wonder, vulnerability and care are important aspects of life and the need for connectedness, and transcendence does justice to them. Humans not only need some control over their lives; they also seek to avoid having everything depend on their decisions. As Christa Anbeek writes, "sometimes I am tired of constantly acting and constantly choosing. Then I want to step back, undergo life, not fulfill possibilities and potentialities, pass all chances, do nothing at all, just be. Such as the grass and the flowers, do not they just grow of themselves?"[25]

According to Baumeister the importance of religion, traditional morality, and tradition as such have decreased strongly by processes of individualization. "Modern Western culture has struggled to establish the self as a major value base. People have always had selves, but selves have not always had to carry the burden of supplying meaning to life in such a far-reaching fashion."[26] The meaningfulness of life has become extremely dependent on the development of a valuable unique self, a personal identity as value of last resort that does not need further justification. One's own death thus becomes enormously disturbing and threatening in that with death all value and meaning associated with one's life disappears.[27] Connectedness, transcendence, and (less traditional more consciously embraced forms of) morality offer options for meaning that in Western culture might be against the grain and not come easily, but they remain important.[28]

We have distinguished seven needs for meaning that together define the concept of a "meaningful life"— the need for purpose, moral worth, self-worth, competence, comprehensibility, connectedness, and transcendence—which can be used to assess the degree to which a person's life is understood as meaningful. If a person succeeds in satisfying all seven needs for meaning sufficiently, then in all probability this person will experience her/his life as meaningful. Problems arise when she/he has not satisfied one or more of these needs. This person will be inclined to restructure life through changes in behavior and so on, until all needs for meaning are fulfilled (again).[29]

A HAPPY OR MEANINGFUL LIFE?

There exists substantial overlap between happiness and meaningfulness, but there are differences as well. Baumeister gives an interesting example in *Meanings of Life* represented by the so-called "parenthood paradox": social scientists in the 1980s discovered that (in a modern society with social security and pension systems) having children makes people less happy.[30] Yet, many people want children. Why do people want children, when having children makes them less happy? According to Baumeister, the solution is found in the difference between a meaningful life and a happy life. Generally, and if all goes well, children provide parents with an enormous amount of purpose, self-worth, moral justification, and competence. That is to say, "people want their lives to be meaningful as well as happy, and sometimes the quest for meaning can override the quest for happiness. Parenthood may be an important instance of this."[31] What, then, is the relationship between happiness and meaningfulness? Baumeister suspects that a meaningful life is a necessary but not a sufficient condition for a life of well-being. The life of a guerilla fighter (or a parent?) can be experienced as meaningful without being happy. On the other hand, few people succeed in being happy when they experience life as meaningless.[32] But, of course, this also depends on the way happiness is defined. If happiness, to a large extent, is defined by a high intensity (high frequency) of pleasant emotions and a low intensity (and low frequency) of unpleasant emotions then meaningfulness clearly is something else.[33] However, if happiness refers to self-acceptance, positive relations with others, personal growth, purpose, environmental control, and autonomy, it is harder to distinguish between happiness and meaningfulness. The most important difference between the two concepts seems to reside in comprehensibility and moral worth.[34]

THE IMPORTANCE OF MEANING

Some researchers emphasize the positive effects of having a meaningful life. In the end, what is important is not that life is meaningful, but that through experiencing life as meaningful people live longer, have better health, or are happier. In a word, "meaning in life is an important variable for human well-being."[35] A meaningful life looks like a means to achieve something else, for instance happiness. However, it is possible to regard a meaningful life as the most important thing. (In the introduction to her book on the emancipation of women Simone de Beauvoir wrote that what interested her in the potential of women as human individuals was not happiness but freedom.[36]) Happiness is not automatically the most important thing in life. One might argue that experiencing life as meaningful is important, whether it makes one happier, or healthier, or not.

MEANING FRAME

At the beginning of this chapter I indicated that the "meaning frames" people use in the daily practice of their lives are largely implicit and incomplete. A meaning frame provides you with a sense of direction, stability, identity, continuity, and with criteria to evaluate situations and one's life course. It is a frame that forces itself by fits and starts and in fragments through the memory of moving experiences and the way one interpreted and digested these. A meaning frame is not a theory of meaning. Each person experiences differently others and objects. Hence, there are as many meaning frames as there are human beings, and any meaning frame is always a context-dependent product of human culture. Yet, because human experiences not only differ but also show similarities, meaning frames can be categorized. And humanism is one of these categories.

THE CORE OF HUMANISM: A PROPOSAL

As children, individuals acquire their meaning frame from people in their environment. But they also encounter conflicting views and learn from their experiences. However, "Normal" adults are themselves responsible for the meaning frame they live by. This leads us to a first central tenet of humanism: *any worldview or meaning frame, including a religious one, is and remains a context-dependent human product.* The first principle—context-dependent product of human culture—could be called epistemological. It expresses the meta-position humanists take towards any ontological or normative position whatsoever. Embedded in this tenet is recognition of historical consciousness, human fallibility, and experience of doubt. It also draws from a critical and dialogical attitude, and requires willingness to account for one's views and actions with openness, tolerance, and an appreciation of diversity.[37] The protestant theologian Harry Kuitert expresses this tenet beautifully: "human statements do not become more true when somebody says that they are based on revelation. All speaking of above comes from below, including the statement that something comes from above."[38] This tenet does not imply that humanism necessarily is in contradiction with a belief in god(s). Yet, it does imply that belief in god(s) will not trump a general human grounding for beliefs and actions. Again, any worldview or meaning frame is a human product and may be critically evaluated by other human beings—using reason, experience, and other human faculties. Meaning frames, of course, can be perceived in a positivist way from an external point of view, but they can only be understood in a hermeneutical way—from the inside, from the interested perspective of a participant. No human is in a position to survey the landscape of different meaning frames from a neutral height and say how—apart from his own experience and history—life and world should be understood.[39] Hence, neither divine revelation nor science provide an unassailable objective position high above human interests, interpretations, and meanings. Of course, free inquiry is very important and produces important results we have to take into account. I cannot agree, however, with the British Victorian scholar William K. Clifford when he writes, "it is wrong always, everywhere, and for anyone, to believe anything upon insufficient evidence."[40] Ludwig Wittgenstein has made clear that anything whatever can be doubted, but it is impossible to doubt everything at the same time.[41] To do scientific research, one always has to take something for granted (at least for the time being). Science also is a context-dependent human product. Moreover—and equally important—not all questions can be answered by empirical scientific research. David Hume has shown how difficult it is to prove or disprove metaphysical/ontological propositions.[42] Twentieth-century philosophers such as the later Wittgenstein, the later Carnap, and Karl Popper have strengthened this skeptical position: a view of the nature of reality as a whole cannot be proven or refuted. The necessary meta-position or meta-language is lacking to be able to decide between competing views.[43] Although more can be said regarding the relationship between science and meaning frame, let it suffice to say that meaning frames always contain elements that go further than is scientifically justified. In view of their function for specific people in the here and now, that is inevitable. Science cannot answer existential questions such as these: What is the proper attitude towards our human mortality? Does human freedom really exist? Can the death penalty be justified? Humanism is not scientism, and involves no plea for technocracy. Whatever meaning frame one adheres to or accepts it has to be accounted for by humans using arguments and giving considerations that do not scientifically prove their case.

Meaning frames are products of human culture that supply meaning and are continuously adapted while doing so. Many worldview authorities and power centers are inclined to deny the historical, contextual, dynamic, and ultimately human element in "their" worldview. Alas, this denial often is successful for some time in a way that hurts people. Nonetheless, in the long run this denial always fails. The meaning frames of human beings exert influence on the way they live, but the challenges people meet in their lives also (re)form their meaning frames. Although meaning frames as a whole cannot be (dis)proven by science, certain aspects or implications of meaning frames can turn out to exist in contradiction to science. In response, some—atheists and theists—might want to keep abreast of advances in the sciences and adjust their meaning frame either superficially or substantively.[44] In a context like this it can be useful to speak of "inclusive humanism" by means of which humanism is conceived as an open, dialogical, and tolerant meaning frame found not only outside of churches, mosques, and the like, but also inside them. Put simply, modern humanism, then, is a worldview which on the one hand stands beside and sometimes in opposition to other worldviews, and on the other hand exists as a non-dogmatic variant of "other" worldviews, religious or not.

A second central tenet of humanism (not quite separate from the first one) is of a moral kind: *all human beings ought to regard and treat each other as equals, with human dignity.* This principle—guided by individual freedom, self-determination, and personal responsibility—connects to the idea that each person is best positioned to assess and determine how he/she should live. Acknowledging our differences, we should approach each other with respect and as equals. Recognition of the dignity of all human beings is related to other characteristics of modern humanism, such as readiness for dialogue and compromise; acceptance of doubt and fallibility; openness and tolerance; appreciation of diversity; choice for democracy; separation of church (life-stance organization) and state; and the fight for justice. Humanism conflicts in principle with all forms of discrimination—racism, sexism, ageism, and discrimination based on sexual orientation. Humanism finds expression in respect of, and in the fight for, human rights. The concept of human dignity is the fundamental idea behind modern human rights.[45] While having a particular look during this historical moment, the thought that all human beings have dignity just and only because they are humans is an idea found with the ancient Greeks (Euripides' *Medea* in 431 BCE, Antiphon, Democritus, Xenophon, the Stoics) and in Cicero's *humanitas*.[46] Basic concepts and concerns originating in earlier periods continued during the American and French Revolutions through fiery debates concerning who qualifies as a human being (deserving to be treated as an equal). Such debates concerning human rights and agency continued past those periods and continue finding expression in our historical moment, as groups demand greater recognition, including all the markers of dignity, such as food, drink, clothing, housing, education, and health care.[47]

Two very central humanist principles have been presented now, and my claim is that these two principles are fundamental to humanism. Are these the only two humanist principles? They, I argue, are part of the minimum conditions for humanism, but do they constitute not only the necessary but also the sufficient minimum? There is reason to believe more is needed. For example, in his beautiful book *Imperfect Garden: The Legacy*

of Humanism, the Bulgarian-French philosopher and theoretician of literature Tzvetan Todorov analyzes the humanism of Montaigne, Rousseau, and
Benjamin Constant as an alternative for conservatism, scientism, and individualism. His conclusion is that humanism is best defined by three—onto-
logically given and normatively desirable—principles: (1) the freedom and
self-determination of the individual (the "autonomy of the I"); (2) the sociability of the human being in his orientation towards unique, irreplaceable
others (the "finality of the you"); and (3) the equality of all human beings (the
"universality of the they").[48] Todorov's "universality of the they" corresponds
to the principle of human dignity noted earlier.[49] His "autonomy of the I" and
"finality of the you," however, might also function as necessary conditions for
humanism:

> The humanists do not claim that human beings are entirely ruled
> by their reason or their conscience. They are not unaware of the
> power of what were formerly called the passions and what we call
> the unconscious or instinct, nor of the constraints exercised on the
> individual by biological givens, economic necessities, or cultural
> traditions. They simply contend that the individual can *also* oppose
> these constraints and act from his will; and this is what they see as
> specifically human.[50]

The "autonomy of the I" is probably one of the most obvious principles to
define humanism.[51] The self-evident importance of it, however, does not
make clear immediately what this value (or principle or postulate) means.
I think that the two principles I have dealt with are already related to the
principle of autonomy. That a worldview always is a human product points
to everyone's responsibility for his or her worldview. And, if all human
beings ought to regard and treat each other as equals, each is accountable
for deciding his/her life direction. Autonomy as negative freedom (others
and the state do not have the right to limit freedom unless there are exceptionally good reasons for it) seems to be implied in the two principles I have
already named.

Autonomy as positive freedom, however, is an important new principle. It concerns what one does with one's freedom. *Self-fulfillment*—self-
development ("*Bildung*" in German), personal growth—constitutes a third
condition necessary for humanism. It can be phrased this way: *one should
consciously create the form and content of life, choose purposes and seriously
try to achieve them, and one should use one's freedom to develop one's personal capacities and talents.*[52] Humanists are of the opinion that human
beings should not let their lives pass by—not "without thought" or "unexam-
ined."[53] This is not a plea for fast running activism. It is not about rejecting

a more contemplative life. Instead, it is about developing personality. For, as Erasmus remarked, horses and other animals are born, while "humans are not born: they are cultivated." Truly human existence demands "a daily commitment which continues your whole life and is never completely finished."[54] This tenet is about consciously deciding what one really wants to do with one's life as a whole. It is about taking responsibility for one's life, taking care of oneself. For this art of living, according to J. Dohmen, one has to get to know oneself; to experiment and to try things; to analyze and interpret one's personal, social, and historical context; to decide what to do first and what can be done later; to choose one's value profile. In all of this one's moral orientation is crucial. By identifying oneself with certain of one's wishes and by rejecting others one creates unity and continuity in life. By one's second-order desires one gets integrity, identity, and what one may call spiritual resilience. In this self-fulfillment one partly discovers and partly creates oneself.[55] It should be noted that fulfillment is not the same as thinking about oneself all the time. With some qualifications, Alan Gewirth thinks that "self-fulfillment, like happiness is attained not by being directly aimed at but rather as a by-product of one's dedicated pursuit of other purposes."[56] An individual can only develop into a person by devoting herself or himself to an external cause.[57] Finally, the social is not a later and secondary addition to the individual self. For instance, in his *Mind, Self, and Society* (1934), George Herbert Mead suggested that an individual only becomes a self through reflection, and that means by looking at herself or himself as if through the eyes of a "generalized" other.[58] When an individual thinks about what he/she really wants with his/her own life, others are already involved in this thinking and these desires. Society does not consist of individuals who are already full-fledged persons *before* they meet and are influenced by other human beings. This is an important insight, but it does not detract in the least from the importance of negative as well as positive autonomy of individuals.

Todorov's "finality of the you" is an interesting candidate for a fourth defining characteristic of a humanist meaning frame. Todorov uses the "finality of the you" not only to distinguish humanism from individualism that does not care about the social lives of human beings, but also to distinguish it from scientistic utopianism (or utopian scientism) and technical scientism. Scientistic utopianism refers to German Nazism and Russian communism in which specific human beings are no longer final ends, but are degraded into means to serve "the new human," that is, the people and the ideal state. Technical scientism refers to the technocratic element in democratic societies. Society incorporates mechanisms that, for example, almost make efficiency and economic growth into ends in themselves. The instruments for achieving anonymous human well-being have become structurally more important than the life purposes chosen by specific, unique human beings. "Finality of the you" means that a human being makes another human being the highest aim of his or her actions. It is crucial here to see that Todorov does not refer to a moral and general love of human beings (such as in the Christian love of one's neighbor, *agapè*, or the Greek *philanthropía*), but to a personal *love of specific, vulnerable, unique, and irreplaceable persons*. Todorov distinguishes between three relational spheres:

> the *humanitarian* [or moral] sphere (for example, I must help a person in danger, whoever it is), the *political* sphere (in some respects, all my fellow citizens are interchangeable, yet they are not interchangeable with foreigners), and the *personal* sphere, in which no substitution is possible: I am attached to my father, to my lover, to my friend, to my child as irreplaceable individuals.[59]

According to Todorov, the difference between the political and the moral sphere on one side and the personal sphere on the other side is to be found in the (im)possibility of substitution:

> As citizens, all members of a society are interchangeable, their relations governed by justice based on equality. As individuals, the same persons are absolutely irreducible, and what counts is their difference, not their equality; the relations that bind them together require preferences, affections, love.[60]

Minding the personal sphere, however, can have large consequences in the moral and political sphere. According to Todorov, equality (the universality of the they) is an important political value, but not the only one.

> To this passive and minimal humanism is added an active, much more ambitious humanism. To make human individuals the finality of our institutions, of our political and economic decisions, might cause a peaceful revolution. ... Resignation to the claimed fatality of social or economic "laws" ... contradicts humanist principles. ... We must remember that the love of a humble human being can be more precious than solemn declarations on the well-being of humanity. Humanism asserts that we must serve human beings one by one, not in abstract categories.[61]

Paying attention to concrete human beings in specific historical situations is connected to the opposition of the Renaissance humanists against the late-Scholastic building of theological–philosophical systems thought to be timeless and eternal and against universities in which metaphysics and juridical texts were central at the expense of fine arts and letters, and of useful insights for practical ethics and politics. Such opposition, in a sense, can also be found in the forms of expression and the opinions of Hume, Diderot, and Voltaire. Todorov's exposition of the love of unique and irreplaceable human beings as an essential element of humanism is very convincing, certainly in view of the horrors of the twentieth century.[62]

I have presented four defining characteristics of humanism now. The last three principles—human dignity, self-fulfillment, and love of unique, irreplaceable human beings—are of an ethical or at least normative kind.

HUMANISM AS A MEANING FRAME: A FIRST REFLECTION ON THE DIMENSION OF COMPETENCE

Instead of dealing with all seven dimensions of meaning very briefly, I will instead confine myself to only one of them as an example, a case study of sorts. And, in my discussion of competence from a humanist point of view, I will mainly refer to the debate about substantial life extension: should we invest billions of dollars in research and development aiming at new biomedical technology to achieve a healthy human life span of 200 years or more?[63] A quote from Michael Lerner makes clear what is involved:

> We ... need to do the spiritual work as we grow older to accept the inevitability of death rather than acting as though aging and death could be avoided if only we had better technology. The enormous emotional, spiritual, and financial cost of trying to hang on to life as long as possible (and to make ourselves look as though we were not aging) is fostered by a marketplace that tries to sell us endless youth. It is also fostered by our cultural failure to honor our elders, provide them with real opportunities to share their wisdom, and combat the pervasive ageism with its willingness to discard people long before their creative juices have dried up, to stigmatize the sexuality of the elderly ... and to provide little in the way of adequately funded and beautifully conceived long-term care facilities.[64]

Aubrey de Grey, Gregory Stock, James Hughes, and other transhumanists do not agree with Lerner that aging cannot be avoided. They admit that immortality is impossible (people can always get killed in many ways that have nothing to do with aging), but they believe "the many lines of converging sciences and technologies and the rapidly escalating pace of medical knowledge suggest that indefinite life extension will be possible in this century."[65] Connected to this, when I told Aubrey de Grey that I am heading a research group called "Aging Well," he said he did not like that. Aging well, according to him, is a contradiction in terms because "aging kills."[66] I think the confusion is on de Grey's part in that he does not realize that aging has different meanings. *Biomedical aging of an individual* means his or her body is deteriorating. The *aging of society* means people grow older than before and that the relative number of elderly persons increases, which demands quite a few changes in society: economically, politically, socially, and juridically. *Existential aging* is about the mental experience of continuing to live in time as a unique and vulnerable individual after social conventions have designated you as an elderly person. Even if aging in the biomedical sense disappeared completely, existential aging would still be there.[67] The research aiming at healthy aging in the biomedical sense is important, but aging well existentially is also important, and it also involves, as Lerner indicates, acceptance of disease, disability, loss, and suffering.

A remark by Clifford Geertz about the religious perspective on suffering is a good starting point for further reflection:

> the problem of suffering is paradoxically, not how to avoid suffering but how to suffer, how to make of physical pain, personal loss, worldly defeat, or the helpless contemplation of others' agony something bearable, supportable—something, as we say, sufferable.[68]

While suffering is and always will be part of the human condition (human competence and control is fundamentally limited), the function of religious and other meaning frames is not only to teach human beings how to accept suffering. Human suffering always has a social, cultural, and historical context that can change. These changes are important and they transform the nature of the moral and existential questions with which we are confronted. For example, the Roman Catholic parents of my mother had five young children in 1918–19. Between December 1918 and January 1920 four of their children died of the contagious bacterial disease known as whooping cough. Now it can be prevented by vaccination (the P in the DTP combination vaccine refers to whooping cough or *pertussis*). I still have the devotional picture commemorating the short lives of these children. The prayer on the back of the little card starts with "Do not weep, parents, over the passing away of your children" and it ends as follows: "Say it now, and say it ever and again: What God does, has been done well." An important aspect of religious and nonreligious worldviews indeed is that they provide a way to accept, endure, and embrace life as it is. However, a dangerous trap for both religious and nonreligious meaning frames and associated moralities is that they become too one-sided. The task for humanists, religious or not, is to find a wise balance between accepting life as it is and striving for the possibility of a higher humanity. Humanity, as the way human beings are and as an ideal, never is just a solid fact to be taken for granted.

Inevitably humanity is always interpreted by human individuals and in cultures and meaning frames, and in an always-changing environment. Humanity also is a context-dependent product of human culture. I think that there is no good reason to suppose that human beings might not be able to live much longer than today. And I think there is no good reason why in principle "we" should not invest billions of dollars in research and development aiming at new biomedical technology to achieve a much longer healthy human life span. But it probably does not deserve the highest priority. We should not forget that average life expectancy at birth in Japan and the US (around 80) is double the life expectancy in Sierra Leone and Zimbabwe (around 40), and within the metropolitan areas of Glasgow (Scotland) and Washington, DC average life expectancies between the poor and the rich differ by twelve and twenty years respectively.[69] Many human lives can be extended without new revolutionary biomedical technology. A lot can be improved, but for the time being quite a lot has to be endured and accepted. There is tension between progress and acceptance, between autonomy and heteronomy,[70] between natality and mortality,[71] between choice and chance,[72] between improving unbearable situations and finding meaning in situations we cannot change (yet). This tension is part of the human condition to which all meaning frames have to respond. Choosing wholly and fully for one of the poles and doing away with the tension is a temptation human beings often find hard to resist. Still, we had better not give in. Humanism as a meaning frame is not only about how to accept suffering, nor is it pure ancient hubris and human arrogance either.

PART II. WHY DOES HUMANISM MATTER?

4. IF WAR IS NOT THE ANSWER: AN ALTERMODERN APPROACH TO POLITICAL ENGAGEMENT

Sharon D. Welch

Political engagement is an arena that could benefit greatly from humanist sensibilities and a humanist posture toward the world. Mindful of this, in what follows, I provide some attention to how humanism as an approach to ethics might serve to enhance the life options of communities.

In the spring of 2005, former US ambassador Jonathan Dean spoke to a gathering of international peace activists in Cuenca, Spain about the work of Global Action to Prevent War. He addressed our hopes for peace, our aversion to war, and our commitment to respond to crimes against humanity with foresight and creativity. He grounded his proposals in a shift begun in the late nineteenth century within the European peace societies. Rather than expecting or seeking a fundamental change in human nature, Dean claimed that "the peace societies ultimately gave priority to mechanisms and measures to constrain war over intellectual [and moral] arguments to end war."[1] This turn to a constructive realism is absent in much of the peace movement today in the United States, and yet, such a stance might have great potential for implementing our proposals for enduring peace and sustainable security.

CONTEXT CONSIDERED

A humanist approach to social ethics and public policy that follows the guidelines of Ambassador Dean echoes many insights of President Obama's Nobel Peace Prize speech without, however, relying on a contrast between the "isness" of the human condition with an eternal "oughtness" that forever confronts us.[2] In contrast to the words of Dr. Martin Luther King, Jr., cited by President Obama, I affirm a humanist ethic resolutely grounded in the "isness" of the human condition. Such an ethic leads to a pragmatic grammar of policy analysis and development, one based in nondualistic understandings of good and evil and a fallibility-based worldview. In this chapter I will give one example of the results of that ethic when applied to international foreign policy and the challenges of strategic peace-building.

As an activist, I have experienced the impact of speaking truth to power: the inspiration and sense of identity evoked by clarion denunciations of injustice and faithful witness to ideals of justice and peace.[3] As first a department chair, and now as a provost, I have, however, confronted personally and collectively the painful fact that to care passionately about injustice does not mean that we are equally skilled in the task of coordinating and managing human and natural resources justly, creatively, and in a way that lasts for the future. As we take up the task of using power truthfully, we recognize that the work is not done when the protests are heard. Rather it is here, it is now, that another, more difficult type of work begins.

The move from knowing what *should* be done to actually getting it done is as great a shift ethically and philosophically as is the move from *is* to *ought*. For here, as we move from *ought* to *how*, we encounter a paradox. Not only does work for constructive, institutional forms of justice take significant amounts of time, but also there are intrinsic differences between prophetic critique, prophetic vision, and democratic leadership. We may critique alone and we may even envision alone, but to implement that vision, to build on that critique, requires the cooperation of other people—other people to actually carry out the work on a daily basis, other people to judge, refine, and criticize new systems and processes. And, as you may have noticed, other people tend to have different ideas—not only different ideas of how to meet shared goals, but possibly better ideas about the most fitting, concrete ways to administer health care, or to support ecologically sustainable forms of energy production.

Pragmatists encourage us to seek the best in any given situation. The reality, however, is that there are multiple and mutually exclusive "bests," and we cannot implement all plausible solutions at a given time. How, then, do we work creatively with profound and seemingly irreconcilable differences in policy, strategy, and tactics among those who share the same social critique and who are moved by the same hopes for justice? As we acknowledge our intrinsic limitations and shortsightedness, we encounter a paradox: *a lack of parity between the moral certainty of our denunciation of existing forms of injustice and our ethically reasonable uncertainty about the justice and long-term feasibility of our cherished alternatives.* For not only are there multiple solutions to singular problems, but any course of action may have devastating unintended consequences. In light of this reality, the ecologists Anna Peterson and Wes Jackson call us to a fallibility-based worldview—an acknowledgment that all that we know, whether through the resources of reason, imagination, intuition, or compassion, is all partial, always vastly exceeded by that which we do not know—the long-term impact, for example, of our agricultural and industrial practices, the ripple effects of changes in social policy, the unpredictable consequences of our attempts to nurture and sustain the generations that depend upon us.[4]

While certainty may at times be a creative delusion, uncertainty is the inescapable matrix of all our problem-solving efforts. As we lead, and as we govern, since we are not tyrants imposing our solutions but participants in a democratic process, it is crucial that we recognize what the philosopher Fred Dallmayr, drawing on Buddhist understandings of emptiness, calls the "hollow or negativity at the heart of democratic practices."[5] Any situation is intrinsically fluid, pregnant with multiple and unpredictable possibilities. Good and ill may emerge from the same action. Even our commitment to justice and peace through the exercise of skillful means may lead in directions and result in consequences we can neither predict nor control.

Let us put these ethical challenges in a larger cultural perspective. I offer a hypothesis for your consideration: we are in a political and artistic moment best characterized not as post-modern but as what Nicolas Bourriaud, the French art critic and curator, and the political theorists Michael Hardt and Antonio Negri call altermodernity. Rather than either the modern imposition of a Western view of human excellence and linear progress, or the multiple fragmentations of post-modern identities and narratives, the altermodern is an emerging global formation, a shift in politics, aesthetics, and culture shaped equally by South America, Asia, Africa, and the West. At the core of the altermodern is a nomadic, dynamic, living out of multiple identities. Many of the ideals of modernity are reclaimed, but are now held in light of postcolonial critiques and in light of the failures of the modernist project.[6]

When Bourriaud introduced the notion of the altermodern and relational aesthetics in 2002, many academics in the US thought that its claims for political relevance were overstated. In a nuanced and insightful essay, Claire Bishop, for example, described Bourriaud's position thoroughly, yet advocated the greater political relevance of antagonistic aesthetics.[7] It is my argument, however, that it is the move from "antagonism" to dynamic, self-critical creativity that is precisely that which is most relevant for humanist ethics and political engagement.

Art and politics in this altermodern moment can be seen as a form of relational aesthetics, an exploration of multiple forms of sociality, of playing the identities that have shaped us, and others. The dynamism of relational aesthetics lies in "learning to inhabit the world in a better way ... The role of artworks is no longer to form imaginary and utopian realities, but *to actually be ways of living and models of action within the existing real*."[8] As Hardt and Negri assert, "the passage from antimodernity to altermodernity is defined not by opposition but by rupture and transformation."[9] This is a political and ethical turn from utopia to microtopias. Drawing on Deleuze and Guattari, Bourriaud claims that microtopias, far from being universal, "serve as the breeding ground for experiments in justice in all its forms."[10] Our political, ethical, and aesthetic task is that of "producing the conditions" where we not only see exploitation and suffering, but where we create alternate, concrete forms of daily practices that embody our ideals of freedom, equality, and flourishing.

Bourriaud names our culture as one shaped by "new intercultural connections" and draws on the botanical analogy of the radicant to describe the dynamism of this global culture. The radicant is "an organism that grows its roots and adds new ones as it advances. To be radicant means setting one's roots in motion, staging them in heterogeneous contexts and formats, denying them the power to completely define one's identity, translating ideas, transcoding images, transplanting behaviors, exchanging rather than imposing."[11]

As we participate, as radicants, in what Felix Guattari calls the "creative uncertainty and outrageous invention" of experiments in justice, we face a stark reality: a shift as big as the switch from an ethic of control to an ethic of risk.[12] The core of our ethical choices is not doing the unambiguously right thing, or, valorizing the prophet as one who points out ethical ambiguities in any course of action. Leadership ethics and political ethics alike call us to a forthright reckoning with the undeniable reality of lesser evils in service of a possible greater good.

Like many other humanists, I understand humanism to be a philosophy and ethos "informed by science, inspired by art, and motivated by human hope and compassion."[13] An altermodern humanist ethics is also grounded in an understanding of creativity itself, whether scientific or artistic, as both foundational to human flourishing, and fundamentally amoral. The energies that ground us, that shape our responses to the opportunities and beauties of life, can be used to heal or harm, to control, exploit or protect and nurture.[14]

THE NATURE AND MEANING OF HUMANISM

I am a mystic, a political activist, a humanist, and an atheist—an odd combination, I grant, but one that I come to naturally.[15] I was raised in a religious tradition in which spirituality was inextricably bound with politics, in which the motive for prayer and service was not guilt or duty, but living fully, deeply, and well. For my parents and grandparents and many members of their churches, life was spirituality and spirituality was life. Service and belief in God did not require sacrifice of individual will, aspirations, or intellect—such religious practice was, rather, the chance to live out the best of one's talents in response to nature, to people, to the particular opportunities for beauty and justice in one's immediate world. Spirituality was that which brought us into full engagement with the world around us.

For my parents, this work took many forms—serving as pastors, farmers, and activists in the liberal wing of the Democratic Party, members of the hospital board, leaders of programs to empower teenagers. Their work was filled with laughter, exuberance, and a delightful absence of fanaticism or self-righteousness. While their political activism and work in the church was grounded in a clear sense of the divine, they were aware that they could be wrong, that it was possible to feel led by the spirit and to misinterpret that leading. They brought two basic criteria, both collective, to their private and communal spirituality: 1) Do these spiritual practices and experiences make us more loving? Do they help us see the worth of everyone? and 2) Do these experiences actually and concretely change how we live?

As a credulous teenager I was fascinated with tales of angels. When I left for college in 1971, one of the stories being commonly recounted was of people picking up a hitchhiker, the hitchhiker telling them that Jesus would soon return to earth, and then the hitchhiker disappearing. I eagerly told my father about these stories, certain that he would be thrilled at the announcement of the imminent return of the messiah. His response, however, was measured and clear. "Well, Sharon, I don't know if people really saw an angel or not. What I would want to know is this—did that encounter change their life? Did it make them a better person?"

I do not believe in God. I know of no concepts, symbols, or images of God, Goddess, gods, or divinity that I find intellectually credible, emotionally satisfying, or ethically challenging in the face of evil and the complexity of life. I do know, however, of spiritual practices that change our lives, that help us see where we are wrong, that propel us to work for justice, that provide a sense of meaning and joy. For my parents and their community, such solace and challenge could be found in daily prayer, in preparing and giving sermons, in individual and collective study and worship, and in physical work with other people—building cabins at the church campgrounds, cooking, cleaning, working together on the concrete tasks that sustain us physically. For me, the same purposes of awareness and gratitude are served through meditation, dance, hearing live music (especially jazz), teaching ethics, and, like my parents, manual labor with and for other people.

Spiritual openness may be sustained by intense physical activity and evoked by meditative awareness. These practices do not guarantee, however, that we will act justly. Profound experiences of connection and spiritual ecstasy can easily fuel self-righteous certainty and exclusivity. But these same experiences may also provide the connections with other people and with nature that motivate us to work for justice, honoring that nature, those people we respect. These practices can enable us to learn where we are wrong in our strategies and actions, can teach us to learn from criticism, and help us to gain the courage to act on our ideals.

HUMANISM IN PRACTICE

There are spiritual practices that are intellectually credible, emotionally comforting, and ethically challenging, habits of individual and collective attention, meditation, reflection, and physical ecstasy that can sustain us as we work for justice, that can promote joy and resilience in the face of life's challenges. I do not think that life makes sense, but I do know that there can be joy and wonder in the service of beauty and justice. I also know that it is possible to respond with wonder, joy, rigor, and creativity to the challenges of enduring security and sustainable peace. Let us now turn to a test case for altermodern humanist ethics, the volatile mix of opportunity, responsibility, and risk in the ongoing uprisings in the Arab world: Arab Spring 2011. Two vignettes and two reports from *The New York Times*:

1. February 20, 2011. Insights into the legacy in Egypt of 18 days in liberation square:

   Omar El-Zuhairy, a 22 year old film director ... [who had] thought of leaving the country, now sees opportunity ... Speaking five days before the ouster of Mubarek, he stated, "My relationship to the country has transformed ... People never used to talk to one another. This has been broken, and this is why I now want to stay—because I have a right to be here. I have a right to my identity, I have a right to this place ... We have already won something."[16]

2. February 15, 2011. Signs of the impact of the Egyptian protests in Bahrain.

   In the village of Beni Jamar, a few hundred demonstrators gathered behind a large sign displaying portraits of Nelson Mandela, the Rev. Dr. Martin Luther King Jr. and Gandhi. They marched toward the road chanting slogans when the police charged in without warning, firing tear gas canisters and rubber bullets into the crowd ... Furious, a young man beside Mr. Mehdi hurled rocks at the police. Mr. Mehdi started screaming: "Don't throw rocks at them. Stop! We have to remain peaceful. We're just here to explain how we feel. We want to make our voices heard. In any case, we don't have a single weapon. The other side has them all."[17]

3. March 20, 2011. European and US forces, with the endorsement of the UN Security Council and the Arab League, begin the imposition of a no-fly zone, and a sustained assault on Libya's air defense systems in order to prevent imminent crimes against humanity.[18]

4. April 7, 2011, Clifford Krauss of *The New York Times* reports on the

increasing repression in Bahrain: "mass arrests, mass firings of government workers, reports of torture and, on Sunday, the forced resignation of the top editor of the nation's one independent newspaper." The
opposition, however, remains committed: "'The people will not give
up,' said Jawad F. G. Fairooz, a leader of Al Wefaq National Islamic
Society, a moderate Shiite party, who resigned in protest last month
from the elected Council of Representatives. 'The government can
keep people silent for a time, but they cannot guarantee that another
uprising will not come at any moment.'"[19]

In the spring of 2011 we witnessed a surge of courageous nonviolence
throughout the Arab world, and have been heartened and inspired by people
standing peacefully for their rights. These struggles are all ongoing, and there
is no quick or easy resolution in sight. It is possible that the forces of nonviolent direct action may lead to a change as momentous and widespread as
the overthrow of repressive Communist governments throughout eastern
Europe. In 2011 there were signs of hope—major reforms in Tunisia, free
elections on March 20 in Egypt to set constitutional reform, and significant
support for the nonviolent protestors by growing numbers of military and
governmental leaders in Yemen.

As the exhilarating work of overthrowing one authoritarian regime is
done, however, the harder work of creating a new, more participatory and
just political order has begun. After the election of Mohamed Morsi of the
Muslim Brotherhood, many of the leaders of the revolt in Egypt acknowledged their failure to have yet initiated such a fundamental political shift.
David Kirkpatrick of *The New York Times* summarized their conclusions:
"Some said they had become too taken with their own fame, distracted by the
news media's attention, and willing to defer to their elders in the Mubarak-
era political opposition. They failed to build a movement that could stand
against either the Muslim Brotherhood or the old elite."[20]

This failure does not mean, however, the end of sustained work for greater
social change. The momentum for transformation that began in the spring of
2011 has been both chastened and deepened. Kirpatrick shares the insights,
and ongoing commitments, of some of the young leaders in Egypt:

"We are the spark that ignites the world; we know how to inflame
things," said Ahmed Maher, 31, a leader of the April 6 Youth
Movement and one of the early organizers. "But when we have a
strong entity that can stand on its own feet—when we can form a
government tomorrow—then we become an alternative." He said
his group was embarking on a five year plan to start building such
a movement.[21]

In spring 2011, while there were signs of promise, there were also signs of ongoing violence. Despite defections, governments continued the violent suppression of peaceful protests in Yemen and Bahrain. There were real threats of grave humanitarian disasters. We heard chilling echoes of Rwanda in the popular dance chants sung by supporters of Colonel Qaddafi: "'House by house, alley by alley,' the catchiest song went, quoting a Qaddafi speech. 'Disinfect the germs from each house and each room.'"[22]

The threats in Libya, in Bahrain, in Yemen were real, and yet, while some supported the use of military force by Europe and the United States, others were unsure if this military intervention was wise. The UN- and Arab League-sanctioned intervention in Libya led to the death of Qaddafi and the overthrow of his government, but the struggle for a more just economic and political order remains. The other options that were in place against Libya—freezing financial assets, sanctions, referral to the International Criminal Court—might they, in time, have also had the desired effects? Are there other options of international intervention that might be created soon, and in our lifetimes?

Let us ponder the truth of President Obama's words, "Peace requires responsibility. Peace entails sacrifice."[23] This is a crucial juncture for the peace movement in the United States. While there is widespread support throughout the world for the "responsibility to protect" and for multilateral humanitarian intervention in the cases of genocide and crimes against humanity, there is an equally widespread dissatisfaction with the legitimacy, morality, and even efficacy of traditional military intervention.[24]

On February 25, 2011, Secretary of Defense Robert Gates unequivocally challenged the wisdom of conventional military action: "In my opinion, any future defense secretary who advises the president to again send a big American land army into Asia, or into the Middle East or Africa should 'have his head examined,' as General MacArthur so delicately put it." Instead, Gates said that the US must foster forms of actions that "prevent festering problems from growing into full blown crises which require costly—and controversial—large scale American military intervention."[25] Gates's stark critique of traditional military action is not unique. It reflects, rather, a growing understanding held by many members of the military. One of the most striking features of the 2007 Army and Marine corps counterinsurgency field manual is a blunt examination of nine "representative paradoxes of counterinsurgency." Colonel Crane, the director of the military history institute at the Army War College and one of the writers of the new doctrine, states that the paradoxes emerge from the ground: "In many ways, this is a bottom-up change ... The young soldiers who had been through Somalia, Haiti, Bosnia, Kosovo, and now Iraq and Afghanistan, understood why we need to do this."[26] Let us examine three of the paradoxes, and ponder their implications:

- *The more force is used, the less effective it is.*
  Using substantial force increases the risk of collateral damage and mistakes, and increases the opportunity for insurgent propaganda.
- *The best weapons for counterinsurgency do not shoot.*
  Often dollars and ballots have more impact than bombs and bullets.
- *Tactical success guarantees nothing.*
  Military actions by themselves cannot achieve success.[27]

In President Obama's Nobel Peace Prize speech, and in his strategy for continued engagement with Afghanistan, we also find a forthright acknowledgment of the limitations of military force. Recall his words from the Nobel speech: "there are two seemingly irreconcilable truths—that war is sometimes necessary, and war at some level is an expression of human folly."[28] Here we have a transformative paradigm shift regarding the nature of power and the limited utility of force: *if we can hear it, if we can hold it, if we can make it real.*

You see, it is not enough for peacemakers to be critics of the cost of war. In my work with conservative students and fellow citizens, I find that many, although they agree with us about the terrible cost of war, are not persuaded by our denunciations of violence and our calls for the peaceful resolution of entrenched conflict. It is not that they doubt either the horror of war, or our compassion and conviction. No—their concerns are more troubling. They suppose that we overestimate the virtue, wisdom, resilience, and competence of peace activists and peacekeepers. They doubt the efficacy and staying power of our alternative approaches to peace. These concerns are not misplaced.

The words of Mahatma Gandhi from 1930 still ring true:

> The law of love will work, just as the law of gravitation will work, whether we accept it or not. Just as a scientist will work wonders out of various applications of the law of nature, even so a man who applies the law of love with scientific precision can work greater wonders ... Only our explorations have not gone far enough and so it is not possible for everyone to see all its workings.[29]

Ponder, as well, these words from 1962, written by the Catholic priest Thomas Merton:

> There can be no question that unless war is abolished the world will remain constantly in a state of madness and desperation in which, because of the immense destructive power of modern weapons, the danger of catastrophe will be imminent ... Christians must become active in every possible way, mobilizing all their resources for the

fight against war ... Peace is to be preached, nonviolence is to be explained as a practical method ... prayer and sacrifice must be used as the most effective spiritual weapons in the war against war, and like all weapons they must be used with deliberate aim: not just with a vague aspiration for peace and security, but against violence and against war.[30]

Although these quotations are familiar to many of us, I wish to highlight an often overlooked aspect of each—Gandhi's advocacy of "scientific precision" and Merton's injunction to use spiritual weapons with "deliberate aim." We saw such aim and precision in many of the nonviolent campaigns in the Arab world. We have yet to see it on a large scale in plausible alternatives to military intervention.

Although the uprisings of the Arab Spring may have seemed spontaneous, they emerged from years of struggle, and from intensive and disciplined study of the techniques of nonviolence. Young activists in Tunisia and Egypt became aware of the strategies of nonviolence through the work of other young activists in Serbia, who themselves had studied and utilized the writing of a venerable scholar of nonviolence, Gene Sharp.

On February 17 *The New York Times* reported the assessment of the importance of Sharp's ideas by Dalia Ziada, an Egyptian blogger and activist who attended trainings led by the International Center on Nonviolent Conflict. Sharp's claim that "advancing freedom takes careful strategy and meticulous planning" is advice that Ms. Ziada said resonated among youth leaders in Egypt. Peaceful protest is best, says Sharp, not for any moral reasons, but because violence provokes autocrats to crack down. "If you fight with violence," Mr. Sharp said, "you are fighting with your enemy's best weapon, and you may be a brave but dead hero."[31]

I first met Gene Sharp in 1981 in Memphis, Tennessee. I was a peace activist, and involved in the nuclear freeze campaign. I had begun the study of nonviolent discipline and tactics, and brought them to the college campus where I was teaching and organizing. In our work, drawing on the teachings of Gandhi and King, we emphasized the moral mandate of nonviolence. Gene Sharp both rattled and deepened our thinking. He made a solidly pragmatic case for nonviolence. He argued that it is folly to use the enemy's best weapon. Repressive regimes want, and even incite violent resistance. Nonviolence, of course, is itself neither easy, nor without risk. What we saw in Bahrain and in Yemen in early 2011 is, tragically, most often the case. Nonviolent resistance is also frequently met with violence and systematic repression. If, however, people are able to remain nonviolent, to have the courage of the protestors in Yemen and Bahrain and Egypt and Tunisia, walking to the police, to the military, chanting, "peaceful, peaceful," they may be able to manifest four striking advantages of nonviolent resistance: "Win national and international sympathy and support; reduce casualties—although hundreds may die, the numbers are less than in all out civil war; induce mutiny of the governments' military and police forces; and attract maximum participation in the nonviolent struggle from all sectors of society."[32]

We saw these advantages as well, with the resignation of governmental officials and newscasters from state controlled newspapers, and military and police forces refusing to fire on their own people. In the long term, nonviolence may well be more practical than violence, for it uses strengths that the opponent lacks. It also builds the internal and external courage and discipline required to transform a repressive society to a more open and democratic system of government.

What is it that gives people the strength to defy a government and congregate in public squares, refusing to disperse, refusing to return to life as normal? What gives military and police officers the strength to defy orders to kill their fellow citizens? Gene Sharp argues that the strength to resist is grounded in basic human nature, not exceptional virtue. In fact, he highlights a central role in nonviolent direct action of simple human stubbornness. In that lecture on nonviolence in 1981 he asked us to ponder the will of a two-year-old child, defiantly refusing to eat some unwanted food, and the inability of a parent to force them to swallow the distasteful meal placed before them. According to Sharp, a people may not be able to overthrow a tyrant directly but they can withhold obedience and thereby remove the sources of power. He challenged us to see and accept our power—our ability to refuse to cooperate in the maintenance and operation of unjust economic and political systems.[33]

How do we take these lessons from the nonviolence of the Arab Spring, and bring them to ongoing threats of genocide and crimes against humanity? What can we do when humanitarian crises seem imminent and international support is essential? Let us return to the words of President Obama: "War is sometimes necessary, and war at some level is always an expression of human folly." I would add to those words another warning: "Criticism of our government's actions may sometimes be necessary, and criticism alone is always an expression of human folly." The question for us is as pointed as for those who advocate the use of military force: "If war is not the answer, what is the answer to genocide, to massacre, to grave threats to human security?"[34]

President Obama, in his speech on March 28, 2011, stated that we were facing an imminent crisis in Libya:

> Gaddafi declared that he would show "no mercy" to his own people. He compared them to rats, and threatened to go door to door to inflict punishment. In the past, we had seen him hang civilians in

the streets, and kill over a thousand people in a single day. Now, we saw regime forces on the outskirts of the city. We knew that if we waited one more day, Benghazi—a city nearly the size of Charlotte—could suffer a massacre that would have reverberated across the region and stained the conscience of the world.[35]

In this situation there were two stark choices. First, do we wait for mass graves and the slaughter of civilians, or, do we act to prevent such atrocities? Second, if we decide to act, whether to prevent or stop mass slaughter, what are our options? William Schulz, President and CEO of the Unitarian Universalist Service Committee and former Executive Director of Amnesty International, poses the question clearly: "How does the international community, within the constraints provided by our religious and ethical traditions, use its power to prevent or stop or punish grievous crimes against humanity?"[36] Are we caught in a struggle between two equally devastating choices—either the tragic human and environmental toll of warfare, or standing by while millions are displaced, and thousands killed? Although the choices may seem grim, there are other options, ways of responding that allow us to act decisively to protect civilians from genocide and crimes against humanity, yet actions that do not take us into the spiral of all-out war, with its devastating toll on civilians as well as military forces.

Given the dangers of armed resistance and military failure, what is the best way to prevent genocide and respond to crimes against humanity? We have an interlocking set of problems, ones clearly manifest in the international response in Libya, Syria, Yemen, and Bahrain: responses that are ad hoc, rather than carefully planned and coordinated, and responses that lack a clear international consensus regarding either the conditions for international intervention or the best means of intervening.

Under the leadership of Kofi Annan, the international community began to address this complex set of issues. When a government cannot or will not protect its citizens from rape, mass murder, and other crimes against humanity, does the international community have the responsibility to protect those peoples from ongoing catastrophe? Within many circles of the international community, the answer is increasingly a resounding "yes." There is, however, an equally widespread and deeply held recognition of the significant dangers in a too-easy rush to humanitarian intervention, such as that it will serve as a mask for neo-colonial intervention. In order to examine these dual concerns, an equal sense of the imperative for, yet the danger of, multilateral humanitarian intervention, the Canadian government established the International Commission on Intervention and State Sovereignty in September 2000. The Commission comprised twelve members from Australia, Algeria, Canada, the United States, Russia, Germany, South Africa, Philippines, Switzerland,

Guatemala, and India. The members were Gareth Evans and Mohamed Sah-
noun, co-chairs, and Gisele Cote-Harper, Lee Hamilton, Michael Ignatieff,
Vladimir Lukin, Klaus Naumann, Cyril Ramaphosa, Fidel Ramos, Cornelio
Sommaruga, Eduardo Stein, and Ramesh Thakur.[37]

The Commission published its findings, *The Responsibility to Protect*, in
December 2001. In this document we find a compelling articulation of an
emerging political consensus about the responsibility of states to protect
their citizens from mass murder, systematic rape, and other crimes against
humanity, and the responsibility of the international community to inter-
vene when they do not. The ground of the consensus was clear: "We want
no more Rwandas."[38]

Once the decision is made that the international community must act,
what are the best means of responding? While there may be both willingness
to act and a widespread international demand for action, as was the case in
Libya, we lack standing peacekeeping forces, ready to be quickly deployed
in a coherent, well-planned manner, suitable to the situation at hand. While
more than 150 heads of state at the UN Summit in 2005 affirmed the responsibility of the international community to protect people from crimes against
humanity, they did not create the institutional means and procedures to
respond to those crimes.[39]

There is increasing international consensus for the imperative of establishing standing, well-trained, multilateral peacekeeping forces. As Kofi
Annan stated so clearly, "The United Nations is the only fire brigade that has
to acquire a fire engine after the fire has broken out."[40] People throughout
the world are now working to rectify this problem. Organizing efforts are
well under way for the creation of a United Nations Emergency Peace Service (UNEPS). Such a service would be constituted by up to 18,000 trained
peacekeepers, and would be capable of being deployed within forty-eight
hours in a crisis situation. This force would be recruited from throughout the
world, and would be characterized by the following seven principles:

1. It will be a permanent standing force based at three UN-designated
   sites.
2. It will be capable of rapid response, able to respond to an emergency
   within 48 hours.
3. It will be coherently organized under a unified UN command.
4. It will involve as many as 18,000 personnel, individually recruited from
   many different countries and demonstrating skills in conflict resolution, humanitarian assistance, law enforcement and other peacekeeping capabilities.
5. UNEPS personnel will receive comprehensive, expert training in
   peacekeeping with an emphasis on human rights and gender issues.

6. UNEPS will supplement existing UN and regional peacekeeping operations, providing another tool to support international efforts to end
genocide and crimes against humanity.
7. UNEPS will be financed through the regular UN budget.[41]

The statute for the creation of UNEPS lays out other essential characteristics of such a standing force. UNEPS will be based in three regions, each
with rigorous training in the culture and history of the area served, and all
members of UNEPS will be required to be fluent in at least two UN languages. While deployment can occur within forty-eight hours, the limits
of such an intervention would be six months. Six months may well not
be enough time to both stop massacres and allow the beginnings of what
is always a lengthy period of political reform. In those cases, the work of
UNEPS may need to be followed by the longer-term deployment of peacekeeping forces, under the auspices of either the UN or regional security
forces. In each case, however, the range of tasks is the same, and it reflects a
paradigm shift in regard to security and the use of armed force. While force
may well be necessary, it is never sufficient. Such operations are, therefore,
significantly different from waging war, where the objective is to destroy the
enemy's military capabilities. Here the goal is to protect human lives with as
little force as possible.

The international response to the humanitarian crises in Libya shows the
need for such planning. We have seen both the imperative and the difficulties in creating an ad hoc response to a grave humanitarian crisis:

- the lack of an established unified command and the need to create
such structures once the response began;
- uncertainty about the best tactics for preventing crimes against
humanity;
- confusion about the distinction between UN-sanctioned international
humanitarian intervention and international military intervention on
the side of the rebel forces;
- lack of clarity about the time limited scope of this type of international
intervention.

UNEPS is designed to circumvent just those problems—standing peacekeeping forces with a clear mandate, with advance preparation, training,
and support. While I concur that it was justifiable for the UN to authorize
an international intervention to prevent a massacre that would, to quote
President Obama, "stain the conscience of humanity," we can craft better
responses for the future. If UNEPS were in place in March 2011, the UN
Security Council would have been able to authorize the deployment within

forty-eight hours of standing peacekeeping forces, based and trained in the Arab region. The peace service would have had a unified command and expert training in the protection of civilians from humanitarian crises. The fact that it was not a military force would give weight to the assertion of NATO and the United States that they were not in Libya to join the rebel struggle against Qaddafi, but were there to protect civilians from assault, whether from rebels or from Qaddafi's forces.

The distinction here is essential to keep in mind and implement in practice: peacekeeping forces do not have the objective of defeating an enemy but have, rather, the complex task of clearing the space where negotiations can either resume or begin. Such interventions are more like community policing than military campaigns, requiring careful coordination with civil society, and in order to restore a society's internal sense of order. And, as is the case with community policing, successful intervention requires knowing well the community in which one protects the lives of civilians and maintains security.

Even with a standing peace service, we must acknowledge a hard truth: it will not be possible to respond with equal force to every humanitarian crisis. Intervention may be blocked by the UN Security Council for political reasons, or there may simply be a lack of resources to respond equally to devastation in the Congo, the Ivory Coast, Syria, Yemen, Bahrain, and Libya.

Furthermore, there is a widespread recognition that the claim of humanitarian intervention could be used as a mask for neo-colonial domination, intervening more for the interest of the intervening state, than to protect people at grave risk. In addition to these salient dangers, the International Commission addressed yet a third risk of international peacekeeping: "Intervention in the domestic affairs of states is undoubtedly often harmful. It can destabilize the order of states, while fanning ethnic or civil strife. When internal forces seeking to oppose a state believe that they can generate outside support by mounting campaigns of violence, the internal order of all states is potentially compromised." And, "here we have a strong assertion of the imperative of the Hippocratic oath: 'First, do no harm.'"[42]

In light of these very real dangers, the Commission provides a clear description of the moral and political dilemma that we face as global citizens:

> If [the international community] stays disengaged, there is the risk of becoming complicit bystanders in massacre, ethnic cleansing, and even genocide. If the international community intervenes, it may or may not be able to mitigate such abuses. But even when it does, intervention sometimes means taking sides in intra-state conflicts. Once it does so, the international community may only be aiding in the further fragmentation of the state system.[43]

Given these very real and ongoing dangers, let us think back on the situations we are addressing: massacre, ethnic cleansing, genocide. In each of these cases, as in the case of the Holocaust, we do well to heed the warning of ethicist David Gushee that the "do no harm of the anguished bystander helps the perpetrator far more than the victim of injustice."[44] If we follow Schulz's challenge, providing ethically and politically rigorous guidance for the use of power, we find ourselves in a moral and political universe limned so clearly by ethicists such as Dietrich Bonhoeffer and political leaders like Nelson Mandela. The Commission itself provided stark guidance, guidance grounded in the imperative of recognizing the dangers and mixed motives that attend multilateral intervention, and the acceptance of a very pragmatic goal:

> National and world politics will never be consistent or pure in heart ... Yet what is the price of recognizing this standard reality? Should selective military interventions be condemned as immoral and in violation of the bedrock principle of the universality of human rights? ... While aspiring to the ideal of consistency ... the inevitable double standards of state practice should not be an excuse for paralysis ... even occasionally doing the right thing well is certainly preferable to doing nothing routinely.[45]

In a letter signed June 11, 2007, thirty-eight organizations wrote in support of the resolution before the United States House that calls for the establishment of a United Nations Emergency Service. Among the non-governmental organizations were several religious organizations: the Unitarian Universalist Association of Congregations; the United Church of Christ, Justice and Witness Ministries; the Global Ministries of the Christian Church (Disciples of Christ and the United Church of Christ); the Presbyterian Church (USA), Washington Office. Such work is also supported by some members of the historical peace churches, long known for their support of nonviolent direct action and opposition to the use of violence. In *Ethics for the New Millennium*, the Dalai Lama advocates the formation of a globally administered police force, with the mandate "to safeguard justice, communal security, and human rights worldwide." He even imagines that there might be a time in which such forces would gradually replace standing armies. He acknowledges that this ultimate goal might not be achieved within our lifetimes, but reminds us that we have initiated this promising work: "Maybe this generation will not live to see it. But we are already accustomed to seeing United Nations troops deployed as peacekeepers. We are also beginning to see the emergence of a consensus that under certain circumstances it may be justifiable to use them in a more interventionist way."[46]

Does this acceptance of the judicious use of force in the case of humanitarian intervention mean that the criticism of violence, its inconsistent application, its grave cost to perpetrators and victims, is irrelevant or invalid? Not at all. In the case of the emerging global security system, while the use of some forms of force is accepted as necessary, this reliance on limited violence does not have the valence and power that it does in either holy war or even just war, where force is seen as the apotheosis of strength and power. In the case of multifaceted, strategic peace-building, while force may at times be necessary, it is never sufficient. The value of peacekeeping is not in resolving a conflict, but in providing the space in which enduring security and sustainable peace may be created through the long-term nonviolent work of obtaining comprehensive political assent and participation.

In our ongoing work as peacemakers, let us return to our core ethical challenge, that of reckoning with the undeniable reality of actual lesser evils as we pursue a possible greater good. We can affirm with Gandhi and King the moral power of nonviolence, and affirm with Sharp the realism that acknowledges the long-term cruelty, folly, and futility of violence. It is extremely difficult to break cycles of violence and counter-violence. In our work for peace, we may be outmaneuvered and overpowered, our efforts to transform a situation derailed by the depth of fear and hatred, and by the terrible beauty of community narratives sustained by exclusion, revenge, and violence.

May we have the discipline to create institutions that move us closer to a genuine rule of law between nations, to a judicious unself-righteous acceptance of the difficult choices before us. May we have the courage to work together for peace.

5. HUMANIST OUTLAWS:
THINKING RELIGION/LIVING HUMANISM

Monica R. Miller

> There are kids committing suicide. They're already being told they're going to
> Hell. They're thinking, well, I might as well finish it ...
> —Alannah Caldwell, 21, The Attic Youth Center

> You know, a lot of people just think it's, you know, "Oh, they're just a bunch
> of rowdy, you know, ghetto, just heathen and thugs." No, what we are, are
> oppressed.   —Dragon, *Rize* (documentary, Lions Gate Entertainment 2005)

Over the past several decades, hip hop culture and its various manifestations have marked out the development of an organic life orientation for young people across the globe. Scholars in the humanities have given deep thought to the religious, spiritual, and existential dimensions of hip hop. Although the recent burgeoning of religion in hip hop scholarship has given this area of study a more "legitimate" and "spiritual" face, analysis has often been confined to Christian theological notions. On the flip side, and with few exceptions, more pragmatic life philosophies, such as humanism, have done little to come to grips with changing contours of religion in culture, especially among communities of color. In other words, few scholars have given thought to humanism as a possible religious option and the types of sources that would benefit the growth and development of such worldview. What does humanism look like today among marginal youth and their cultural productions?

This chapter explores the new look of humanism through cultural productions such as hip hop and youth culture (here I am exploring the "effects" of humanism; I do not suggest that young people are making conscious commitments to a philosophy of humanism). In essence, through cultural production, I carve out the new look of humanism today, what it is (that which I call an "outlaw humanism"), and why it matters.

The two quotations above emerge from within radically different contexts, yet speak to the burgeoning realities of the austere sociopolitical conditions in which marginal youth of color find themselves today. On one hand, a young person of color highlights recent attention to the proliferation of suicide among gay teens, suggesting that when one is told they're going to hell why not go ahead and finish it? On the other, a young black male who is part of a growing dance culture called "krumping" in South Central, Los Angeles, gives voice to the dominant perception of postindustrial urban youth bodies as nihilistic and out of bounds. The concept of "difference" affects these competing narratives, where the seemingly connected signifiers of sexuality, race, and class both separate and bind. What is clear is that these two marginalized bodies are not only aware of their social positioning but express similar understandings of the dangers and perils of hegemonic ideologies, often religious in nature. Between the place of "Hell" and the embodiment of the "Heathen," young black and brown bodies, bearing the marks and traces of the effects of social inequality, have been condemned to social and physical death before their time. This should spark both concern and alarm—could refiguring and rethinking what humanism is and why it matters assist in addressing these social concerns? In a recently published article for *Religion News Service* I suggested "overwhelmingly" that non-theism is flourishing among young African Americans today, adding that many of them express "'an inherited religiosity' that pays lip service to faith to appease family members and maintain status in their communities, which are sometimes overwhelmingly religious."[1]

Throughout the religious, social, and political institutions of our society youth bodies and the cultural life-worlds which they inhabit are perpetually othered in areas such as theology, policy, and the law, to name a few. LGBTQ (lesbian, gay, bisexual, transgender, and queer) teens are told "It Gets Better," to proffer hope in the midst of darkness, yet many find resolution not in the law, cliché slogans, or institutions of religion, but rather through the cultural ingenuity produced in and through their own bodies—a sort of "faith in the flesh." In other words, bodies become the main instrument of cope and release among emergent cultural practices and productions. While youth such as these are often unaware of their humanist sensibilities in rhetoric and practice, their hope more often than not resides in their flesh alone. Remixing humanism (as faith in the flesh) matters because young black and brown bodies are dying way to quickly—way too young. In other words, I am suggesting that we give attention to humanism not only a rational philosophy of the mind (as suggested by Enlightenment ideations), but also, a way of being in the world that is *embodied* and culturally relevant for our contemporary moment. If we truly want to understand the new face and look of humanism today and why it matters, we must shift our attention to under-interrogated cultural spaces and milieus.

For the purposes of this chapter, I'd like to suggest that we think about humanism as a form of survival: an orientation to the world that sometimes occurs in unintentional and unconscious ways, especially for marginalized subjects. I refer to this embodied human-centered philosophy as "faith in the flesh": a type of faith highly visible in material cultural production. While academicians and the larger public alike show much investment in conversations such as "The Black Church Dead",[2] the titillation and obsession with the state of Christianity within and among African American communities not only often sidetracks more pressing concerns, but does little justice to the changing contours of black faith, especially among young people today. Studies across the board show that while youth of color (over and against white and Hispanic youth) espouse high rates of subjective religiosity (often expressed as Christian in nature), attention to non-institutional cultural practices has been slim (by "espouse," I mean that these studies often point towards a certain kind of "lip service" to religious beliefs, such as "I believe in God" or "I attend church often"). A peek into the life-worlds of young people offers a glimpse into a thugged-out human-centered philosophy and practice of life that highlights a "faith in the flesh," where the utmost importance and utility is placed in the raw ingenuity of the body. This faith in the flesh is not consciously articulated as a coherent guiding orientation among youth (that is, if you are looking for certain young people to "confess" or "come out" as humanists, atheists, agnostics, or freethinkers), but their cultural practices often point towards a growing shift in orientation: one that moves away from their traditional inheritances of Christian faith (or belief in god) towards a human-centered philosophy of life that is difficult to isolate as entirely one worldview or another. Within and among the shape-shifting, tricky, and witty cultural economy of youth culture—humanism abounds in the fleshy materiality of the body—I would argue that contemporary expressions of humanism, for marginal communities, is faith in the flesh; not faith in a theological sense, but faith in corporeality itself.

This chapter addresses the manner in which this "thugged-out" humanism emerges from the constraints of postindustrial urban environments. In these spaces of constraint and possibility, shit is often turned into sugar by the power of both mind and body. This chapter gives attention to the dizzying world of material culture among marginal youth of color and considers the possible subjugated humanist dimensions of such modalities.

WHY CULTURAL PRODUCTION FOR THE STUDY OF HUMANISM?

The landscape of youth religious participation is an under-engaged area across both the humanities and the social sciences. On the humanities side, we lack empirical data on the changing religious life-worlds of youth and religion, while existing empirical work in the social sciences suggests that institutional religion buffers criminality and delinquency[3]—a brand of engagement I refer to as "buffering transgression," a process that both

conceives and privileges religion as an institutional and moral force responsible for creating pro-social behavior.[4] Social science literature on youth and
religion often keeps the concept of religion arrested to institutional confines, yet, on the other hand, there persists a common "legitimation" trend
that collapses youth cultural forms with hopes of democratic and prophetic
sensibilities (such as constructing rappers as Christian agents of liberation).
More often than not this approach is couched within a "prophetic" understanding of black faith. These types of claims are often rooted in a linear
understanding of progress and placed within a constructed propheticism of
African American origins, rooted in Christian thought.

Scholars such as Anthony B. Pinn have worked hard to give articulation
to alternative religious options, such as humanism, within African American communities. He has given consistent consideration to the humanist
sensibilities of the rugged terrain of black cultural production and popular culture, especially rap music. Dominant interpretations emanating from
religious and theological studies often analyze religious dimensions of youth
culture in a Christian fashion (sometimes explicitly, and other times implicitly through the reliance on Christian themes and categories), thus giving
little attention to the kind of work that Pinn, among others, has so consistently argued for. That is, as Pinn suggests:

> a theological stance on moral evil requires an alternate religious
> system—African American humanism. This is not meant to dismiss
> Christian approaches out of hand, rather, to broaden the possibili-
> ties, the religious terrain, and to foster conversation concerning lib-
> erating ways of addressing the problem of evil.[5]

Taking up cultural production for the study of black religion in public life is
not a new approach: creative and ingenious musical and artistic sensibilities
such as the blues and gospel have proved a solid and relevant way to study
the changes and patterns of black religiosity across time and space.

Despite recent attention to cultural productions such as hip hop, notions
of respectability and moral panics[6] have often prevented sustained attention to what some sectors of society have labeled deviant and criminal in
nature. Relaxing moral judgment (such as deviance) of such cultural forms
allows for a more robust peak into the humanist sensibilities of "outlaw"
cultural practices. And while the law—both judicial and theological—continues to depict black popular culture in general as being aberrant and void
of any moral edges, a refocused vision proves otherwise. Youth across racial,
ethnic, classed, gendered, and geographical lines of difference are continually declining in dominant religious membership and participation, but
this does not suggest that new ways of being, seeing, and believing are not

cultivated, or have persisted in unexcavated ways. On the contrary: although religious rhetoric sometimes contradicts the logic of their cultural practices in fragmented ways, youth cultural practices seemingly highlight a growing humanist tendency and orientation, albeit not succinctly articulated.

The tricky part of researching the life-worlds of youth is that sometimes what they claim to "believe" (rhetoric) is proved otherwise in close attention to their lived realities. Earlier in this chapter, I suggested that current empirical data reveals higher rates of "religiosity" and claims to belief for African American youth compared to their white and Hispanic counterparts. While such data may prove true, such statements do not tell the whole story of how belief is practiced and performed outside of institutions (which often defies or challenges their very own claims to belief). What is more, empirical research on youth and religion argues that religious participation in an institutional sense buffers and militates against delinquency, criminal activity, and immoral behavior, particularly for African American youth.[7] Studies such as these do not account for alternative cultural practices such as hip hop, the mode of cultural production with global reach. For example, Christian Smith's National Study of Youth and Religion[8] suggests that youth attending churches have lower rates of teen pregnancy, sex before marriage, and alcohol and drug consumption; that is, religious activity in churches become responsible for creating pro-social behavior using the practice of Christianity as the moral police. While many, such as policy-makers, applaud the "buffering transgression" hypothesis as affirmative and inherently positive, I suggest that studies such as these are limiting and symbolically violent and ultimately deny the range of youth cultural production. These one-sided evangelical studies continue in the denial of human flourishing and revolution. They seek to make docile those bodies that have been othered and labeled as out of bounds. These types of claims maintain dominance of Christian churches and force a rather narrow view of what constitutes the religious. What researchers do not realize is that religious rhetoric (talk about belief) does not always connote belief, as such. For young people, belief and religiosity are not articulated in a vacuum; it very much reflects the political economy of social inequality through familial and societal inheritance.

The performativity of religion in culture extends beyond the walls of faith institutions. This kind of stretching is a must in order to include nontraditional rituals and cultural practices. Rhetorical claims to belief are often residual products of earlier forms of socialization inherited in the home, community, and larger society. This is best understood more generally through the process of inheritance: a young person born into a religious household adopts religious language to describe their social world. This process, especially at younger ages, is passively consumed as tradition and habit; this is the process referred to as social inheritance. As one is born into the world, beliefs and practices become inscribed onto the child: this is the process of appropriation that allows for possibility, but also a process that through life becomes utilized, recast, doubted, revisited, and remade. It is the latter which I find not only interesting but compelling for the study of cultural production and religion in general.[9]

I want to suggest that a motif of "faith in the flesh," as a remixed humanist orientation (a *thugged-out* humanism), is a growing trend across African American youth culture today. Attention to marginal cultural production robustly highlights this reality.

GIVE 'EM FAITH: HUMANISM AS COVERT/OVERT PROTECTION FOR LGBTQ YOUNG PEOPLE

I would be remiss to discuss "marginal" youth without mentioning LGBTQ youth of color, not only because of their marginality *within* marginality (in terms of race and sexuality), but also for the ways in which a long tradition of cultural practices continues to provide community. Humanism, as a life orientation, has ability to create resilience among LGBTQ youth of color and potential to change the political landscape from which they come. While black youth may espouse higher rates of religiosity, we can infer that a large number of queer young people are included in these numbers. The seldom recognized, rugged humanism embedded in youth culture is connected to the ways in which humanism is understood and defined. In other words, as humanism continues to thrive, it must likewise develop cultural relevance to constituents outside of its normative purview. In 2010, the American Center for Progress reported that, "There are approximately 1.6 million to 2.8 million homeless young people in the United States, and estimates suggest that disproportionate numbers of those youth are gay, lesbian, bisexual, or transgender";[10] disproportionate numbers also remain alarmingly high within the context of schools. One could infer the plethora of struggles these young people face in traversing faith institutions such as black churches. Using their cultural life-worlds and creative practices, how might humanism as "faith in the flesh" provide a religious option to young people who struggle to find a more equitable and relevant faith or religiosity? A "faith in the flesh" notion of humanism not only holds possibility as one such option, but also provides a space by which to address pressing political concerns of this community.

As a prior board member of The Attic Youth Center in Philadelphia, Pennsylvania, it is my experience that many LGBTQ young people have troubled relationships with religious institutions in our society through lack of affirmation of their sexuality or through symbolically violent theologies that are unwelcoming to their sexual lives. This type of marginalization has potential to exacerbate disproportionate rates of suicide, a type of nihilism related to self-worth, increase in drug use, or homelessness. As the afore-mentioned quotation from a young lesbian at the start of this chapter implies, once you internalize the futile fight for your own righteousness, what then is left to live for? As a strategy of survival hoards of LGBTQ youth of color may be forced to leave religion behind. Community then becomes forged in other ways through cultural practices specific to the community, such as drag or ballroom culture. That is not to say that these practices are solely confined or relegated to the "queer" community. We must, however, raise the question of the type of psychological displacement that these young people experience and face, and the ways in which religious options have failed in light of their social circumstances. Scholars such as Susan Driver have argued that distinct cultural practices and performances (such as ballroom culture) have carved out a unique and robust space of resistance and play for LGBTQ youth.[11] It is undeniable that institutions of American society have failed "the least of these": religious spaces, symbolically violent media, and het-eronormative educational institutions (by proxy) have contributed towards the social death of queer youth (and people) in general. Yet resilience still abounds, and making do takes over in cultural forms: the body and the per-formance of the body remain central. Cultural practices such as ballroom[12] and drag culture provide more than community and belonging; they also manufacture a type of faith (not in a theological sense, but faith understood as possibility) that possibly provides cathartic release and hope. In my own experience of working with LGBTQ youth of color in Philadelphia alone, these young people, despite their negative experiences with religion, yearn for something of its kind.

Across the United States, particularly in urban areas, ballroom culture remains an energetic beat that gives shape to the LGBTQ youth of color: whether onlooker or participator, this culture continues to thrive in signifi-cance. Documentaries such as *In the Life: Documentary Stories from the Gay Experience* suggest that ballroom culture not only provides community and aspiration, but also assists in political mobilization. This is testimony to the ways in which marginal youth of color in general have struggled to carve out spaces of "play" among cracks of oppression in a world of concrete. At The Attic Youth Center for example, Creative Action Groups (CAGs) are offered free of service to LGBTQ young people and provide opportunities to take part in art forms like "vogueing." In ballroom culture, the body is the main prop and costumes and make-up allow young people to perform and to remake and embrace identity. While certain institutions in society have dealt LGBTQ youth social death by way of exclusion, emergent cultural art forms have, in some ways, provided life, recognition, and acceptance. It is possible that some young people have traded and replaced the burdens of faith institutions with more flexible, sex-positive, life-affirming cultural spaces. This could, perhaps, be religious for some.

Again, the body is central here and the freedom to express oneself sensually is not prohibited. The abundance of life determination is present in ballroom culture. These types of cultural practices performed by LGBTQ youth of color exemplify a type of embodied humanism as "faith in the flesh" by encouraging creativity, resilience, and the use of their own imaginations without the restrictive boundaries of heteronormativity and other hegemonic ideologies.

These ideas are, of course, not divorced from the political: there is a way in which this brand of humanism, as described in this chapter, can be read as the *effects* of larger structures of denial and violence (a forced space). I'd like to suggest that humanism, as a "faith in the flesh," can result out of default by exclusion while also providing a space of creativity, possibility, and flexibility.

In a land of plurality it is ludicrous that religion be central to any debate surrounding the most important political issues facing us today. And yet, religion must not be discounted as a valid way in which marginalized bodies have sought resolution and liberation, especially among communities of color. Perhaps a reformulation of healthier visions and options of the religious, such as humanism, could prove fruitful as a space that takes seriously political issues such as LGBTQ youth homelessness while also providing a sense of cohesion. Making concerns of the body central to humanism might be a more equitable way of addressing perennial issues of LGBTQ young people of color. Attention to alternative expressions of humanism—even those that remain implicitly embodied and practiced— holds the possibility of attention to concerns of under-represented constituents, more generally.

While youth of color may espouse the highest rates of religiosity (rhetorical and subjective) among their peers,[13] what is often practiced in the body through cultural production defies and challenges the very religious sentiments they seem to express. A focus on the "body" invariably expresses, exposes, and critiques the political sphere and constricting measures such as religion. The body not only becomes a sphere of mobility, utility, and expression, but it likewise affords an opportunity to express a rugged hope in materiality. The opportunity to rethink a culturally relevant iteration of humanism subsequently allows for a rethinking of its divergent expressions across lines of difference. This community, I believe, has without explicit and conscious articulation acknowledged that when community functions as a guiding concern and ethos, a sense of self and belonging begin to take shape. A reflexive and contemporary humanism that takes seriously the cultural contexts and products of marginalized sectors of society—even those that do not consciously articulate humanism as a guiding principle—holds great potential for the relevance of humanism in the twenty-first century.

DO FOR SELF: KRUMP CULTURE AS EMBODIED HOPE AND CATHARTIC RELEASE

In and around 2005, world-renowned fashion photographer David La-Chapelle, while on set for a Christina Aguilera video shoot in Hollywood, stumbled upon a new hip-hop-inspired urban dance form taking South Central, Los Angeles by storm. Curious about what large groups of young black men and women were doing with the twisting and contorting of their bodies at lightning speed, LaChapelle embarked on a journey that would culminate in a documentary entitled *Rize* (2005). This emerging dance culture from the worn concrete of Los Angeles, California reflects both creativity and constraints of oppression. In other words, youth in this film talk about krump dancing as a spontaneous and not so calculated art that emerges from social inequality and structural limitation. With few resources to create spaces of supplementary education, such as art and dance classes, these youth take matters in their own hands by creating a dance form that would not only radically change their social environment, but would, in unexpected ways, philosophically alter their existential and religious sensibilities away from dominant perceptions of empirical studies that suggest a majority of young black people find their hope in black churches. Here hope remains in the body housed in the urban concrete of America's ghettos.

Krump dancing appears to occur spontaneously. The youth in this film suggest that this form cannot be rehearsed nor learned: an ethic of "authentic struggle" houses and grounds the motivation for getting "krump." In other words, they suggest that one has to live a particular kind of struggle and structural limitation, even existential absurdity, in order to be "krump." They mention that almost every social space in society has rejected them, so they make use of the only element left: their bodies as a response to evil, pain, hurt, and despair. The infrastructure of the urban concrete has replaced the "safety" of church pews, the very space where violence and social death lurks. In krump culture, black and brown bodies become the main instrument in channeling anger, rage, and the hurts of life. Not only is this dance form articulated as a mechanism of release, but it is also scripted as the main site and terrain of struggle. In this sense, the hope produced by dancing black bodies doesn't just become a mode of cathartic release of social anxiety; likewise, it performs a theatrics of struggle and injustice. The dance form is, then, both ingenious and an effect, concurrently.

No fancy theological or religious codes govern this dance culture, only a sense of "making do."[14] The fast-paced and in-your-face warrior-like style of krump dance is a reminder that while such bodies may be fixed by inequity, these very same bodies are not pathologically nihilistic nor fully condemned to social death. Dance then becomes a reminder and critique of marginalization, and yet through rugged movement and knee-jerk body movements, new possibilities are created. This possibility, however, is rooted in the body where survival and hope abound (and yet, remain threatened) across the landscape of the urban ghetto. Dancing in the streets, at parks, and on corners is a visceral embodied protest of failing policy, political systems, and social spaces such as faith-based institutions.

The human-centered manufactured zones of significance of krumping are indeed, to borrow from social theorist Michel de Certeau, a poetic way of "making do."[15] The raw materials that make up the uniqueness of this subculture are not necessarily chosen freely; they are products of social inequality and the raced and classed struggle of American society. In the beginning of the film, one krumper, Dragon, articulates his notion of "do for self" when he states:

> If you're drowning and there's nothing around for help but a board floating, you're gonna reach out for that board floating, you're gonna reach out for that board and this was our board. We floated abroad and we built us a big ship and we are going to sail into the dance world, the art world, and we are gonna take it by storm.[16]

When Dragon explicates this art of "doing for self" he uses the metaphorical analogy of krumping as a "board"—a raw material from which they would sail—he continues by saying, "this is our belief, this is not a trend, let me repeat, this is not a trend."[17] Dragon's use of belief here is curious and telling; he wants the world to know that krumping holds a considerable amount of weight in his life. While Dragon might have something more in mind through his use of belief, he is also aware that the body, if only for a moment, can provide relief from the angst of social life on the underside of capitalism. This momentary relief is in *Rize* channeled through flesh and human activity. I would not suggest that krump culture has metaphysical dimensions that point beyond human activity—krump culture is, I believe, a highly humanist art form. Traditional religious language might sometimes be used to give shape to their thoughts about what krump is and means for their lives; I suggest, at best, this dance form provides a mode of survival and coping.

Herein emerges the humanist dimensions of this dance phenomenon where the black body is front and center as a response to social misery and lack of neighborhood resources. Krump culture does not provide an alternate realm of reality that takes these youth outside of their social conditions of existence: nothing metaphysical or supernatural occurs. On the flip side, humanism abounds as that which places the body, and therefore community, at the center locus of practice. While god, churches, mosques, and schooling perhaps have failed these young people, they look to the body for hope, acknowledging and safeguarding that which remains perpetually threatened. The social contagion and antagonism of the black body provides a social resolution to life's hurts, pains, and sorrows. And while faith institutions such as black churches across the American landscape conjure new ways to maintain youth membership, these youth are, alternatively, finding expression of societal constraints in the very materiality of their own flesh. For example, Dragon suggests in the film:

> There is a spirit in the midst of krumping. We don't have after school programs when you don't want to do football, because that's pretty much the only thing that you can do in the inner-city … we're all thought of to be sports players. … Is there something else for us to do? So what we did is a group of us got together and we invented this [krump dancing] … A lot of people think it's just "Oh, they're just a bunch of rowdy, you know, just ghetto, heathen, thugs." No, what we are, are oppressed."[18]

While Dragon uses the language of "spirit" to describe the kind of kinetic energy felt when krumping, he boldly states that krumping was created in response to societal perceptions (and realities) often racial in nature. I suggest that the body in *Rize* takes on multiple meanings, such as creating new products in the face of little resources, a way to release life's hurts, sorrows, and pains, and lastly, an embodied critique and performativity of social inequality and constraint. Above all, krumping is about surviving against all odds and releasing social pain through the materiality of one's body. Despite the title of the film, krumpers are not able to "rise" above their social circumstances; rather, they are able to creatively express in and through their bodies the struggles they face in everyday life. The floating board that Dragon reached out for was a glimpse of hope in the holler—this board was possibility, creativity, and vision—seeing "something" out of "nothing."

In a June 22, 2005 interview with Charlie Rose, krump participant Lil' C suggests that "The youth gravitated towards this because it was, it was an alternative to what was being offered to us, spoon fed to us, so I was like 'you know I gotta get into this,' ended up joining the crew."[19] Again, similar to Dragon's "creating something out of nothing," Lil' C is able to articulate the "difference" between what krump represents and what society has tried to force feed marginalized youth. The "outlaw humanism" expressed in *Rize* is one that can come to grips with social inequality and the lack of means in an embodied way—realizing that hope or "faith" doesn't and cannot go beyond the material reminder of flesh. There is a war raging in the streets for young people such as these; their weapons of war become their bodies, undying resilience, hope against hope, and face paint. The vignettes highlighted in this film—featuring other cast members such as Tight Eyez, who talks at length about the significance of krumping in his life—clearly express just how important krumping is for them. Moreover, there is no wool over these young people's eyes; they know that resources abound in plentitude just forty-five minutes from their ghetto paradise (Hollywood). After Tight Eyez expresses his hope in krumping, Lil' C adds, "In better neighborhoods they have performing arts schools, they have ballet, they have modern, you have jazz, you have tap, and just all those prestigious academies you can go to, it's nothing like that available to you, when you live where we live."[20] Krumping isn't solely a physical reminder of inequality: there is a certain kind of motivation that draws these young people to get krump; for example, Dragon boldly proclaims, "You know, a lot of people just think it's, you know, 'Oh, they're just a bunch of rowdy, you know, ghetto, just heathen and thugs.' No, what we are, are oppressed."[21] The art of "do for self" doesn't provide liberation from such oppression: rather, krumping becomes a way to cope through creative cultural production. It is this type of creativity that I refer to in my work as "cathartic release from social anxiety." Lil' C says it best when he states:

> Say if people have problems, you know, didn't get this, didn't get that, short on this bill, short on that bill, the fact that you can get krump, you can channel that anger, anything negative that has happened in your life, you can channel that into your dancing, and you can release that in a positive way because you are releasing that through art—the art of dance.[22]

To this, Dragon adds, "This is our ghetto ballet, this is how we express ourselves, this is the only way we see fit of storytelling, this is the only way of making ourselves feel like we belong."[23] This ghetto-laden storytelling is a performativity of everyday struggle, the body becomes a canvas by which to tell or paint the narrative. This canvas, however, is always changing, always in flux with the movement of life's hurts and pains. The aggression of the bodily movements are embodied expressions of struggle; as situations in life change according to this struggle, aggression might become heightened. On this note, Lil' C explains how:

> before you know it we were dancing to much more aggressive music, we were experiencing turmoil and anguish in our lives, and

the dance style began to change, became more aggressive, we would just turn the music on real loud … just real rugged music … we would just hype each other up and feed off of each other's kinetic energy, and it was crazy, before you know it, three people in a room, seven people in a room, ten people in a room, fifteen, thirty, sixty … then you have a krump session, we called it krump, it just came to us … . You feel so serene after you get it all out, it's nothing like it, nothing at all.[24]

The language of "kinetic energy" used here describes the affective qualities of this dance form.

Krumpers might not express a coherently articulate philosophy of humanism; in fact, many often note that krumping has Christian roots. This is not, however, a quagmire or contradiction. Beyond the durable religiosities often inherited in the home during early processes of socialization, there is, in fact, a multiplicity at play here—one that is very much humanist in nature: a certain kind of humanism that understands that the only saving grace that might abound in the face of austere social conditions in fact resides within ourselves and not something beyond. The *embodied* dimensions of emergent cultures such as Krump give shape to the manner in which humanism as a sort of faith in the flesh abounds in postindustrial spaces of urbanity within American made ghettos.

50 CENT AND THE LAW OF "FEARLESSNESS": THE THUG'S GUIDE TO SELF-HELP

In addition to krumping, there is another hip hop inspired brand of humanism taking shape through rapper-produced texts, such as gangster rapper 50 Cent's *The 50th Law*, co-authored with self-help guru Robert Greene. Packaged as a holy bible, *The 50th Law* is anything but Christian in orientation. In this text, Greene and 50 Cent take the life lessons of 50's experiences as a thug and gangster, who escapes death nine times, and fashions them as "hard lessons of life" based on realism and a law of fearlessness. The main theme of this text is *fear nothing* and put hope not in a higher power, but rather, the power of the mind; this text is about "do for self" and "trust in self." Greene describes his life's work:

> GREENE: I take the most powerful people in their field and kind of break them down, what is the essence, what's the core of their success … I call it their power sense of gravity. So I decided that I would do that with you [50 Cent]. After a couple of months following you around, I decided the secret to your success … is your

> fearlessness ... you're the one that has less fear than they do, and
> that gives you a constant strategic advantage ... adapt, take risks
> ... this is to me the source of your power ... this is the subject of
> our book *The 50th Law* ... . Were you sort of just born this way?
> Or did you have to develop this attitude on the streets as a kid?
> 50 CENT: ... It's absolutely something I had to develop ... I think I have
> the same emotions as everyone else does ... I can kind of adjust.[25]

One has to wonder, with the abundance of well-respected self-help authors whose lives reflect the positive messages they often write and speak about, how could anything of value come from a rapper, shot nine times, who is anything but shy about using his thug experience to garner power and wealth in the belly of capitalist America? What can 50 Cent possibly teach business students about climbing the walls of capitalism and rising to the top of their corporate hustle? Throughout *The 50th Law*, as the back of the book declares, the main message of this text is *nihil timendum est*, fear nothing. The philosophy of *fearlnessness* and "doing for self" was harnessed throughout 50's dangerous life of thugging, gangbanging, and selling drugs on the dangerous streets of Queens, New York. Suspending and re-altering ethical norms, these authors together suggest that, "if you were to have any power as a hustler, you had to overcome this emotion [fear] ... testing and proving his courage in this way gave him [50 Cent] a feeling of tremendous power."[26] A metaphysics of self-help is advanced in this text: together they suggest a new-age centered sensibility of a hip hop humanism, one that describes feelings such as fear as emotions that lead humans to irrational endeavors such as the search for help in higher powers. In this text, the evils of life are dealt with through the power of the mind, the battleground where life and death decisions are made. This text suggests that while we are all constrained in varying ways, there is ultimate freedom in the mind: a type of alchemy and realism that assist in social mobility and advancement. Using the dangerous and risky thug ethics procured over 50's life, they argue that the idea of cultural, social, emotional, and human *flow* can assist individuals in traversing any hardship they might face. One of the aspects of this hip hop new-age styled humanism is an embrace of mortality: an understanding that we get one life to live, and death will inevitably be an outcome for all, across various lines of social difference. Moreover, *The 50th Law* proposes that we not look for help in constructs such as God; rather, we are to embrace our own human potentiality and possibilities by putting the battlefield of the mind to work. Greene and 50 write, "Your fears are a kind of prison that confines you within a limited range of action. The less you fear, the more power you will have and the more fully you will live. It is our hope that *The 50th Law* will inspire you to discover this power for yourself."[27]

Again, much like krumpers, 50 does not (consciously) articulate a coherent humanist platform or agenda; rather, this rugged brand of humanism emerges, almost unexpectedly, in and through the marketing and content of *The 50th Law*. While there are certainly some dangers in denying structural disadvantage and limitations of this type of new-age ideology (where a mythology of capitalist meritocracy grounds the power of the mind), what this vignette speaks to is the growing reality of humanist leanings and sensibilities among African American cultural productions. This reality has been an untapped resource for the doing and thinking of alternative visions of African American religiosities.

WHAT IS HUMANISM AND WHY DOES IT MATTER? NEW POSSIBILITIES

The stories above bring us back to the main query of this chapter: what is humanism and why does it matter? Humanism matters because, as the stories above suggest, marginal youth constrained by inequalities of all sorts, whether recognizable or not, make use of humanist sensibilities as a way to cope with very real social inequalities. Attention to the cultural productions of these demographics reveals that an ethic of "faith in the flesh" abounds as a guiding philosophy of life. The issues facing these youth are very much indeed about life and death; the resolutions they are developing as responses to societal evil are indeed humanist in nature, whether acknowledged or not.

In the crucible of everyday struggle, humanism is not a fancy intellectual option for pontification. In fact, here there is little conscious reflection on their humanistic leanings. It is possible that humanist ideals persist in cultural practices even when rhetorically shrouded in the structures of dominant religion (described as something else). For communities on the margins of dominant culture, emergent cultural humanism is about survival, coping: in other words, a strategy for surviving the odds against them. In this sense, humanism, while unacknowledged, provides hope where there is little. This brand of humanism may not appear traditional in nature, as it is often a blended street corner philosophy with traces of the very marginalization they seek to escape. In fact, many youth from these populations probably have little understanding of what humanism as a philosophy of life is; they probably can offer little by way of explication. However, attention to their practices and cultural life-worlds reveals that a type of reworked humanism might be emerging in cracks of fixity, constraint, and inequality.

Thugged-out humanism is faith in the flesh, where *outlawish*, thuggish, and rugged codes of life alter traditional understandings of how humanism is being unconsciously (and spontaneously) practiced across geographies of difference. Attention to these kinds of emergent ideas necessitates a shift in

91

what we claim humanism to be and why it matters in the world in which we live. New modes of humanist practice require new frames of thought and approach. The outlawish look of humanism among marginal communities (where experts say it seldom exists) extends beyond and seemingly rebels against our textbook, encyclopedic, and dictionary definitions of what we often claim it to be.

PART III. WHAT DO WE DO WITH HUMANISM?

6. BEYOND KUMBAYA: CULTURALLY RELEVANT HUMANISM IN AN AGE OF "POSTS"

Sikivu Hutchinson

In 1781, black and brown women and men founded the city of Los Angeles. In this so-called city without a history, legend has it that undocumented Anglos were the real "o.g. illegals."[1] A few years before, a "new" revolution in what it meant to be human unfolded on the opposite shore in the British colonies. My students know the "romance" of the American Revolution but not the secret of Los Angeles. In the prison house of textbook history, they know each other as enslaved "niggers" and wetback interlopers. Growing up in the same neighborhoods, elbow to elbow, cheek by jowl, they are taught to believe that black and Latino culture can be distilled down to media stereotypes: get rich or die tryin', hip hop and ghetto dysfunction; big Catholic families and "job-stealing illegals." As kindergartners they were taught to cite the pledge of allegiance as sacred chapter and verse, hand solemnly over heart, in homage to royal theft. Founding myths of heroic white men bootstrapping to liberty are intimately bound to their imagination of the classroom, to its rhythm of shrill discipline and stench of ground chalk, to a regime of time in which white supremacy and narratives of progress are the currency of American faith. Over the past few decades, progressive education reform activists have reshaped the dialogue about the so-called achievement gap in public schools. Culturally relevant or culturally responsive pedagogy that builds on the lived experiences, cultural knowledge, language, and worldviews of children of color have become a standard, if still controversial, approach to redressing race and class disparities in education. Culturally relevant pedagogy rejects myths of meritocracy, colorblindness, and exceptionalism. At its most radical it critiques institutional structures of racist power and control that render children of color invisible within mainstream curriculum and instruction. It is based on the view that the question of what it means to be moral, to be a citizen, and to be human is implicit within the politics of education. So how does cultural relevance relate to radical humanism? And what is at stake for black atheists/humanists in "post-racial" America? What is the connection between humanism and social justice in this so-called post-racial era? What is the connection between humanism and black liberation struggle?

RACE AND BLACK LIBERATION

Black liberation struggle disrupts the process by which only certain bodies of knowledge are privileged within the national moral compass. After President Obama's election the mainstream media giddily trumpeted post-racialism as the new norm. There was much speculation about whether Black History Month, long commodified and domesticated as a quick and dirty way to pay homage to the black other, was still relevant; was it redundant now that there was an African American first family in the White House and Sasha and Malia were the new girls next door?

But of course, no one ever called Bill Clinton—rib-eating, sax-playing, back-slapping, philandering, good ol' boy Bill Clinton—a bone-in-the-nose, bongo-playing savage or the son of apes. And no one ever caricatured Hillary Clinton as an ape or a missing link. Yet these were some of the prevailing images after the 2008 election. These images underscored the fact that America is still deeply divided and deeply segregated by race. They belied the media's bromides about post-racialism, exceptionalism, and colorblindness. And they fatally trashed the soothing Kumbaya message of American unity that Barack Obama himself evoked in his pivotal speech at the 2004 Democratic National Convention. Indeed, galvanized by the far right Tea Party, some white folks even woke up the day after the election, staggered into the new dawn of a black president, and proclaimed that the dark clouds of apocalypse were descending. They used millennialist language to pronounce that the End Times—the so-called Rapture in which Christian true believers will be swept up to heaven, away from Earth's cesspit of sin—were near. They exhorted the American electorate to see that "we" needed to take back "our" nation.

Assessing this phenomenon, some white liberal and progressive pundits dubbed this backlash a populist uprising rather than a white nationalist insurgency. Commentators like Sean Wilentz and Robert Scheer caution that dismissing the Tea Party as a white racist insurgency is too simplistic.[2] Wilentz locates the Tea Party lineage in the Cold War hysterics of the ultraright John Birch Society. Scheer identifies the Tea Partyers as an "authentic" populist response to the recession. The mainstream media's aversion to characterizing these uprisings as a racial phenomenon was part of the insidious narrative of colorblindness and exceptionalism. According to a 2010 Public Religion Research poll, a majority of Americans believe God has "granted Americans a special role in history."[3] This belief informs American exceptionalism, the idea that the US represents the pinnacle of First World democracy, liberty, and opportunity. It has been a recurring theme in Tea Party rhetoric. Slamming Obama in a speech to a group of home schoolers, former Pennsylvania Senator Rick Santorum succinctly captured the sense of betrayal that fuels this belief: "You have been given a great gift in living in the greatest country in the history of the world ... but that freedom, that equality, that exceptionalism, is at stake right now ... if we do not replace the current president."[4] Certainly the white conservative backlash against health care reform, public employee unionism, undocumented immigrant rights, abortion rights, and family planning—in short, the very foundation of social welfare—can be seen as part of this belief in an Obama-driven threat to American exceptionalism. Thus, this view is closely linked to a resurgence of white nationalism that has dominated the political landscape since the 2008 election. Again according to the Public Religion Research Institute, 44 percent of Americans believe that discrimination against whites is just as pressing as that against so-called minorities. Seventy-five percent of the Tea Party "populists" believe that this is the case, as do a majority of evangelical Christians. A recent study by researchers from Tufts University and Harvard University found that a majority of whites now believe that anti-white racism has increased while racism against blacks has decreased.[5]

Both polls underscore the nexus of white nationalism, white supremacy, and Christian evangelical activism. It is no revelation that this nexus continues to have a profound influence on the direction of American politics. White voters abandoned the Democratic Party in droves when it became associated with civil rights, that is, the "black" platform in the 1960s.[6] The white-dominated Christian evangelical movement emerged in response to the passage of the Civil and Voting Rights Acts of 1964 and 1965. Consequently, Democratic presidential candidates have consistently lost the "white vote" in every election since that of Jimmy Carter in 1976. During the blood and guts battle of the 2010 mid-term elections, 60 percent of white voters backed GOP, or Republican Party, candidates. Thus, the far right birther movement's zealous fixation on Barack Obama's citizenship is the perverse corollary to white backlash against the civil rights gains of the post-Vietnam era.

As an African American feminist, I subscribe to humanism because it is a belief system based on the view that humanity defines morals, ethics, and notions of justice. Scientific inquiry and reason are the best vehicles for explaining the emergence of the universe and all life forms, rather than recourse to supernatural causes and explanations. Thus, rather than privilege redemption or eternal reward in an afterlife, humanism reveres human potential, ingenuity, and creativity in the material world and the *here and now*. A radical humanist vision eschews religious and social hierarchies of race, gender, sexuality, and class because they undermine the universal human rights and self-determination of oppressed peoples. For communities of color, radical humanism reinforces the cultural legitimacy, visibility, and validity of non-believers of color within the context of a white supremacist, heterosexist, patriarchal, economically disenfranchising ideological regime that equates morality with Abrahamic religious paradigms and beliefs. Radical humanism rejects the notion that there is only one way to be black or Latino, and that women and the LGBT (lesbian, gay, bisexual, and transgender) community are marginal and morally aberrant.

ATHEISTIC HUMANISM IN THOUGHT AND ACTION

So what does a godless morality based on social justice look like in this toxic climate of political hysteria? What does it mean to be an African American atheistic humanist? And what role do race, gender, sexuality, and power play in shaping public morality? To put this assessment in historical and intellectual context, in 1927, the socialist civil rights organizer and humanist activist A. Philip Randolph sponsored an essay contest called "Is Christianity a Menace to the Negro?" for the radical journal the *Messenger*. As publisher and editor of the *Messenger*, Randolph was an ardent critic of what he dubbed "orthodox Christianity." Randolph was widely believed to be an atheist because of his radical political stance on organized religion. However, there is still considerable speculation among historians about whether or not he actually identified as such.[7] Nonetheless, Randolph's apostasy played out during a period when "Commies" were plotting behind every bedpost and it was better to be dead than red. Political radicals were associated with godlessness and vice versa. Throughout his career Randolph was under close watch by the FBI for his allegedly seditious activities. Openly challenging the role of religion in civil society was part of the heady political upheaval ushered in by the Russian Revolution of 1918. Randolph and black activist "fellow travelers" like Chandler Owen and Hubert Henry Harrison were deeply influenced by the revolutionary foment of the era.

While Randolph and his compatriots were organizing protest rallies and developing their oratorical chops on the soapboxes of Harlem street corners, Harlem Renaissance author Nella Larsen published her landmark 1928 novel *Quicksand*. *Quicksand* was perhaps the first explicitly skeptical black feminist critique of the stifling gender norms of the black Church. It laid a foundation for feminist criticism of the way religion domesticated and marginalized black women. Like Randolph, Larsen's protagonist Helga Crane was considered an oddball non-conformist who bucked the black authenticity police. In one vivid passage, Helga decries the absurdity of blacks' slavish devotion to the "white man's god." Black devoutness struck her as odd given the depth of black poverty. Religious devotion was dysfunctional for black people because it "blunted the perceptions. Robbed life of its crudest truths. [religion] Especially had its uses for the poor—for the blacks. How the white man's God must laugh at the great joke he played on them. Bound them to slavery, then to poverty and insult, and made them bear it."[8]

Larsen alludes to the sentiments of seventeenth-century Puritan orator Cotton Mather's treatise on the benefits of "Christianizing" the Negro. Exhorting planters to treat their slaves like they were their brothers, Mather also wrote:

> Yea, the pious masters, that have instituted their servants in Christian Piety ... the more serviceable, and obedient and obliging behavior ... unto them, will be a sensible and a notable recompence. ... Your servants will be the better servants, for being made Christian servants. ... Were your servants well tinged with the spirit of Christianity, it would render them exceeding[ly] dutiful unto their masters, exceeding[ly] faithful in their business, and afraid of speaking or doing any thing that may justly displease you.[9]

For Larsen, the God concept was rooted in the deep disenfranchisement and class struggle of poor black people. Larsen's critique encapsulated many of the themes of apostasy that Randolph would explore early on in his career as an organizer and intellectual. For the young Randolph, religion was a dangerous opiate, a sop to the potential radicalism of African American communities. As Randolph biographer Jervis Anderson notes, "it was his dim sense that ... getting religion was a way of escaping their social condition ... and if that kind of emotion were translated into politics, it would represent 'the awakening and even the uprising of the masses.'"[10] In the *Messenger's* 1919 Thanksgiving issue Randolph declared: "We wish to give thanks. We do not wish to thank God for anything nor do our thanks include gratitude for the things which most persons give thanks at this period. With us, we are thankful for different things and to a different Deity. Our Deity is the toiling masses of the world."[11]

Yet as he emerged as a union leader Randolph had to downplay his secularism in light of the reality of racial apartheid in America.[12] Because African Americans were excluded from white political, social, and economic institutions the black Church played a powerful role in community organizing and social welfare. After decades of fighting against white supremacy in the trade union movement, Randolph and his colleagues founded the Brotherhood of Sleeping Car Porters (BSCP). The BSCP was the most influential black trade union in American history. It worked strenuously to overcome the black community's misgivings about trade unionism.[13] In the BSCP's early years many prominent black congregations were openly hostile to it and even supported the Pullman Company's official union. In an attempt to undermine the BSCP, the Pullman Company routinely smeared Randolph as a godless atheist and a communist. As a result, Randolph vehemently denied both charges. According to Cynthia Taylor's 2006 biography,[14] Randolph retreated from many of his more radical critiques of organized religion. By the 1940s Randolph and the BSCP had adopted a "social gospel" message that was in line with the founding traditions of the African Methodist Episcopal church.

Randolph was part of a vanguard of twentieth-century black activists and intellectuals who subscribed to secular humanist principles of social justice and liberation struggle. This vanguard included W. E. B. DuBois, the towering rationalist, skeptic, and critic of the US's imperialist Christian missionary policies in the Third World, and one-time Student Nonviolent Coordinating Committee (SNCC) head James Farmer, who was an outspoken critic of redemptive suffering and black religious hypocrisy and venality. During the 1970s Farmer challenged a prominent white congregation over its alleged complicity in the African slave trade. The writers Richard Wright, James Baldwin, Nella Larsen (as aforementioned), and Zora Neale Hurston also criticized black religious indoctrination and the role it played in undermining liberation struggle and free thought.[15]

Fast forward to the twenty-first century, and the far right demagogues of Fox News have made secularism a dirty word again. Given this climate it is hardly surprising that no prominent black leader or elected official would dare raise the humanist, much less atheist, flag. Michele Bachman, Newt Gingrich, Glenn Beck, and Sarah Palin have all sought to link political liberalism with socialism/communism, godlessness, and anti-Americanism. For example, Newt Gingrich has smeared the very centrist, very corporate and very Christian Obama as the architect of a secular socialist machine.[16] Lurking not too far behind this demonization is the taint of racial otherness. As a black man who is already othered by his "anti-colonial" Kenyan heritage, Obama has worked the language of Christian national solidarity as best he can. He has bent over backwards to portray himself as a moral *über*-Christian. He has courted hard-line evangelicals like Rick Warren, green-lit Bush's Faith-Based Initiative ruse, and salted many of his public addresses with scripture. But if one were to nakedly deconstruct the demonization of Obama he will never be Christian enough for the heartland, nor secular or American enough for the birthers. Hate-mongering Christian evangelist and bestselling author Tim LaHaye has consistently questioned Obama's Christian bona fides and used "End Times" language to describe the impact of his policies.[17] So even though some claim Obama's white heritage makes it just as legitimate for him to claim whiteness as blackness, he will never be white enough to pass. In the white supremacist logic of American cultural ideology, if you are a black-appearing person in the US (whether or not you daydream about calling yourself Lithuanian, Swedish, Irish, or Russian), one drop still makes you fully black.

Obama will never be Christian enough for inveterate racists. He will never be so because the US's status as a so-called Christian nation has a very distinct racial provenance. Although many of the framers of the Constitution were deists and did not invoke God or a divine authority in the Constitution, the tenor of American national identity is in fact Christian in nature. The American public's rank disdain for non-believers, the absence of non-believing politicians, and the religious right's successful campaign against global warming, evolution, stem cell research, and science literacy suggests that the US is effectively a Christian nation in many respects. From the torturous battles over abortion and choice, to the continuing divide between American imperialism and human rights, American public morality has consistently been defined through a repressive Christian lens.[18] Here, white supremacy and public morality have always been closely linked. For example, it was not until the institutionalization of racial slavery in the late seventeenth century that the terms Christian, white, and free became synonymous. Prior to that there were laws against enslaving Christians, and whites did not primarily identify as white. They identified as freemen or by their class status. Slavery radically transformed the way whites classified and identified their emergent racial selves. As Toni Morrison notes in her work *Playing in the Dark: Whiteness and the Literary Imagination*, "Black slavery enriched the country's creative possibilities, for in that construction of blackness and enslavement could be found not only the not-free ... but the not-me."[19] Drawing moral boundaries of racial self and nationhood were critical to this enterprise.

I was reminded of this legacy when an African American and a white teacher got into an argument about whether or not the US is a Christian nation during one of my teacher-training workshops. The school where the workshop was being held is predominantly black and Latino, with a high dropout rate and a low four-year college going rate. After a high-profile incident in which a gun that a young man had brought to school accidentally went off in a classroom, the school was widely stereotyped by the local media as a dead end repository of lawless black and brown youth. Nonetheless, there are many students at the school who are achieving and showing leadership, contrary to the stereotype. During the discussion, the African American teacher staunchly defended the notion that the US is a Christian nation. The white teacher, who is notorious for making racist paternalistic comments about his students, swaggeringly proclaimed his non-belief and declared that the US has always been defined by the separation of church and state. Listening to this exchange, I was acutely aware of the nuances of race and gender privilege. The reality is that even the most abject disreputable white non-believer does not suffer any racial consequences for his non-belief. There might be political consequences; but even disreputable white men do not surrender their universal subject status over a little matter of heathenism. You might be a godless "freedom-hating" (in the mind of the Fox mafia) "flag-burning pinko commie infidel," but you were still human and still a citizen until proven otherwise. And this has been the paradox for African American non-believers: the fact that being Christian was a de facto pathway to becoming moral, to becoming American, and to becoming a provisional citizen. At the height of the Jim Crow era there was nothing more intensely American than that old time Christian religion. On a hot summer night, white kids could get that old time religion and a taste of American justice in one bloody serving. When their congregations moseyed on down with picnic baskets and binoculars to watch that Sunday's public lynchings like they were theatre, performance art, or sport, they could learn the gospel of being white and free, because the family and congregation that lynched and prayed together, stayed together.

In her 1970s short story "The Flowers," humanist womanist writer Alice Walker evokes the horror of a young African American girl's discovery of the decomposing corpse of a lynching victim while she is out picking flowers.[20] Walker's story powerfully exposes the savage contradiction of a nation that has always portrayed itself as the global paradigm of justice and democracy, but has done so through the erasure of this legacy of racial disenfranchisement and terrorism. The parting salvo of the story is "and then the summer was over." She contrasts the lightness and innocence of the girl's walk with the weight of her discovery, suggesting that to be a black child is to never be innocent. This phrase not only signals the figurative end of summer, but also the brutality of a nation in which black children are always othered, racialized, "pathologized," and criminalized. It underscores the savagery of a free land where feminine innocence has never been afforded to black girls who wear pink and have pigtails and pick flowers. And it indicts the myth of meritocracy in a nation in which my students have a greater opportunity to spend most of their childhood and adolescence in and out of prisons than they have to go to a four-year college or university. The writer Michelle Alexander has dubbed this regime the "New Jim Crow." In her book of the same name, she documents how there are more black males in prison, on parole, or probation than were enslaved in 1850.[21] So when many people of color hear exhortations about restoring honor or taking back the country in the name of God, guns, lower taxes, and bloody fetuses, it conjures up this history. It evokes the bloated body of fifteen-year-old Emmett Till, dragged from his bed in the middle of the night and murdered by a lynch mob of white men for the crime of whistling at a white woman. It conjures up the image of the parallel universe in which thousands of people of color from the ghettos and barrios of East LA, Detroit, New York, and Chicago stormed the Capitol for an explicitly anti-government demonstration or to exercise their right to "2nd Amendment solutions." How would this "act of patriotism" be greeted by the nation? By Capitol police? By the feds? James Baldwin once wrote, "In the United States, violence and heroism have been made synonymous except when it comes to blacks."[22] How long would this ghetto insurrection have been tolerated before the military started cracking heads and jailing everyone in sight? Not long, given the history of violent suppression of revolutionary movements led by people of color from the Black Power movement to the American Indian Movement. There's a reason why blacks and Latinos are disproportionately incarcerated from cradle to grave. It has everything to do with cultural perceptions of black and Latino criminality and the subtext of white innocence, humanity, and citizenship.

Thus, the notion of humanist social justice must begin here, with an unflinching assessment of American racial history. It must also be based on a reckoning with the paradoxes of this era of "posts." For example, the US is post-racial and post-Jim Crow in much the same way that it is "post-feminist." Despite the fact that there are greater numbers of women in college and in the workplace, sexism and misogyny in popular representation, in TV, film, and music imagery, continue unabated. In this supposedly post-feminist era, young women of color continue to be taught to marginalize, question, and devalue themselves. They are still taught that their ultimate social worth lies in being desirable to a man. They are still socialized to believe that being a caregiver means backbreaking self-sacrifice that men and boys are not held accountable for. They are still indoctrinated to view hyper-sexuality, rather than organized resistance against patriarchal domination in the home and workplace, as a feminist statement. They are still socialized to view female sexuality and reproduction as proprietary objects that should be controlled and exploited by patriarchy, the state, and organized religion. They are not so subtly led to believe that they are worthy of punishment should they breach the terms of "proper" subservient femininity. Women who buck this regime of authoritarian power and control are still regarded as "bad bitches."

On the other hand, the dominant culture still trains boys to be predators. Mainstream media and the US's imperialist culture of incessant global warfare socializes boys to believe that in order to be a real man you need to be hard, aggressive, emotionally invulnerable, competitive, and violent toward other men and boys, as well as objectifying and violent toward women. After all, when mainstream culture thinks of a "gender lens" it means women's issues; ghettoized and marginalized. Even within many social justice

organizations there is little concerted attention to humanist notions of transforming masculinity. There is no engaged discourse around how men and
boys are trained and socialized to systematically dehumanize women. No
one thinks to ask how the minds of men and boys are colonized by sexism
and heterosexism. Writing on the US's culture of hyper-masculine violence,
feminist social commentator Kevin Powell asks, "How do we socialize our
boys? How do we assign certain attitudes and behaviors as 'normal?' And,
ultimately: What does it mean to be a man in 21st century America? For too
many young men, communal rituals of sexism perpetuate negative notions
of manhood."[23]

Powell's query is at the heart of a humanist transformation of masculinity.
Deconstructing binary notions of masculinity and femininity based on Abrahamic religious ideology is a key part of humanist struggle. In mainstream
American culture normative gender roles are closely linked to heterosexism.
Heterosexism dictates that men learn how to be dominant, controlling and
competitive in pursuit of women's attentions and sexuality. Men have unlim-
ited access to women's bodies as sexual territory, reproductive "vessels," and
family property. Despite the myth of post-feminism, mainstream media such
as cartoons, films, and, especially, the multi-billion-dollar toy industry, with
its "pink princesses and blue commandos" marketing, reinforce these gender
regimes. Given that black and Latino men are themselves disproportionately
impacted by violence (homicide being a leading cause of death for young
black and Latino males), humanist notions of masculinity would have even
deeper resonance for communities of color.

But tragically, there has been no social movement that builds on the courageous examples of feminist men of color like Powell. I'm thinking specifically of the work of cultural critic Mark Anthony Neal, filmmaker Byron
Hurt (author of the widely influential documentary *Hip Hop: Beyond Beats
and Rhymes*), and community-based organizations like Los Angeles' Peace
over Violence, which trains young men to be anti-violence prevention and
intervention advocates.[24] For example, incorporating anti-sexist feminist
work into urban anti-gang violence prevention and intervention programs
could critically challenge the hyper-masculine culture that underlies sky-
rocketing black homicide rates.

But this is a radical concept in a nation in which black death is sexy and
lucrative for both global media and the prison industrial complex. It is a
radical concept when there is no grassroots humanist vision about the intersection of gender justice and social justice. Within the past two years the
GOP's relentless attacks on American family planning provider Planned
Parenthood, family planning, and abortion access have led the media to
characterize them as a war on women. Indeed, the war on social welfare
and the war on women are informed by white supremacy, theocracy, and

capitalist economic policies. But these national currents are also reflected in the way social justice organizations do not deem reproductive justice or intimate partner violence to be urgent enough causes for national mobilization. This is despite the fact that black women rely disproportionately on family planning preventive care and are increasingly the primary breadwinners in their households. Gender injustice is just as important as mass incarceration, police brutality, racial profiling, and unemployment, yet it is not a burning priority for many social justice organizations. In fact, in their silence, social justice organizations of color tacitly endorse the conservative reactionary line of the black religious right. According to this agenda black women should sacrifice their bodies, destinies, and their right to self-determination in service to black patriarchy. African American LGBT folk should stay marginalized, silent, and invisible vis-à-vis the overall arc of black liberation struggle. This narrow vision of liberation struggle is still based on a heterosexist masculinist model of authentic black community.

These tensions are exemplified by the "abortion as black genocide" billboard campaign that has spread its tentacles across inner-city communities over the past year. The campaign is sponsored by the ultra-conservative Radiance Foundation and Life Always group. It evokes the most reductive plantation era caricatures of black femininity. By charging black women who get abortions with orchestrating "genocide," these billboards suggest that women who do not surrender their wombs to patriarchy are hyper-sexual irresponsible black matriarchs hell-bent on undermining the black family. In essence, these billboards reinforce plantation era notions of black women as vessels, instant wombs ready to pop out babies on demand for "massa," the Church, black men, and the state. This intersection between black hyper-religiosity, black nationalism, and white supremacy is destructive for black women, but it is also destructive for black families and black communities. Even more insidiously, this propaganda gives the impression that the greatest threat to black communities is bad black women who make immoral choices by using abortion as "birth control." The demonization of black women and black female sexuality via these billboards is part of the dominant culture's continuing narrative of black pathology.

Of course, science and superstition have always gone hand in hand when it comes to the social construction of race and sexuality in America. Black women's bodies have historically been the battleground for this regime of cultural knowledge. For example, the secularist hero, slaveholder, and amateur scientist Thomas Jefferson routinely decried "religious slavery" and the tyranny of religious dogma. But as a man of his times, Jefferson also deemed the inferiority of blacks to be part of the natural moral order.[25] In her book *Medical Apartheid*, Harriet Washington recounts how Jefferson experimented with the smallpox virus on slaves.[26] According to Washington,

Jefferson tried to cover up this experimentation by claiming that he had used members of his own (white) family as subjects. In Jefferson's universe, Sally Hemings, the widely accepted slave mother of several of Jefferson's children, was bound deterministically to slavery because it was ordained by God and enshrined by nature. Her status was transparent. It was self-evident, natural, and immutable.

In the "post-racial" era, the media myth of colorblindness seeks to obliterate the contemporary implications of these legacies. It makes inequality and racism appear to be an aberration. It transforms racism and inequality into embarrassing faux pas that the US has "evolved" out of. Yet in this Christian, colorblind, up-by-our-bootstraps nation the reality of residential segregation, black mass incarceration, race-based achievement, wealth gaps, and dehumanizing media representations of people of color says otherwise.

A humanist morality based on social justice goes beyond deconstruction of religious hierarchies. It should expose the structures of oppression that promote religion as an enterprise. It should go beyond mere tolerance and Kumbaya notions of diversity towards the articulation of a Freirian critical consciousness.[27] It should be based on the view that racism is not just the "problem" of people of color but is as American as baseball, apple pie, and "in God we trust." Racism is an integral part of what it means to be a white American citizen in a twenty-first-century global context in which white children grow up seeing Sasha and Malia scampering on the White House lawn. While this is hardly revelatory, unlearning and fighting against racism and white supremacy amid such paradoxical conditions is a battle that critically conscious white people should be prepared to engage in.

In this regard, teaching invisible histories and developing critical pedagogy among young people is a humanist strategy for mental liberation. Humanist ethics lies in both valuing difference and understanding how difference radically shapes power, privilege, and identity. For example, in 2010 a university researcher appointed by CNN revisited the 1947 doll test experiment developed by psychologists Kenneth and Mamie Clark.[28] The Clarks conducted this experiment to assess the self-esteem of black youth. Elementary school children were asked a series of questions about a black doll and a white doll. When the children were asked to choose which doll was smart, attractive, and more like them they chose the white doll. The Clarks' research was used to buttress the landmark 1954 Brown vs Board of Education school desegregation decision. In the new study the CNN researcher used white and black children. They were shown a range of children's images from very dark skinned to very light or white skinned. The white children overwhelmingly identified the darker-skinned images as less attractive, less intelligent, less desirable, bad, and mean. In a follow-up discussion on the implications of the findings, CNN filmed a tearful white mother responding to the experiment with dismay. Like many liberal white parents she couldn't understand why her child expressed negative views of darker-skinned children when she "never talked about race" at home and taught her to be colorblind. In fact, researchers Po Bronson and Ashley Merryman, authors of *Nurture Shock*, in addition to researchers Louise Derman-Sparks, Carol Tanaga Higa, and Bill Sparks, found that not talking about race actually predisposed white children to being more prejudiced toward people of color.[29] As Derman-Sparks *et al.* contend:

> A considerable body of research demonstrates that children are aware, at a very early age, of physical and cultural differences among people, and that they learn the prevailing social attitudes toward these differences whether or not they are in direct contact with people different from themselves ... the "colorblind" thesis is not only untrue; it has several pernicious aspects ... colorblindness is a perspective that implies that differences are bad because it focuses exclusively on the universality of humans. Further, the ideology of colorblindness permits people to deny the role of institutional racism.[30]

Small wonder, given that the average white child associates being white with being normal. Being normal means never having one's basic humanity questioned. White children intuitively know that they are normal and that they are valued because the media (from the Disney Channel to mainstream Hollywood film), the educational system (because they see people who look like them when they open any textbook), government (because they see people who look like them controlling the US Congress), and law enforcement (because they are not constantly being pulled over by the police) tell them so every day, even if they do not consciously recognize it. Moral value, worth, and universal subject status are automatically ascribed to whiteness.

For example, when I spoke at the 2009 Atheist Alliance International Convention in Burbank I was approached by a white man who proceeded to tell me in a hushed confidential tone that religion was the primary cause of intimate partner violence among African Americans. He said that it was a tragedy that more blacks didn't realize it. He was clearly an expert on all things black because he had taken black history classes in college, a tidbit that he revealed in parting. After the exchange I resisted the temptation to approach random white people and inform them that if "your kind" stopped practicing evangelical Christianity there would be fewer out-of-wedlock births among you white people. This is why the New Atheist science and reason as magic bullet shtick is reductive. Atheists/humanists of color have a broader mandate because many see intimate partner violence as connected to conditions of sexist oppression in the dominant culture, as well as black patriarchy. Further, the social construction of black women as racial other has been crucial to the articulation of scientific discovery. In the 1950s the cancerous cells of a black woman named Henrietta Lacks were used to develop the polio vaccination, and advance cancer research and numerous other medical cures. Lacks's case was the legacy of a long history of scientific racism dating back to the use of black women's bodies for slave-era experimentation. Constructing the racial and sexual other to define what is "human" is as much a part of the legacy of Western rationalism as individual liberty. So science without social justice can be dangerous. Progressive or radical humanism without insight into America's apartheid history is an oxymoron. The flower girl in Alice Walker's lovely field bore witness to the special savagery of American justice, where "due process" meant the bullet and the bullwhip. And without a radical vision of culturally relevant humanism it will continue to be so.

7. HUMANISM AND THE BIG PROBLEM

Dale McGowan

Once in a great while, a single sentence rockets off the page and brands itself permanently on my mind. One such gift appears early in Jennifer Michael Hecht's book *Doubt*—a simple sentence that captures the central human problem: "We live in a meaning-rupture because we are human and the universe is not."[1]

I am both conscious and mortal. That's a bad combination that puts me—and, incidentally, you—in a rather desperate fix. It's not unreasonable to see traditional religion as first and foremost a response to this galling conundrum, solving the Big Problem of death by declaring it unacceptable, and therefore untrue. Religion repairs Hecht's meaning-rupture by denying it, giving the universe a brain and a heart after all, so we in turn can have courage and a home.

A neat and useful trick if you can manage it. I never quite could.

It's not that I care less than most about this predicament. My own feeling about death is straightforward: I am opposed to it. True, there is beauty to be found in my return to the universe whence I came, even real consolation in the idea of utter, untroubled annihilation. My own children have been fascinated by the knowledge that every atom in their bodies has been here since the beginning of time, part of planets and suns and animals and plants and people before coming together to make them. That every bit of us returns to the earth to fuel the ongoing story of life is a gorgeous natural symmetry that never ceases to move them when they are reminded of it.

An unexpected reminder came in 2010 at the burial of their great-grandmother. My daughter Delaney, eight at the time, suddenly pointed at the casket and whispered, "What is that thing on the outside?"

I'd been wondering too. The coffin was sitting in what looked to be a solid metal outer box. As Laney spoke, the cemetery workers closed the lid of what I've since learned is called a burial liner (a fairly recent innovation used in the US and almost nowhere else), cranking down hard on four handles, sealing it tight.

Erin (12) looked at the sealed apparatus, appalled. "So much for returning to the earth," she said. "She's *never* gettin' out of there."

After all of our talk about the beauty of going back into the system, of being a link in an endless chain, Great-Grandma's atoms end up bicycling in a cul-de-sac. Until this impressive bit of denial cracks open, or the sun goes nova, her license to dance is revoked.

So yes, there is beauty in the physical return, made clearest by the ugliness of that cul-de-sac. But it must be admitted that the beauty falls well short of solving the problem for the conscious vanisher. Consciousness, especially one that natural selection has imbued with a feverish love of life, will naturally recoil at the sober consideration of its non-negotiable end.

This inbred revulsion presents a serious challenge for humanism, which embraces the startling suggestion that we can live honestly, then ventures into value by saying we *should* do so, no matter how difficult that may be. One might define humanism as "the focused attempt to live honestly."

When I tell other humanists that I fear death, some shrug and say that death is a non-issue. As Epicurus put it, while I'm here, death is not. When death is here, I will not be. Why fear something you will never meet?

On first hearing, I'm sure I found that honest, humanistic answer intellectually thrilling. But I knew even then it didn't come close to feeding the bulldog. And I find the glib denial of the fear of death to be at least dishonest, if not downright inhuman.

It's not that I think the answer is wrong. From an objective, naturalistic point of view, I understand that the dead themselves surely aren't all that impressed with death. Emotionally, though, *subjectively*, to the living, Epicurus provides nothing but empty calories, a kind of linguistic shell game that solves the problem only by moving the goalpost.

One enormous consolation of a naturalistic humanist outlook is that the annihilation of me also annihilates the possibility of anything to fear. That's Epicurus's point, of course, and he's right. And once you stop thinking of oblivion as *me-floating-in-darkness-forever*, the usual way a conscious brain conceives of oblivion, death loses its sting. But still I am afraid, because, as Michel de Montaigne put it four centuries ago, "It is not death but *dying* that alarms me." The end of my conscious existence: *that* is what I can't stand to think about. Five minutes after that, yes, I understand how little I'll care. But from this side of the turnstile, the problem is all too real. I've been bred by natural selection to want desperately to stay alive, and coming to grips with the end of the only state I've ever consciously known is the single greatest challenge of a worldview that dispenses with supernatural solutions.

I have contemplated mortality more directly and relentlessly than most, due in equal parts to my humanism and to the unexpected death of my father when I was thirteen. In addition to my undiminished natural contempt for

death, I've come to consider the fact that life ends the most profound fact of
our existence, rivaled only by the fact that it begins. It is both repelling and
compelling. A naturalistic humanist outlook allows me to join the very small
circle of humans who have honestly contemplated one of the most aston-
ishing parts of being human, something for which I'm immensely grateful.
Mortality seen clearly changes *everything*, often for the better. That's why, far
from averting my gaze, I seize every opportunity to accept the invitation of
humanism to look my situation squarely in the eye.

Sometimes this means looking through the eyes of others.

In the middle of the sixteenth century, in the middle of his country's third
civil war, Montaigne went riding with friends near his estate in the valley of
the Dordogne. A party of his servants rode nearby as well, likewise enjoying
the spectacular weather. One of the servants, a very large man, lost control
of his powerful horse. Horse and rider careened down the path, finally slamming into the much smaller horse and person of Montaigne.

The philosopher's horse lay stunned in a heap. Montaigne himself lay
unconscious on his back where he had landed, ten yards down the path, his
face bruised and skinned, his entire body having no more sensation than a log.

His companions tried everything to revive him, deciding at last that he
was dead. With heavy hearts, they bore him up and began to carry him
toward his house, more than a mile away.

After being thought dead for over two full hours, Montaigne began to
move and breathe. With much excitement his companions helped him to
sit up. He began to bring up great volumes of blood from his stomach. They
would move him another hundred yards, then stop again as he lost what
seemed more blood than his body could possibly hold, over and over.

"When at last I began to see anything," he later wrote in his journal:

> it was with vision blurred and weak. I could perceive only light. I
> did not have any idea what had happened. I had a sensation for a
> time of my very life hanging at the tip of my lips, and a strange idea
> floated into my head: I had a choice to breathe my life back in or to
> push it off my lips and away. Most strange, that feeling. And I chose,
> quite without distress, to push it out. I tried to do so, coaxed by that
> sweet sensation one feels when about to drift into sleep.
>
> It seems to me that what I describe must be the common feeling
> one has on death's door, a feeling of naturalness and repose. We fear
> death because we view it from a condition of vigor and strength, a
> condition we cannot bear to relinquish. But the act of dying, I now
> believe, must be most often a gradual one, a gentle resignation, pro-
> ceeding by stages so incremental that each seems a more natural, even
> a more desirable step than a jolting return to the full vigor of life.[2]

Montaigne's experience at death's door is anything but unusual. It mirrors the most common near-death experience in every culture and time: a sense of overwhelming peace and calm, the total absence of fear. "The remembrance of this accident, which is very well imprinted in my memory, so naturally representing to me the image and idea of death, has in some sort reconciled me to it," he wrote.[3] His experience and response are personal, naturalistic, and humanistic, without reference to anything beyond death, only to the experience itself and his lessened fear of it.

In *Lives of a Cell*, biologist and essayist Lewis Thomas described a similar scene:

> In a nineteenth-century memoir on an expedition in Africa, there is a story by David Livingston about his own experience of near-death. He was caught by a lion, crushed across the chest in the animal's great jaws, and saved in the instant by a lucky shot from a friend. Later, he remembered the episode in clear detail. He was so amazed by the extraordinary sense of peace, calm, and total painlessness associated with being killed that he constructed a theory that all creatures are provided with a protective physiologic mechanism, switched on at the verge of death, carrying them through in a haze of tranquillity. I have seen agony in death only once, in a patient with rabies; he remained acutely aware of every stage in the process of his own disintegration over a twenty-four-hour period, right up to his final moment. It was as though, in the special neuropathology of rabies, the switch had been prevented from turning.[4]

There's a symmetrical loveliness to the fact that my body's lifelong tendency to cling to survival is apparently reversed once it's time to go: that the gears that now keep me impelled toward existence will, when the time is right, shift ever so gently, and impel me no less confidently toward nonexistence. I'm consoled by the way that underlines the naturalness of death, and by the further realization that this body of mine, yet again, seems to know what it's doing. I can relax a bit further into my seat and enjoy the ride.

So why is it that those who die (or nearly die, depending on your definitions) and are revived, regardless of culture, religious beliefs or age, so often describe the near-death experience in the same way: as a journey through a tunnel toward increasingly bright light, accompanied by out-of-body sensations, flashes of memory, visions of loved ones, and feelings of overwhelming peace and contentment?

The traditional answer, of course, is that the dying person has glimpsed a paradise beyond death. And the universally paradisaic nature of that moment seems to suggest that we all make the grade in the end. Who ever heard of people coming back on the operating table with stories of flames?

Imagine my surprise to learn that not one of the commonly reported phenomena—tunnel of light, out-of-body sensations, hearing what others in the room said after you've died, memory flashes, contentment—not *one* of them is the least bit mysterious. We know why they *all* happen.

An intense test through which the US Air Force puts its high-altitude pilots offers a window on the near-death experience. The pilot is placed in the world's largest centrifuge and spun at high velocity until all of the blood runs out of the brain into the blood vessels on the periphery. The pilots lose consciousness, at which point the centrifuge slows, the blood returns to the brain—and they very often wake up laughing and woohooing.

And what else? Tunnel, bright light, memories, loved ones, contentment. These pilots report experiences that are essentially identical to the "near-death" experience. Why?

When the human heart stops beating, the blood, not surprisingly, drains from the brain. The Air Force centrifuge simulates that blood-starved brain without stopping the heart. And we know, from these and other experiments, what happens when the blood drains out of the brain: billions of cortical neurons begin to fire randomly. Neurons in the visual cortex are more densely packed toward the center (fovea), so when those neurons begin to fire randomly, the person "sees" darkness at the periphery and increasing brightness toward the center. As more and more neurons fire, the bright center grows in size. The effect is one of moving toward a bright light down a long tunnel.

The neurons firing randomly in the prefrontal cortex trigger random flashes of memory, giving the effect of "life flashing before your eyes." As the sensory neurons connecting us to our bodies fail, an out-of-body feeling naturally kicks in. Again, these aren't guesses, a competing hypothesis to put next to heaven in the lineup. We *know* they happen, and how, and when, and why.

Hearing is the last sense to go, which explains reports of having heard what others have said after apparently being demised.

And the laughing of the pilots, the woohooing? This is the loveliest part, the experience that cured Montaigne of his fear of dying. As our head loses its lunch, the anterior pituitary gland, our private little opium den, floods the brain with endorphins. Whenever the body is stressed—and having the blood sucked out of your brain apparently qualifies as stress—these endorphins, powerful opiates that they are, suffuse us with feelings of tremendous happiness and well-being, an adaptive response that helps us make the best possible decisions in dangerous circumstances. We feel wonderful, peaceful, contented. This contentment combines with the fireworks in the prefrontal memory to produce scores of our happiest memories, like loved ones embracing us, accepting us, welcoming us.

It is not death but dying that alarms me. But by learning about the experiences and knowledge described above, the humanistic embrace of naturalistic explanations once again leads not to despair but to genuine comfort in the fact of our most difficult reality. We're never going to be free of our natural, adaptive fear of losing the magnificent experience of being alive. But the thoughts of other mortals like Epicurus, Montaigne, and Lewis Thomas—who all had the same personal stake in the subject that you and I do—lead me further away from fear and closer to acceptance and understanding. The more knowledge I gather about the two profound bookends between which I find myself, the more I seem to settle into my seat.

Most religious attempts to think about or characterize death, while well meaning, are incurious, dishonest, and unprobing to the greatest possible degree. They tend to answer the difficult question of mortality by simply declaring us immortal, which is a bit like trying to heal a cancer patient by erasing "cancer" from the dictionary. Humanism keeps me searching for ways to both understand and accept my situation.

For humanist parents, the urgency is intensified. It's one thing to ponder my own mortality with cold-eyed honesty over the course of a lifetime. But what do I tell my beloved six-year-old child when she expresses fear of death?

I was confronted with exactly that question when Delaney was six and a wide-ranging bedtime conversation of ours wound its way unexpectedly to a question: "Does everybody die?"

I answered yes, everything that lives eventually dies.

"Am *I* going to die?"

She "knew" the answer to this, of course, but most likely in a way both abstract and incomplete. In his brilliant classic *The Tangled Wing*, Emory neurologist Melvin Konner notes that "from age three to five [children] consider [death] reversible, resembling a journey or sleep. After six, they view it as a fact of life but a very remote one."[5] Though rates of development vary, Konner places the first true grasp of the finality and universality of death around age ten: a realization that includes the first dawning deep awareness that it applies to them as well. So grappling with the concept early, *before* we are paralyzed by the fear of it, can go a long way toward fending off that fear in the long run.

I said very gently, "Sweetie, everything that lives eventually dies."

She began to cry. *"But I don't wanna die!"*

Let's freeze this tableau for a moment and make a few things clear. The first is that I love this child so much I would throw myself under a bus for her. She is one of just four people whose health and happiness are vital to my own. When she is sad, I want to make her happy. It's one of the simplest equations in my life.

I say such obvious things because it is often assumed that nonreligious parents respond to their children's fears of death by saying, in essence, *deal with it.* In fact, I am convinced that there is not just honesty but also real comfort to be found in a naturalistic view of death, that our mortality lends a new preciousness to life, and that it is more humane and more loving to introduce the concept of a life that truly ends, even to a six-year-old, than it is to proffer an immortality that their inquiring minds will have to painfully discard later.

But all my smiling confidence threatens to dissolve under the tears of my children.

"I know," I said, cradling her head as she convulsed with sobs. "Nobody wants to die. I sure don't. But you know what? First you get to live for a hundred years. Think about that. You'll be older than Great-Grandma Huey!"

It's a cheap opening gambit. It worked the previous time we'd had this conversation, when Laney was four. Not this time.

"But it *will* come," she said, sniffling. "Even if it's a long way away, it will come, and I don't want it to! I want to stay alive!"

I took a deep breath. "I know," I said. "It's such a strange thing to think about. Sometimes it scares me. But you know what? Whenever I'm scared of dying, I remember that being scared means I'm not understanding it right."

She stopped sniffling and looked at me. "I don't get it."

"Well, what do you think being dead is like?"

She thought for a minute. "It's like you're all still and it's dark forever."

A chill went down my spine. There it was, my childhood image of death *precisely.* It's the most awful thing I can imagine. Hell would be better than an eternal, mute, insensate limbo.

"That's how I think of it sometimes too," I said. "And that frrrrreaks me out! But that's not how it is."

"But how do you *know*?" she asked pleadingly. "How do you know what it's like?"

"Because I've already been there."

"What! Haha!" she laughed. "No you haven't!"

"Yes I have, and so have you."

"What? No I haven't."

"After I die, I will be nowhere. I won't be floating in darkness. There will be no Dale McGowan, right?"

"I guess so."

"Okay. Now where was I a hundred years *ago*? Before I was born?"

"Where were you? You weren't anywhere."

"And was I afraid?"

"No, becau ... OMIGOSH, IT'S *THE SAME!*"

She bolted upright with a look of astonishment.

"That's right, it's *exactly* the same. There's no difference at all between not existing before you were born and not existing after you die. None." This is Lucretius enlarging on Epicurus. My life is bounded by two eternities of nonexistence. Why should I fear the nonexistence after my life if I didn't fear the one before it? There's real consolation there.

"So if you weren't scared then, you shouldn't be scared about going back to it. I still get scared sometimes because I forget that. But then I try to really understand it again and I feel much better."

The crisis was over, but she clearly wanted to keep going. I took the opportunity to step into what I see as one of humanism's single greatest contributions: the inversion of our usual perspective on life and death.

One of the most unusual concepts on which my children have been raised is, to paraphrase Monty Python, how amazingly unlikely was their birth. Far from being preordained, they were much, much more likely to have never been born at all. Instead of taking life for granted, we should each see ourselves for what we really are: the unlikely winners of the biggest lottery of all time. And it's here that I see the greatest power of humanism and naturalism to revolutionize our understanding of ourselves by flipping the question of life and death on its head. Yes, it takes courage to look improbability and uncertainty straight in the eye, but it can also lend life a whole new deliciousness. Instead of whining because life doesn't go on forever—something I have done plenty of, believe me—a humanistic perspective makes it possible to see yourself as plenty lucky to have been here at all.

"You know something else I like to think about?" I asked Laney. "I think about the egg that came down into my mommy's tummy right before me. And the one before that, and before that. All of those people never even got a chance to exist, and they never will. There are billions and trillions of people who never even got a chance to be here. But *I made it!* I get a chance to be alive and playing and laughing and dancing and burping and farting ..."

(Brief intermission for laughter and sound effects.)

"I could have just not existed forever—but instead, I get to be alive for a hundred years! And you too! Woohoo! We made it!"

"Omigosh," Laney said, staring into space. "I'm the luckiest thing *ever.*"

"Exactly. So sometimes when I start to complain because it doesn't last forever, I picture all those people who never existed, like they're standing over my shoulder, trillions of them, all telling me, 'Hey, wait a minute, bucko. At least you got a chance. Don't be piggy.'"

More sound effects, more laughter.

Coming to grips with mortality is a lifelong process, one that ebbs and flows for me, as I know it will for them. Delaney was perfectly fine going to sleep that night, and fine the next morning, and the morning after that. It will catch up to her again, but every time it comes it will be more familiar and potentially less frightening. We'll talk about the other consolations: that every bit of you came from the stars and will return to the stars, the peaceful symphony of endorphins that usually accompanies dying, and so on. If all goes well, her head start may help her come up with new consolations to share with the rest of us.

Delaney, thanks to the humanistic perspective of our family, is ahead of the curve. All I can do is keep reminding her, and myself, that knowing and understanding something helps tame our fears. It may not completely feed the bulldog—the fear is too deeply ingrained to ever go completely—but it's a bigger, better milk-bone than anything else we have.

As my children have grown, so too has our exploration of this theme of personal improbability. When my son was eleven, he announced that he needed boxer shorts right away. The reason was the usual hash of peer pressure and arbitrary norms and middle school locker rooms. I drove him to the mall and we bought a few pairs. On the way home, I turned and asked Connor if he knew that he owed his existence to (among many other things) boxer shorts.

What follows is, I submit, a definitively secular exchange of wonder.

This was news to the boy. Not the general idea of owing his existence to countless small happenstances, mind you. He has long enjoyed the knowledge that several hundred things could have prevented his parents from meeting, from finding each other attractive, from dating, from marrying, and from staying married long enough to spring off. He understands that one *particular* sperm and one *particular* egg had to meet for him to ever exist. And he vibrates with dawning excitement as he extends these "had-tos" back through the generations, back to his Confederate great-great-great-great-grandfather who was felled by a Yankee bullet through the neck at nineteen and bled profusely—almost, but not quite, enough to erase the great-great-great-great-grandson he would one day have. Connor has worked his way back through a couple million generations of humans and prehumans to imagine two rat-like creatures mating at the precise moment the asteroid slammed into Chicxulub 65 million years ago, further clinching the existence of their great-great-great etc. grandson.

But boxer shorts—that was a new one. He demanded to know what I was talking about. I told him that sperm can get sluggish if they are too warm, that briefs hold the testicles against a man's warm body, and that four months after his mom and I started trying to create him, without luck, I saw this article that suggested switching to boxer shorts, and *boom* ...

His eyes were wide. "You got pregnant."

"Well *Mom* did, technically, but I ..."

He clutched his head, then turned toward me with an electric look, the look of a person who just missed getting hit by a train. "What if you saw that article a month EARLIER?"

116

He understood. "Or later." We'd added another casual causal coincidence to the march of time: his father stumbling over a random magazine article while waiting for a haircut ...

"While you waited ..." He sputtered, incredulous at the implications. "What if ... WHAT IF SHE FINISHED THE OTHER HAIRCUT BEFORE YOU SAW THE ... ?"

Boy did he get it.

I have several religious friends who think that God fixes these things for us. He put the magazine there and kept the other gentleman's haircut going until I could read it. We each have one ideal mate, and God works things out so we meet, fall in love, have the children we're supposed to have when we're supposed to have them. Setting aside the revolting idea that God wanted an abused woman to marry her abuser, and so on, we still end up with a world that makes me yawn, a world with a good measure of the wonder stripped out. In that world, we are Jehovah's chess pieces, moving in preordained patterns. In addition to believing it false, I find that world exceptionally tedious. It seems to repair the meaning-rupture by removing meaning entirely.

Meditating instead on how amazingly unlikely was your birth: well, if you haven't done it, please be my guest. It's hard to take existence quite so much for granted once you realize how very, very, *very* close you came to missing the dance entirely. And it's a perspective that can lend humanistic parenting a deliciously different flavor from religious parenting.

The most eloquent defense I've heard of this radically new perspective is offered by Richard Dawkins in *Unweaving the Rainbow*:

> We are going to die, and that makes us the lucky ones. Most people are never going to die because they are never going to be born. The potential people who could have been here in my place but who will in fact never see the light of day outnumber the sand grains of Arabia. Certainly those unborn ghosts include greater poets than Keats, scientists greater than Newton. We know this because the set of possible people allowed by our DNA so massively exceeds the set of actual people. In the teeth of these stupefying odds it is you and I, in our ordinariness, that are here ...[6]

Death, not life, is our natural condition. *This* is the extraordinary moment, the departure from the norm. Far from bemoaning our return to nonexistence, we should, for as long as we live, never stop dancing and singing about our current reprieve from it. Humanism is no guarantee that I'll dance. But thanks to that honest and ennobling perspective, I can at least hear the music. And that's a brilliant start.

8. GROWING HUMANISM IN A FAITH-DOMINATED SOCIETY

Maggie Ardiente and Roy Speckhardt

Dialogue concerning, and embrace of, secularization in general and humanism in particular, within the European context, has come to represent something of a litmus test for marking out a compelling framing of life that challenges the myopic and reified framing of the public and the private marking of religious discourse. Much of what stems from this attention to secularization involves battle over ideas, a rethinking of the language and grammar of the public sphere. Unfortunately, certain ways to enhance humanist agendas have given less systematic attention to the development of solid strategies that might be applied across various communities. We bring this to the fore because developing societies committed to secular values and sensibilities have clear strategies and implementation plans that can be used by humanist organizations. What this chapter proposes involves one way of thinking about such strategies for advancing humanist societies. Although we frame much of this conversation regarding the United States as a case study, we believe the general principles and strategies can have value and find application in other areas of the world as well.

In 2007 the Pew Forum conducted the US Religious Landscape Survey, the largest nationwide survey to date on religion in the United States, with a sample of more than 35,000 adults.[1] This survey found that the percentage of people unaffiliated with a particular faith is at 16 percent, more than double the percentage of those who said they were not affiliated with a particular religion as children. Even more interestingly, one in four Americans between the ages of eighteen and twenty-nine say they are not currently affiliated with any religion. Digging deeper, the survey found tremendous diversity within the "unaffiliated":

> Like the other major groups, people who are unaffiliated with any particular religion (16.1%) also exhibit remarkable internal diversity. Although one-quarter of this group consists of those who describe themselves as either atheist or agnostic (1.6% and 2.4% of the adult

population overall, respectively), the majority of the unaffiliated population (12.1% of the adult population overall) is made up of people who simply describe their religion as "nothing in particular." This group, in turn, is fairly evenly divided between the "secular unaffiliated," that is, those who say that religion is not important in their lives (6.3% of the adult population), and the "religious unaffiliated," that is, those who say that religion is either somewhat important or very important in their lives (5.8% of the overall adult population).[2]

So in honing in on the likely non-theist portion of the survey respondents, one can see that 10.3 percent (16.1% less 5.8%) are those who are both unaffiliated and find religion to be unimportant in their lives. In contrast, how are the Protestant and Catholic movement doing? Not so well:

The Landscape Survey confirms that the United States is on the verge of becoming a minority Protestant country; the number of Americans who report that they are members of Protestant denominations now stands at barely 51% ... Catholicism has experienced the greatest net losses as a result of affiliation changes. While nearly one-in-three Americans (31%) were raised in the Catholic faith, today fewer than one-in-four (24%) describe themselves as Catholic.[3]

This is positive news for the future of humanism and the freethought movement, a group made up of national and local organizations and individuals who identify as atheist, humanist, rationalist, agnostic, freethinker, and other terms that imply life without a belief in a god or traditional religion. Not only are the numbers of Americans unaffiliated with any major traditional religion growing, but traditional religion—populous religions such as Protestantism and Catholicism—is declining.

Humanism must be prepared to address the changing religious landscape of the United States. How do we get the 12 percent among the unaffiliated that describe their religion as "nothing in particular" to see the value in affiliating with humanism?

DEFINING HUMANISM

According to the American Humanist Association, the organization that drove the development of modern humanism in the twentieth century, humanism is defined as "a progressive philosophy of life that, without theism or other supernatural beliefs, affirms our ability and responsibility to lead ethical lives of personal fulfillment that aspire to the greater good of humanity."[4] In short, humanism is the idea that you can be good without a belief in a god. Greg Epstein, humanist chaplain at Harvard University, sums it up nicely in his 2009 book *Good Without God: What a Billion Nonreligious People Do Believe*:

> If you identify as an atheist, agnostic, freethinker, rationalist, skeptic, cynic, secular humanist, naturalist, or deist; as spiritual apathetic, nonreligious, "nothing"; or any other irreligious descriptive, you could probably count yourself what I call a Humanist. Feel free to use whatever terminology you prefer—that's not important. We don't believe a god created perfect religions or sacred texts, so why would we believe he or she created one perfect, sacred name that all doubters were required to adopt?[5]

Humanists distinguish themselves from atheists—simply defined as those who do not believe in the existence of a god or gods—based on values described in 2003's Humanist Manifesto III, a successor to the original Humanist Manifesto in 1933 (see the appendix). Humanism goes beyond non-belief in a god or gods because it also defines values and morality rooted in human experience and reason-based knowledge. According to Humanist Manifesto III:

> Knowledge of the world is derived by observation, experimentation, and rational analysis. Humanists find that science is the best method for determining this knowledge as well as for solving problems and developing beneficial technologies. We also recognize the value of new departures in thought, the arts, and inner experience— each subject to analysis by critical intelligence ... Ethical values are derived from human need and interest as tested by experience. Humanists ground values in human welfare shaped by human circumstances, interests, and concerns and extended to the global ecosystem and beyond. We are committed to treating each person as having inherent worth and dignity, and to making informed choices in a context of freedom consonant with responsibility.[6]

Today's freethought movement (freethought defined as "a phenomenon running the gamut from the truly antireligious—those who regarded all religion as a form of superstition and wished to reduce its influence in every aspect of society—to those who adhered to a private, unconventional faith revering some form of God or Providence but at odds with orthodox religious authority"[7]) includes dozens of humanist, atheist, agnostic, secular, and liberal religious groups, such as American Atheists, American Ethical Union, Atheist Alliance International, Camp Quest, Center for Inquiry, Freedom From Religion Foundation, The Richard Dawkins Foundation for Reason and Science, the Secular Coalition for America, and the Society for Humanistic Judaism. While each organization is unique and caters to a particular segment of the movement based on preferred identity or support of the organization's causes, many of these groups work together in common cause. For example, a number of organizations are working in coalition to support efforts to provide humanist chaplains for military service men and women, and many work together to support same-sex marriage.

THE NEED FOR HUMANIST ACTIVISM

More Americans are considering the idea that ethics can be derived from human need and interest, not from ancient texts or divine revelation. And this idea has merit. Some of the credit for this shift in thinking is due to religious right leaders like Pat Robertson and Ralph Reed in the 1990s, followed by those like Tom Delay and Rick Santorum, and now by creationists who want to teach the so-called debate on the merits of evolution, or Biblical literalists who see the United States as a "Christian nation." For example, in his 1992 book, *The New World Order*, prominent American evangelist and host of the Christian television show *The 700 Club*, Pat Robertson wrote:

> When I said during my presidential bid that I would only bring Christians and Jews into the government, I hit a firestorm. "What do you mean?" the media challenged me. "You're not going to bring atheists into the government? How dare you maintain that those who believe in the Judeo-Christian values are better qualified to govern America than Hindus and Muslims?" My simple answer is, "Yes, they are."[8]

Robertson's comment implies that atheists and other non-Christians or non-Jews lack the moral capacity to hold public positions in the United States government. It is a sentiment not argued by the general public: according to a 2007 Gallup poll, only 45 percent of Americans would vote for an atheist who was an otherwise qualified candidate, keeping atheists firmly in last place behind gays, Mormons, and candidates who have been divorced twice.[9] In light of such comments, it became necessary for more prominent atheists to speak out about morals and ethics without the need of a god or divinely revealed text such as the Bible. Unapologetic atheists lodged arguments for non-theistic morality and ethics in a growing body of texts. While many authors have written about atheism and humanism in the twentieth century, there was an explosion in the interest in atheist books with the release of Sam Harris's *The End of Faith*,[10] Daniel Dennett's *Breaking the Spell: Religion as a Natural Phenomenon*,[11] Richard Dawkins's *The God Delusion*,[12] and Christopher Hitchens's *God is Not Great*.[13] All four books, released between 2005 and 2009, became best-sellers.

These books have served as an important shift in the public challenge of taboos about criticizing traditional religious beliefs and questioning the existence of God. For instance, in the words of Harris one gets a sense of this comfort with critiquing ideas and beliefs long assumed beyond critical engagement. He writes:

> Many religious moderates have taken the apparent high road of pluralism, asserting the equal validity of all faiths, but in doing so they neglect to notice the irredeemably sectarian truth claims of each. As long as a Christian believes that only his baptized brethren will be saved on the Day of Judgment, he cannot possibly "respect" the beliefs of others, for he knows that the flames of hell have been stoked by these very ideas and await their adherents even now. Muslims and Jews generally take the same arrogant view of their own enterprises and have spent millennia passionately reiterating the errors of other faiths. It should go without saying that these rival belief systems are all equally uncontaminated by evidence.[14]

In past decades, to publish a forthrightly non-theistic book one needed to go through a freethought publisher, so these books are particularly noteworthy. As recently as early 2004 New York City author Susan Jacoby noted that we have not seen success for non-theist authors since the late 1800s, when a freethought orator like Robert G. Ingersoll could be wildly popular.[15]

Besides written texts such as those mentioned above, another stream of critique and assertion of humanist ethics and morals was seen in the provocative billboards going up on major highways, placed by the American Humanist Association, Freedom From Religion Foundation, and the United Coalition of Reason. One exemplary campaign included a billboard in North Carolina that read "One nation indivisible."[16] Though the campaign cost was just fifteen thousand dollars, it earned millions of dollars in publicity through the overwhelmingly positive media coverage it received around the globe,[17] including a report by Dan Harris on *ABC World News Report with Diane Sawyer*:

> Deep in the heart of the Bible Belt, a dispute over God and country is being waged very publicly.

It all started when an atheist group decided to remind people of the history of the Pledge of Allegiance by putting up six billboards around the state of North Carolina, in honor of the July Fourth holiday. One was placed even on Billy Graham Parkway in Charlotte.

The signs read "One nation indivisible," a reference to the Pledge of Allegiance but deliberately omitting the words "under God."

The billboards, paid for by the North Carolina Secular Association, a coalition of groups including the Western North Carolina Atheists, were intended to show that even Americans who don't believe in God can be patriotic and to promote a sense of unity.[18]

These billboards in North Carolina, like those put in place by the United Coalition of Reason, have brought together non-theistic organizations to do more than just put up billboards. The group in Philadelphia, for instance, went on to do work for the homeless jointly with a Baptist church, and another group in West Virginia worked with a food bank to demonstrate how you can be good without God. In fact, a significant number of humanist groups at the local level are making service and volunteer projects a part of their regular meetings. Other, smaller streams have come together as well:

- In 2006 Julia Sweeney's one-woman show, *Letting Go of God*, received a positive *New York Times* theater review for being "refreshingly unrancourous, lucid and, yes, inspirational."[19]
- The American Humanist Association ran the first national radio adverts that were clearly non-theist on Air America in 2007.
- Camp Quest, the summer camp for freethinking kids, today has six branches in North America and one in Europe.[20]

Figure 8.1 American Humanist Association billboard campaign.

- The year 2009 marked the 200th anniversary of Charles Darwin's birth; the American Humanist Association, as the administrator for the website DarwinDay.org, held high-profile events across the country, including a special series on scores of college campuses, where it screened *Becoming Human*, a series that aired on PBS.
- In 2010, the Secular Coalition for America arranged the first ever meeting of non-theistic leaders at the White House.[21]
- Even more recently, the Supreme Court took the advice provided in a joint amicus brief on behalf of six organizations including the American Ethical Union and others, allowing universities to require funded clubs to follow their non-discrimination policies.[22]

Finally, the conclusion of the second term of President George W. Bush, a committed born-again Christian who regularly invoked God and religious language in his public addresses, and the election of President Barack Obama, whose values, he states, come from his mother, who was "a lonely witness for secular humanism,"[23] provided optimism for humanists and atheists. During his presidential inauguration speech on January 20, 2009, he stated, "For we know that our patchwork heritage is a strength, not a weakness. We are a nation of Christians and Muslims, Jews and Hindus—and nonbelievers."[24] This would be the first time a United States president would refer to atheists and humanists in a positive way, categorizing them as "nonbelievers." But political changes aren't enough to guarantee progress. Further strategy on humanist activism is needed to realize a significant change in how the general public sees humanists and atheists.

CASE STUDIES ON HUMANIST ACTIVISM

Now that there is an established need to grow humanism in the United States, strategies are needed to accomplish the goal of seeing a larger percentage of the population understanding what humanism means and identifying as humanists in their philosophical or religious outlook. The first step is effectively communicating to the public what humanism is and why it matters. The second step is to build a human rights movement by identifying when atheist discrimination occurs and combating it in the legislative or legal system. And finally, the third step is to encourage individuals to "come out" as a humanist and identify as a nonreligious person.

Strategy 1: Effective communication
What stance should humanists and other freethinkers take toward effectively communicating with the public? Herb Silverman, in addition to being

a math professor at the College of Charleston in South Carolina, is the president of the Secular Coalition for America, the organization that represents the American Humanist Association, the American Ethical Union, the Society for Humanistic Judaism, and other collegial groups in the halls of Congress. Herb's activism in the freethought movement began when he challenged a South Carolina state constitution law that prohibited atheists from running for public office. After nine years, he was able to hold the office of notary public and declared the law illegal.[25] Writing for the *Washington Post*, Silverman said,

> Theist or non-theist, we are all evangelists for issues that matter to us. The question isn't whether we should proselytize, but how and how often? ... I think we shouldn't be screaming atheists, nor should we go door-to-door spreading the word that there are no gods. But many of us are comfortable writing letters to the editor, participating in forums or debates, writing to members of Congress, or coming out of our atheist and humanist closets at appropriate times. For all of us, religious or not, people are likely to respect our worldview more for what we do, than for what we preach.[26]

So, when one considers Silverman's approach toward outreach and activism, it is easy to see that something must be done to raise the positive profile of the humanist worldview. This has led to more national organizations presenting themselves to the general public through advertising. For instance, the holiday advertising campaigns that the American Humanist Association ran in Washington, DC, New York, and elsewhere beginning in 2007 featured the text: "Just be good for goodness' sake," alongside "Why believe in a god?" or alongside "No god, no problem." Most people see these campaigns for what they are: an attempt to raise the flag for non-theists who focus on doing good, and thus attract likely humanists. The reactions from religious and nonreligious are mostly positive.[27] But as absurd as it sounds, a surprising number of conservative religious people are convinced that the adverts are aimed at them, and are an underhanded attempt to convert them to atheism during their sacred holiday season.

During an appearance on CNN Headline News, Catholic League President Bill Donohue had the audacity to call the American Humanist Association's open-ended question "Why believe in a god?" "hate speech," while simultaneously comparing humanists to the serial killer Jeffrey Dahmer and to Adolf Hitler. He said that it was impossible to be good for goodness' sake, and that the advert was a personal attack on his faith and that of other religious people. Fox News's Bill O'Reilly even asked, "Why do they loathe the baby Jesus? You don't sell atheism by running down a baby!"[28] While this phenomenon of fundamentalists misinterpreting non-theist intent with these adverts may have more to do with selling a religious conservative image for more viewers, it does raise some interesting questions: Is it worth risking offense to spread the freethought message? Can humanists be clear about our identity without alienating our progressive religious allies? As humanists and freethinkers are seeking to expand a positive impact on the world and increase the respect and acceptance of the humanist worldview, the answer to both these questions must be "yes." That, however, doesn't mean non-theists are being called upon to offend purposely the mainstream religious people by burning Bibles or flushing Korans down the toilet. To raise our profile humanists need to continue outreach and activism and should be clear about identity, not for the purpose of offending people, but *regardless* of whether the very existence of non-theists does cause offence.

Strategy 2: Building a humanist rights movement

Philip K. Paulson, a humanist who served in the Vietnam War, wrote about his experiences in the September–October 1989 issue of *The Humanist* magazine, particularly on sharing his atheism to others:

> I knew that proclaiming to be an atheist while on duty in South Vietnam could likely prejudice promotions and possibly cause harmful reprisals. An atheist was perceived as tantamount to being a communist. Our army chaplain was a fundamentalist Christian who saw the devil in virtually everything he didn't believe in. Army chaplains wielded a lot of power; their opinions could make the difference between whether or not you got promoted. So, I was quiet about my nonbelief in God.[29]

Paulson's story is common, not just in the military but in everyday job practices—business, teaching, medicine, and so on. In addition to the pressure to keep one's non-belief private, is actual discrimination against atheists. In one Tennessee school a pagan girl discovered she was the only student in the school to show up the day they held a Christian revival nearby. While she had been private about her pagan identity in the past, she faced such harsh harassment that the family was forced out of town.[30] In Bastrop, Louisiana, Damon Fowler was ostracized by his fellow classmates and parents for objecting to a religious prayer planned for his public high school's graduation.[31] In Cranston, Rhode Island, Jessica Ahlquist was called a "stupid atheist" for filing a lawsuit with the American Civil Liberties Union to remove a banner containing a religious prayer that had been hanging in the school since the 1960s.[32] And in Hardesty, Oklahoma, Nicole Smalkowski was kicked off her school's basketball team and nearly driven out of town for refusing to participate in group prayer before games.[33] In response, national organizations like the American Humanist Association, American Atheists, and Freedom From Religion Foundation have made it a priority to represent humanists in the courts when they are discriminated against based on their viewpoint. There are clear instances where humanists have been fired from their jobs,[34] been passed on promotions,[35] seen their taxpayer money support religious schools,[36] been forced to listen to inappropriate religious proselytizing in public settings,[37] and many others. It is clear that what is happening is a drive toward a humanist rights movement.

Furthermore, one area where change is overdue is in the nation's court system as it pertains to the rights of the non-theists' growing minority. Humanists are held captive to the will of Christian conservatives who emphasize their superior position by using the power of government to enforce laws that put truth claims about religion in front of us at every turn. Humanists must endure statements about the nation's trust in a fictional god on money,[38] on public buildings, and in ceremonies for public office—from census worker to president. Children and grandchildren have to hear a statement that excludes them and their family every day at school, and they are asked to stand and recite the statement along with the majority.[39] Humanists have to watch on as neighbors go unpunished for child abuse because they claim a religious exemption to certain laws.[40] And such exemptions may also apply to vaccinations that leave all children more vulnerable to disease.[41] It is critical for national humanist organizations to lead the fight against atheist discrimination and protect religious freedom in the United States. In addition, humanists and atheists must recognize discrimination when it happens and speak out.

Strategy 3: "Coming out" as a humanist

In 1978, Proposition 6 was the California ballot measure aimed at preventing gay people from working as teachers in public schools. On election night that year, Harvey Milk said the following:

> To the gay community all over this state, my message to you is: so far a lot of people joined us and rejected Proposition 6, and we owe them something. We owe them to continue the education campaign that took place. We must destroy the myths once and for all, shatter them. We must continue to speak out, and most importantly, most importantly, every gay person must come out.
>
> As difficult as it is you must tell your immediate family, you must tell your relatives, you must tell your friends, if indeed they are your friends, you must tell your neighbors, you must tell the people you work with, you must tell the people in the stores you shop in,

and once they realize that we are indeed their children, that we are indeed everywhere, every myth, every lie, every innuendo will be destroyed once and for all.

And once you do, you will feel so much better.[42]

Milk's strategies were controversial and edgy, but they laid the groundwork for dramatic progress for the LGBT (lesbian, gay, bisexual, and transgender) movement. As Milk exemplified with respect to LGBT struggles for justice, it is clear that progress in the humanist movement can only be made when humanists, atheists, and other freethinkers are open about their non-belief and identify as a nonreligious person. When religious people see that non-religious people are good people with morals and ethics, then myths about nonreligious people being immoral will diminish.

Yet, individual outreach is just as critical, if not more important, than support of freethought groups. Frequently, for example, the New York City Atheists[43] have a table on Columbus Circle where they invite passers-by to learn more about what it means to lack a belief in a god. The act of sitting there is both empowering and a little scary, but it is an opportunity as well. Whenever we come out of non-theist closets and voice secular pride, there is a chance to challenge such stereotypes. When religious people see humanists and atheists performing community service projects, or getting involved in the electoral process, or serving as their doctors, teachers, friends, and neighbors, it destroys negative myths about non-theists in America.

CONCLUSION

There is no doubt that prejudice persists against non-theists. We want to move along the path from that current intolerance, to tolerance of our non-theist perspective. And then from tolerance, to a mutual respect for our humanist viewpoints, to a day when there is a common appreciation for our reason-based, science-oriented approach to solving problems.

By working individually and together, humanists can mobilize for change through public outreach, activism, advocacy, and efforts to change hearts and minds one person at a time. If the freethought movement is willing to work with natural allies, the dozens of organizations in this orbit can seize this moment, and move society in a direction of progress.

There was a time when it seemed the only way to progress was through gradual social evolution, which too often stagnated, or, even worse, experienced backslides. But now humanists are riding a dramatic wave of change. All humanists and freethinkers should join together to bolster this wave and give it the energy it needs to last.

APPENDIX: HUMANIST MANIFESTOS

The first document in the appendix is the Humanist Manifesto I, produced in 1933, by Roy Wood Sellars and Raymond Bragg. It takes into consideration the value of humanism in light of world conditions during that historical moment—racial discrimination, the underbelly conditions of industrial life, and so on. After the trauma of war, the struggle for social transformation on a variety of fronts including race, gender, sexuality, and nuclear weapons, and other world conditions, a second manifesto was produced (1973), the primary authors being Paul Kurtz and Edwin Wilson. The appeal to humanism as an important corrective to traditional thinking and action is carried through both manifestos. A third manifesto—Humanist Manifesto III—was published in 2003. It offers ongoing support for the structure of humanism as having value on the levels of rational thought, ethics, and policy. Readers should pay careful attention to the transformation in the use of "religion" in the progression from the first to the third.

The final document is the Neo-Humanist Statement of Secular Principles and Values, written by Paul Kurtz in 2010. This document seeks to recognize but advance humanism beyond traditional formulation (hence, "Neo-") through attention to sixteen principles or recommendations that cover a variety of aspects of individual and collective life.

While there are numerous other documents that provide an outline of humanist belief and practice, space restraints make it impossible to include them all here. However, readers may be interested in additional materials such as:

- "Amsterdam Declaration 2002," World Humanist Congress, www.iheu. org/adamdecl.htm
- "An African-American Humanist Declaration," *Free Inquiry*, Council for Secular Humanism (Amherst, NY). Available in Anthony B. Pinn, *By These Hands: A Documentary History of African American Humanism* (New York: New York University Press, 2001), 319–26.

- "A Secular Humanist Declaration," Council for Democratic and Secular Humanism, 1980, www.secularhumanism.org/index.php?page=declaration&section=main

HUMANIST MANIFESTO I

The Manifesto is a product of many minds. It was designed to represent a developing point of view, not a new creed. The individuals whose signatures appear would, had they been writing individual statements, have stated the propositions in differing terms. The importance of the document is that more than thirty men have come to general agreement on matters of final concern and that these men are undoubtedly representative of a large number who are forging a new philosophy out of the materials of the modern world.

Raymond B. Bragg (1933)

The time has come for widespread recognition of the radical changes in religious beliefs throughout the modern world. The time is past for mere revision of traditional attitudes. Science and economic change have disrupted the old beliefs. Religions the world over are under the necessity of coming to terms with new conditions created by a vastly increased knowledge and experience. In every field of human activity, the vital movement is now in the direction of a candid and explicit humanism. In order that religious humanism may be better understood we, the undersigned, desire to make certain affirmations which we believe the facts of our contemporary life demonstrate.

There is great danger of a final, and we believe fatal, identification of the word religion with doctrines and methods which have lost their significance and which are powerless to solve the problem of human living in the Twentieth Century. Religions have always been means for realizing the highest values of life. Their end has been accomplished through the interpretation of the total environing situation (theology or world view), the sense of values resulting therefrom (goal or ideal), and the technique (cult), established for realizing the satisfactory life. A change in any of these factors results in alteration of the outward forms of religion. This fact explains the changefulness of religions through the centuries. But through all changes religion itself remains constant in its quest for abiding values, an inseparable feature of human life.

Today man's larger understanding of the universe, his scientific achievements, and deeper appreciation of brotherhood, have created a situation which requires a new statement of the means and purposes of religion. Such a vital, fearless, and frank religion capable of furnishing adequate social goals and personal satisfactions may appear to many people as a complete break

130

with the past. While this age does owe a vast debt to the traditional religions, it is none the less obvious that any religion that can hope to be a synthesizing and dynamic force for today must be shaped for the needs of this age. To establish such a religion is a major necessity of the present. It is a responsibility which rests upon this generation. We therefore affirm the following:

FIRST: Religious humanists regard the universe as self-existing and not created.

SECOND: Humanism believes that man is a part of nature and that he has emerged as a result of a continuous process.

THIRD: Holding an organic view of life, humanists find that the traditional dualism of mind and body must be rejected.

FOURTH: Humanism recognizes that man's religious culture and civilization, as clearly depicted by anthropology and history, are the product of a gradual development due to his interaction with his natural environment and with his social heritage. The individual born into a particular culture is largely molded by that culture.

FIFTH: Humanism asserts that the nature of the universe depicted by modern science makes unacceptable any supernatural or cosmic guarantees of human values. Obviously humanism does not deny the possibility of realities as yet undiscovered, but it does insist that the way to determine the existence and value of any and all realities is by means of intelligent inquiry and by the assessment of their relations to human needs. Religion must formulate its hopes and plans in the light of the scientific spirit and method.

SIXTH: We are convinced that the time has passed for theism, deism, modernism, and the several varieties of "new thought".

SEVENTH: Religion consists of those actions, purposes, and experiences which are humanly significant. Nothing human is alien to the religious. It includes labor, art, science, philosophy, love, friendship, recreation—all that is in its degree expressive of intelligently satisfying human living. The distinction between the sacred and the secular can no longer be maintained.

EIGHTH: Religious Humanism considers the complete realization of human personality to be the end of man's life and seeks its development and fulfillment in the here and now. This is the explanation of the humanist's social passion.

NINTH: In the place of the old attitudes involved in worship and prayer the humanist finds his religious emotions expressed in a heightened sense of personal life and in a cooperative effort to promote social well-being.

TENTH: It follows that there will be no uniquely religious emotions and attitudes of the kind hitherto associated with belief in the supernatural.

ELEVENTH: Man will learn to face the crises of life in terms of his knowledge of their naturalness and probability. Reasonable and manly attitudes will be fostered by education and supported by custom. We assume that humanism will take the path of social and mental hygiene and discourage sentimental and unreal hopes and wishful thinking.

TWELFTH: Believing that religion must work increasingly for joy in living, religious humanists aim to foster the creative in man and to encourage achievements that add to the satisfactions of life.

THIRTEENTH: Religious humanism maintains that all associations and institutions exist for the fulfillment of human life. The intelligent evaluation, transformation, control, and direction of such associations and institutions with a view to the enhancement of human life is the purpose and program of humanism. Certainly religious institutions, their ritualistic forms, ecclesiastical methods, and communal activities must be reconstituted as rapidly as experience allows, in order to function effectively in the modern world.

FOURTEENTH: The humanists are firmly convinced that existing acquisitive and profit-motivated society has shown itself to be inadequate and that a radical change in methods, controls, and motives must be instituted. A socialized and cooperative economic order must be established to the end that the equitable distribution of the means of life be possible. The goal of humanism is a free and universal society in which people voluntarily and intelligently cooperate for the common good. Humanists demand a shared life in a shared world.

FIFTEENTH AND LAST: We assert that humanism will: (a) affirm life rather than deny it; (b) seek to elicit the possibilities of life, not flee from them; and (c) endeavor to establish the conditions of a satisfactory life for all, not merely for the few. By this positive morale and intention humanism will be guided, and from this perspective and alignment the techniques and efforts of humanism will flow.

So stand the theses of religious humanism. Though we consider the religious forms and ideas of our fathers no longer adequate, the quest for the good life is still the central task for mankind. Man is at last becoming aware that he alone is responsible for the realization of the world of his dreams, that he has within himself the power for its achievement. He must set intelligence and will to the task.

HUMANIST MANIFESTO II

Preface

It is forty years since Humanist Manifesto I (1933) appeared. Events since then make that earlier statement seem far too optimistic. Nazism has shown the depths of brutality of which humanity is capable. Other totalitarian regimes have suppressed human rights without ending poverty. Science has sometimes brought evil as well as good. Recent decades have shown that inhuman wars can be made in the name of peace. The beginnings of police states, even in democratic societies, widespread government espionage, and other abuses of power by military, political, and industrial elites, and the continuance of unyielding racism, all present a different and difficult social outlook. In various societies, the demands of women and minority groups for equal rights effectively challenge our generation.

As we approach the twenty-first century, however, an affirmative and hopeful vision is needed. Faith, commensurate with advancing knowledge, is also necessary. In the choice between despair and hope, humanists respond in this Humanist Manifesto II with a positive declaration for times of uncertainty.

As in 1933, humanists still believe that traditional theism, especially faith in the prayer-hearing God, assumed to live and care for persons, to hear and understand their prayers, and to be able to do something about them, is an unproved and outmoded faith. Salvationism, based on mere affirmation, still appears as harmful, diverting people with false hopes of heaven hereafter. Reasonable minds look to other means for survival.

Those who sign Humanist Manifesto II disclaim that they are setting forth a binding credo; their individual views would be stated in widely varying ways. This statement is, however, reaching for vision in a time that needs direction. It is social analysis in an effort at consensus. New statements should be developed to supersede this, but for today it is our conviction that humanism offers an alternative that can serve present-day needs and guide humankind toward the future.

Paul Kurtz and Edwin H. Wilson (1973)

The next century can be and should be the humanistic century. Dramatic scientific, technological, and ever-accelerating social and political changes crowd our awareness. We have virtually conquered the planet, explored the moon, overcome the natural limits of travel and communication; we stand at the dawn of a new age, ready to move farther into space and perhaps inhabit other planets. Using technology wisely, we can control our environment, conquer poverty, markedly reduce disease, extend our life-span, significantly modify our behavior, alter the course of human evolution and cultural development, unlock vast new powers, and provide humankind with unparalleled opportunity for achieving an abundant and meaningful life.

The future is, however, filled with dangers. In learning to apply the scientific method to nature and human life, we have opened the door to ecological damage, over-population, dehumanizing institutions, totalitarian repression, and nuclear and bio-chemical disaster. Faced with apocalyptic prophesies and doomsday scenarios, many flee in despair from reason and embrace irrational cults and theologies of withdrawal and retreat.

Traditional moral codes and newer irrational cults both fail to meet the pressing needs of today and tomorrow. False "theologies of hope" and messianic ideologies, substituting new dogmas for old, cannot cope with existing world realities. They separate rather than unite peoples.

Humanity, to survive, requires bold and daring measures. We need to extend the uses of scientific method, not renounce them, to fuse reason with compassion in order to build constructive social and moral values. Confronted by many possible futures, we must decide which to pursue. The ultimate goal should be the fulfillment of the potential for growth in each human personality—not for the favored few, but for all of humankind. Only a shared world and global measures will suffice.

A humanist outlook will tap the creativity of each human being and provide the vision and courage for us to work together. This outlook emphasizes the role human beings can play in their own spheres of action. The decades ahead call for dedicated, clear-minded men and women able to marshal the will, intelligence, and cooperative skills for shaping a desirable future. Humanism can provide the purpose and inspiration that so many seek; it can give personal meaning and significance to human life.

Many kinds of humanism exist in the contemporary world. The varieties and emphases of naturalistic humanism include "scientific," "ethical," "democratic," "religious," and "Marxist" humanism. Free thought, atheism, agnosticism, skepticism, deism, rationalism, ethical culture, and liberal religion all claim to be heir to the humanist tradition. Humanism traces its roots from ancient China, classical Greece and Rome, through the Renaissance and the Enlightenment, to the scientific revolution of the modern world. But views that merely reject theism are not equivalent to humanism. They lack commitment to the positive belief in the possibilities of human progress and to the values central to it. Many within religious groups, believing in the future of humanism, now claim humanist credentials. Humanism is an ethical process through which we all can move, above and beyond the divisive particulars, heroic personalities, dogmatic creeds, and ritual customs of past religions or their mere negation.

We affirm a set of common principles that can serve as a basis for united action—positive principles relevant to the present human condition. They are a design for a secular society on a planetary scale.

For these reasons, we submit this new Humanist Manifesto for the future of humankind; for us, it is a vision of hope, a direction for satisfying survival.

Religion

FIRST: In the best sense, religion may inspire dedication to the highest ethical ideals. The cultivation of moral devotion and creative imagination is an expression of genuine "spiritual" experience and aspiration.

We believe, however, that traditional dogmatic or authoritarian religions that place revelation, God, ritual, or creed above human needs and experience do a disservice to the human species. Any account of nature should pass the tests of scientific evidence; in our judgment, the dogmas and myths of traditional religions do not do so. Even at this late date in human history, certain elementary facts based upon the critical use of scientific reason have to be restated. We find insufficient evidence for belief in the existence of a supernatural; it is either meaningless or irrelevant to the question of survival and fulfillment of the human race. As nontheists, we begin with humans not God, nature not deity. Nature may indeed be broader and deeper than we now know; any new discoveries, however, will but enlarge our knowledge of the natural.

Some humanists believe we should reinterpret traditional religions and reinvest them with meanings appropriate to the current situation. Such redefinitions, however, often perpetuate old dependencies and escapisms; they easily become obscurantist, impeding the free use of the intellect. We need, instead, radically new human purposes and goals.

We appreciate the need to preserve the best ethical teachings in the religious traditions of humankind, many of which we share in common. But we reject those features of traditional religious morality that deny humans a full appreciation of their own potentialities and responsibilities. Traditional religions often offer solace to humans, but, as often, they inhibit humans from helping themselves or experiencing their full potentialities. Such institutions, creeds, and rituals often impede the will to serve others. Too often traditional faiths encourage dependence rather than independence, obedience rather than affirmation, fear rather than courage. More recently they have generated concerned social action, with many signs of relevance appearing in the wake of the "God Is Dead" theologies. But we can discover no divine purpose or providence for the human species. While there is much that we do not know, humans are responsible for what we are or will become. No deity will save us; we must save ourselves.

SECOND: Promises of immortal salvation or fear of eternal damnation are both illusory and harmful. They distract humans from present concerns, from self-actualization, and from rectifying social injustices. Modern science discredits such historic concepts as the "ghost in the machine" and the "separable soul." Rather, science affirms that the human species is an emergence from natural evolutionary forces. As far as we know, the total personality is a function of the biological organism transacting in a social and cultural context. There is no credible evidence that life survives the death of the body. We continue to exist in our progeny and in the way that our lives have influenced others in our culture.

Traditional religions are surely not the only obstacles to human progress. Other ideologies also impede human advance. Some forms of political doctrine, for instance, function religiously, reflecting the worst features of orthodoxy and authoritarianism, especially when they sacrifice individuals on the altar of Utopian promises. Purely economic and political viewpoints, whether capitalist or communist, often function as religious and ideological dogma. Although humans undoubtedly need economic and political goals, they also need creative values by which to live.

Ethics

THIRD: We affirm that moral values derive their source from human experience. Ethics is autonomous and situational needing no theological or ideological sanction. Ethics stems from human need and interest. To deny this distorts the whole basis of life. Human life has meaning because we create and develop our futures. Happiness and the creative realization of human needs and desires, individually and in shared enjoyment, are continuous themes of humanism. We strive for the good life, here and now. The goal is to pursue life's enrichment despite debasing forces of vulgarization, commercialization, and dehumanization.

FOURTH: Reason and intelligence are the most effective instruments that humankind possesses. There is no substitute: neither faith nor passion suffices in itself. The controlled use of scientific methods, which have transformed the natural and social sciences since the Renaissance, must be extended further in the solution of human problems. But reason must be tempered by humility, since no group has a monopoly of wisdom or virtue. Nor is there any guarantee that all problems can be solved or all questions answered. Yet critical intelligence, infused by a sense of human caring, is the best method that humanity has for resolving problems. Reason should be balanced with compassion and empathy and the whole person fulfilled. Thus, we are not advocating the use of scientific intelligence independent of or in opposition to emotion, for we believe in the cultivation of feeling and love. As science pushes back the boundary of the known, humankind's sense of wonder is continually renewed, and art, poetry, and music find their places, along with religion and ethics.

The Individual

FIFTH: The preciousness and dignity of the individual person is a central humanist value. Individuals should be encouraged to realize their own creative talents and desires. We reject all religious, ideological, or moral codes that denigrate the individual, suppress freedom, dull intellect, dehumanize personality. We believe in maximum individual autonomy consonant with social responsibility. Although science can account for the causes of behavior, the possibilities of individual freedom of choice exist in human life and should be increased.

SIXTH: In the area of sexuality, we believe that intolerant attitudes, often cultivated by orthodox religions and puritanical cultures, unduly repress sexual conduct. The right to birth control, abortion, and divorce should be recognized. While we do not approve of exploitive, denigrating forms of sexual expression, neither do we wish to prohibit, by law or social sanction, sexual behavior between consenting adults. The many varieties of sexual exploration should not in themselves be considered "evil." Without countenancing mindless permissiveness or unbridled promiscuity, a civilized society should be a tolerant one. Short of harming others or compelling them to do likewise, individuals should be permitted to express their sexual proclivities and pursue their lifestyles as they desire. We wish to cultivate the development of a responsible attitude toward sexuality, in which humans are not exploited as sexual objects, and in which intimacy, sensitivity, respect, and honesty in interpersonal relations are encouraged. Moral education for children and adults is an important way of developing awareness and sexual maturity.

Democratic Society

SEVENTH: To enhance freedom and dignity the individual must experience a full range of civil liberties in all societies. This includes freedom of speech and the press, political democracy, the legal right of opposition to governmental policies, fair judicial process, religious liberty, freedom of association, and artistic, scientific, and cultural freedom. It also includes a recognition of an individual's right to die with dignity, euthanasia, and the right to suicide. We oppose the increasing invasion of privacy, by whatever means, in both totalitarian and democratic societies. We would safeguard, extend, and implement the principles of human freedom evolved from the Magna Carta to the Bill of Rights, the Rights of Man, and the Universal Declaration of Human Rights.

EIGHTH: We are committed to an open and democratic society. We must extend participatory democracy in its true sense to the economy, the school, the family, the workplace, and voluntary associations. Decision-making must be decentralized to include widespread involvement of people at all levels— social, political, and economic. All persons should have a voice in developing the values and goals that determine their lives. Institutions should be responsive to expressed desires and needs. The conditions of work, education, devotion, and play should be humanized. Alienating forces should be modified or eradicated and bureaucratic structures should be held to a minimum. People are more important than decalogues, rules, proscriptions, or regulations.

NINTH: The separation of church and state and the separation of ideology and state are imperatives. The state should encourage maximum freedom for different moral, political, religious, and social values in society. It should not favor any particular religious bodies through the use of public monies, nor espouse a single ideology and function thereby as an instrument of propaganda or oppression, particularly against dissenters.

TENTH: Humane societies should evaluate economic systems not by rhetoric or ideology, but by whether or not they increase economic well-being for all individuals and groups, minimize poverty and hardship, increase the sum of human satisfaction, and enhance the quality of life. Hence the door is open to alternative economic systems. We need to democratize the economy and judge it by its responsiveness to human needs, testing results in terms of the common good.

ELEVENTH: The principle of moral equality must be furthered through elimination of all discrimination based upon race, religion, sex, age, or national origin. This means equality of opportunity and recognition of talent and merit. Individuals should be encouraged to contribute to their own betterment. If unable, then society should provide means to satisfy their basic economic, health, and cultural needs, including, wherever resources make possible, a minimum guaranteed annual income. We are concerned for the welfare of the aged, the infirm, the disadvantaged, and also for the outcasts—the mentally retarded, abandoned, or abused children, the handicapped, prisoners, and addicts—for all who are neglected or ignored by society. Practicing humanists should make it their vocation to humanize personal relations.

We believe in the right to universal education. Everyone has a right to the cultural opportunity to fulfill his or her unique capacities and talents. The schools should foster satisfying and productive living. They should be open at all levels to any and all; the achievement of excellence should be encouraged. Innovative and experimental forms of education are to be welcomed. The energy and idealism of the young deserve to be appreciated and channeled to constructive purposes.

We deplore racial, religious, ethnic, or class antagonisms. Although we believe in cultural diversity and encourage racial and ethnic pride, we reject separations which promote alienation and set people and groups against each other; we envision an integrated community where people have a maximum opportunity for free and voluntary association.

We are critical of sexism or sexual chauvinism—male or female. We believe in equal rights for both women and men to fulfill their unique careers and potentialities as they see fit, free of invidious discrimination.

World Community

TWELFTH: We deplore the division of humankind on nationalistic grounds. We have reached a turning point in human history where the best option is to transcend the limits of national sovereignty and to move toward the building of a world community in which all sectors of the human family can participate. Thus we look to the development of a system of world law and a world order based upon transnational federal government. This would appreciate cultural pluralism and diversity. It would not exclude pride in national origins and accomplishments nor the handling of regional problems on a regional basis. Human progress, however, can no longer be achieved by focusing on one section of the world, Western or Eastern, developed or underdeveloped. For the first time in human history, no part of humankind can be isolated from any other. Each person's future is in some way linked to all. We thus reaffirm a commitment to the building of world community, at the same time recognizing that this commits us to some hard choices.

THIRTEENTH: This world community must renounce the resort to violence and force as a method of solving international disputes. We believe in the peaceful adjudication of differences by international courts and by the development of the arts of negotiation and compromise. War is obsolete. So is the use of nuclear, biological, and chemical weapons. It is a planetary imperative to reduce the level of military expenditures and turn these savings to peaceful and people-oriented uses.

FOURTEENTH: The world community must engage in cooperative planning concerning the use of rapidly depleting resources. The planet earth must be considered a single ecosystem. Ecological damage, resource depletion, and excessive population growth must be checked by international concord. The cultivation and conservation of nature is a moral value; we should perceive ourselves as integral to the sources of our being in nature. We must free our world from needless pollution and waste, responsibly guarding and creating wealth, both natural and human. Exploitation of natural resources, uncurbed by social conscience, must end.

FIFTEENTH: The problems of economic growth and development can no longer be resolved by one nation alone; they are worldwide in scope. It is the moral obligation of the developed nations to provide—through an international authority that safeguards human rights—massive technical, agricultural, medical, and economic assistance, including birth control techniques, to the developing portions of the globe. World poverty must cease. Hence extreme disproportions in wealth, income, and economic growth should be reduced on a worldwide basis.

SIXTEENTH: Technology is a vital key to human progress and development. We deplore any neo-romantic efforts to condemn indiscriminately all technology and science or to counsel retreat from its further extension and use for the good of humankind. We would resist any moves to censor basic scientific research on moral, political, or social grounds. Technology must, however, be carefully judged by the consequences of its use; harmful and destructive changes should be avoided. We are particularly disturbed when technology and bureaucracy control, manipulate, or modify human beings without their consent. Technological feasibility does not imply social or cultural desirability.

SEVENTEENTH: We must expand communication and transportation across frontiers. Travel restrictions must cease. The world must be open to diverse political, ideological, and moral viewpoints and evolve a worldwide system of television and radio for information and education. We thus call for full international cooperation in culture, science, the arts, and technology across ideological borders. We must learn to live openly together or we shall perish together.

Humanity As a Whole

IN CLOSING: The world cannot wait for a reconciliation of competing political or economic systems to solve its problems. These are the times for men and women of goodwill to further the building of a peaceful and prosperous world. We urge that parochial loyalties and inflexible moral and religious ideologies be transcended. We urge recognition of the common humanity of all people. We further urge the use of reason and compassion to produce the kind of world we want—a world in which peace, prosperity, freedom, and happiness are widely shared. Let us not abandon that vision in despair or cowardice. We are responsible for what we are or will be. Let us work together for a humane world by means commensurate with humane ends. Destructive ideological differences among communism, capitalism, socialism, conservatism, liberalism, and radicalism should be overcome. Let us call for an end to terror and hatred. We will survive and prosper only in a world of shared humane values. We can initiate new directions for humankind; ancient rivalries can be superseded by broad-based cooperative efforts. The commitment to tolerance, understanding, and peaceful negotiation does not necessitate acquiescence to the status quo nor the damming up of dynamic and revolutionary forces. The true revolution is occurring and can continue in countless nonviolent adjustments. But this entails the willingness to step forward onto new and expanding plateaus. At the present juncture of history, commitment to all humankind is the highest commitment of which we are capable; it transcends the narrow allegiances of church, state, party, class, or race in moving toward a wider vision of human potentiality. What more daring a goal for humankind than for each person to become, in ideal as well as practice, a citizen of a world community. It is a classical vision; we can now give it new vitality. Humanism thus interpreted is a moral force that has time on its side. We believe that humankind has the potential, intelligence, goodwill, and cooperative skill to implement this commitment in the decades ahead.

We, the undersigned, while not necessarily endorsing every detail of the above, pledge our general support to Humanist Manifesto II for the future of humankind. These affirmations are not a final credo or dogma but an expression of a living and growing faith. We invite others in all lands to join us in further developing and working for these goals.

HUMANIST MANIFESTO III

Humanism and Its Aspirations: Humanist Manifesto III, a successor to the Humanist Manifesto of 1933

Humanism is a progressive philosophy of life that, without supernaturalism, affirms our ability and responsibility to lead ethical lives of personal fulfillment that aspire to the greater good of humanity.

The life stance of Humanism—guided by reason, inspired by compassion, and informed by experience—encourages us to live life well and fully. It evolved through the ages and continues to develop through the efforts of thoughtful people who recognize that values and ideals, however carefully wrought, are subject to change as our knowledge and understandings advance.

This document is part of an ongoing effort to manifest in clear and positive terms the conceptual boundaries of Humanism, not what we must believe but a consensus of what we do believe. It is in this sense that we affirm the following:

Knowledge of the world is derived by observation, experimentation, and rational analysis. Humanists find that science is the best method for determining this knowledge as well as for solving problems and developing beneficial technologies. We also recognize the value of new departures in thought, the arts, and inner experience—each subject to analysis by critical intelligence.

Humans are an integral part of nature, the result of unguided evolutionary change. Humanists recognize nature as self-existing. We accept our life as all and enough, distinguishing things as they are from things as we might wish or imagine them to be. We welcome the challenges of the future, and are drawn to and undaunted by the yet to be known.

Ethical values are derived from human need and interest as tested by experience. Humanists ground values in human welfare shaped by human circumstances, interests, and concerns and extended to the global ecosystem and beyond. We are committed to treating each person as having inherent worth and dignity, and to making informed choices in a context of freedom consonant with responsibility.

Life's fulfillment emerges from individual participation in the service of humane ideals. We aim for our fullest possible development and animate our lives with a deep sense of purpose, finding wonder and awe in the joys and beauties of human existence, its challenges and tragedies, and even in

142

the inevitability and finality of death. Humanists rely on the rich heritage of human culture and the life stance of Humanism to provide comfort in times of want and encouragement in times of plenty.

Humans are social by nature and find meaning in relationships. Humanists long for and strive toward a world of mutual care and concern, free of cruelty and its consequences, where differences are resolved cooperatively without resorting to violence. The joining of individuality with interdependence enriches our lives, encourages us to enrich the lives of others, and inspires hope of attaining peace, justice, and opportunity for all.

Working to benefit society maximizes individual happiness. Progressive cultures have worked to free humanity from the brutalities of mere survival and to reduce suffering, improve society, and develop global community. We seek to minimize the inequities of circumstance and ability, and we support a just distribution of nature's resources and the fruits of human effort so that as many as possible can enjoy a good life.

Humanists are concerned for the well being of all, are committed to diversity, and respect those of differing yet humane views. We work to uphold the equal enjoyment of human rights and civil liberties in an open, secular society and maintain it is a civic duty to participate in the democratic process and a planetary duty to protect nature's integrity, diversity, and beauty in a secure, sustainable manner.

Thus engaged in the flow of life, we aspire to this vision with the informed conviction that humanity has the ability to progress toward its highest ideals. The responsibility for our lives and the kind of world in which we live is ours and ours alone.

(Permission to reprint Humanist Manifestos I–III was granted by the American Humanist Association.)

NEO-HUMANIST STATEMENT OF SECULAR PRINCIPLES AND VALUES: PERSONAL, PROGRESSIVE, AND PLANETARY

Preamble
Humanism has been transforming the modern world. We introduced the term "Neo-Humanism" to present a daring new approach for dealing with common problems. Neo-Humanist ideas and values express renewed confidence in the ability of human beings to solve the problems we encounter and to conquer uncharted frontiers.

For the first time in history our planetary community has the opportunity to peacefully and cooperatively resolve any differences that we may have. We use the term "community" because of the emergence of global consciousness and the widespread recognition of our interdependence. The worldwide Internet has made communication virtually instantaneous, so that whatever happens to anyone anywhere on the planet may affect everyone everywhere.

While most decisions that concern human beings are made by them on the local or national level, some issues may transcend these jurisdictions. These include emergency concerns such as regional wars and gross violations of human rights as well as more stable developments such as new ideas in science, ethics, and philosophy. Of special significance today is the fact that we inhabit a common planetary environment. In this context, activities in any one country may spill over to others, such as resource depletion and the pollution of the atmosphere and waterways. Of particular concern is the phenomenon of global warming, affecting everyone on the planet. Similarly, the possible outbreak of an epidemic or plague (such as the swine flu, tuberculosis, and wide-reaching malaria) can have global consequences. Here it is vital to coordinate activities for the distribution of vaccines, application of common quarantine policies, and so forth.

Increasingly, many other issues are of concern to the planetary community and may require cooperative action, such as the preservation of unique species and ecosystems, prevention of excessive fishing on the high seas, management of economic recessions, development of new technologies with their promise for humankind, amelioration of poverty and hunger, reduction of great disparities in wealth, seizing the opportunities to reduce illiteracy, addressing the need for capital investments or technical assistance in rural areas and depressed urban centers, and providing for public sanitation systems and fresh water. Of special concern is the need to liberate women from ancient repressive social systems and attitudes and to emancipate minorities, such as the untouchables in India, who suffer from religious prejudice and caste systems. Similarly gays and other sexual minorities need to be liberated wherever they suffer harsh punishment because of their sexual orientations. The list of indignities is long indeed and a constant campaign for education and improvement is essential.

We submit that science and technology should be used for the service of humanity. We should be prepared to reconstruct human values and modify behavior in the light of these findings. In a rapidly changing world, fresh thinking is required to move civilization forward. We are concerned with reconstructing old habits and attitudes in order to make happiness and wellbeing available for every person interested in realizing the good life for self and others. Accordingly, this Neo-Humanist Statement of Secular Principles and Values is offered as a constructive contribution to the planetary community.

The Next Step Forward

There are various forms of religious belief in the world today. Many of these (though surely not all) stand in the way of human progress. This Neo-Humanist Statement aims to provide an agenda for those who are skeptical of the traditional forms of religious belief, yet maintain that there is a critical need to bring together the varieties of belief and unbelief and provide a positive outlook for the benefit of the planetary community.

Believers include all of the major religions (Christianity, Islam, Judaism, Hinduism, Confucianism, Taoism, Shinto, and some forms of Buddhism, etc.) and also the many denominations within each. It is estimated that there are 4200 religions or faith groups, ranging from dogmatic extremists who are certain that they are right to religious liberals who are receptive to new ideas and dialogue. Where creeds are deeply entrenched, rooted in faith and tradition, it may be difficult to reconcile differences. Historically, believers have often attempted to suppress dissent and persecute heretics. The conflicts between Protestants and Roman Catholics, Sunni and Shiites, Hindus and Muslims, continuing to this day, have at times erupted into violence.

At the other end of the spectrum of unbelief stand the atheists, historically a small minority, who focused primarily on the lack of scientific evidence for belief in God and the harm often committed in the name of religion. The "New Atheists" have been very vocal, claiming that the public has not been sufficiently exposed to the case against God and his minions. We agree that the lack of criticism is often the rule rather than the exception. We point out, however, that the community of religious dissenters includes not only atheists, but secular and religious humanists, agnostics, skeptics, and even a significant number of religiously affiliated individuals. The latter may be only nominal members of their congregations and may infrequently attend church, temple, or mosque, primarily for social reasons or out of ethnic loyalty to the faiths of their forbearers, but they do not accept the traditional creed. *Ethnic identities can be very difficult to overcome,* and may linger long after belief in a given body of doctrine has faded—sometimes for many generations. Although such individuals may be skeptical about the creed, they may believe that without religion the moral order of society might collapse.

Religious identity has been instilled in children, at the earliest ages, so much so that it may define a person; as such it may be difficult to say that one is no longer an Irish Roman Catholic, Jewish, or a Greek Orthodox Christian—even though he or she may reject the religion per se and no longer believe in its creedal tenets. For religion not only entails a set of beliefs, but a way of life, a commitment to cultural traditions, and institutionalized moral practices and rituals. Critics of religion may only focus on its beliefs which are taken literally, whereas many believers interpret them metaphorically or symbolically, and judge them functionally for the needs that they appear to satisfy.

Perhaps the strongest case against religions today is that they are often *irrelevant* to the genuine solution of the problems faced by individuals or societies. For the major religions are rooted in ancient premodern nomadic or agricultural cultures that, in many ways, render them no longer applicable to the urban, industrial, and technological planetary civilization that has emerged.

In our view of the current scene, not enough attention has been paid to Humanism as an alternative to religion. Humanism presents a set of principles and values that began during the Renaissance and came to fruition during the modern era. It marked a turning point from the medieval concern with the divine order and salvation to an emphasis on this life here and now, the quest for personal meaning and value, the good life and social justice in modern democracies and economies that served consumer tastes and satisfactions.

Humanists today sometimes differ as to its meaning. Some humanists have attempted to appropriate the term "religious," using it in a metaphorical sense. Among the self-described religious humanists, we may find people identified with liberal Protestant denominations, Unitarian Universalists, secular Jews, lapsed Catholics, Muslims, or Hindus, and even some who wish to distinguish the "religious" quality of experience from religion. Although they are naturalistic humanists rather than supernaturalists and do not believe in a transcendent God, they wish to encourage a new humanist cultural identity based primarily on ethical ideals that are humanistic.

Humanism

On the other side of this debate stand the *secular humanists* who are wholly nonreligious and naturalistic. They do not consider their stance *religious* at all; they think this term obfuscates matters; so they differ with liberal religious humanists. They draw their inspirations primarily from modern sources: preeminently science but also philosophy, ethics, secular literature, and the arts. Moreover, many may even wish to join secular-humanist communities and centers in order to share bonds of human kinship and friendship. The term "Neo-Humanism" best describes this new posture, which aims to be more outgoing and receptive to cooperation with a broader network.

What then are the characteristics of Neo-Humanism as set forth in this Statement? *First,* Neo-Humanists aspire to be more inclusive. They will cooperate with both religious and nonreligious people to solve common problems. Neo-Humanists recognize that countless generations of human beings have been religious and that we often need to work together with religious people to solve common sociopolitical problems. But Neo-Humanists themselves are *not religious,* surely not in the literal acceptance of the creed.

Nor do they generally adhere to a religious denomination, except nominally. They look to science and reason to solve human problems and they wish to draw upon human experience to test claims to knowledge and values. On the other hand, Neo-Humanists are *not* avowedly antireligious, although they may be critical of religious claims, especially those that are dogmatic or fundamentalist or impinge upon the freedom of others. They understand that neither emotion, intuition, authority, custom, nor subjectivity by itself can serve as a substitute for rational inquiry.

Science and Skepticism

Second, Neo-Humanists are skeptical of traditional theism. They may be agnostics, skeptics, atheists, or even dissenting members of a religious tradition. They think that traditional concepts of God are contradictory and unsubstantiated. They do not believe that the Bible, the Koran, the Book of Mormon, or the Bhagavad Gita are divinely revealed or have a special spiritual source. They are skeptical of the ancient creeds in the light of modern scientific and philosophical critiques, especially, the scholarly examination of the sources of the so-called sacred texts. They are critical of the moral absolutes derived from these texts, viewing them as the expressions of premodern civilizations. Nevertheless they recognize that some of their moral principles may be warranted, and in any case deserve to be appreciated if we are to understand their cultural heritages. They consider traditional religion's focus on salvation as a weakening of efforts to improve this life, here and now. They firmly defend the separation of religion and the state and consider freedom of conscience and the right of dissent vital. They deplore the subservience of women to men, the repression of sexuality, the defense of theocracy, and the denial of democratic human rights—often in the name of religion.

Neo-Humanists, however, are aware of the dangers of an overly zealous atheism such as emerged in Stalinist Soviet Union and Eastern Europe under totalitarian communism or Maoist China, where totalitarian atheists responded to the conservative Orthodox Church in Russia by closing churches, synagogues, and mosques and persecuting ministers of the cloth. Neo-Humanists believe in freedom of conscience, the right to worship or not, and they abhor any kind of repression whether at the hands of atheists in the name of the state or theological inquisitors in the name of the Bible or Koran.

Third, Neo-Humanists are best defined by what they are for, and not by what they are against. They aim to be *affirmative*. Although they are able and willing to critically examine religious claims that are questionable, their focus is on constructive contributions, not negative debunking. They are turned on by positive possibilities, not negative criticisms.

Fourth, Neo-Humanists use critical thinking to evaluate claims to knowledge by reference to evidence and reason. Claims to knowledge are most effectively confirmed by the methods of science where hypotheses are tested objectively. In those areas where scientific inquiry has not been effectively applied, every effort should be made to bring the best methods to bear so that beliefs are considered reliable if they are rationally justified. Thus claims to knowledge in principle are open to modification in the light of further inquiry, and no belief is beyond reexamination. The reflective mind is essential in evaluating the beliefs of people.

Human Values

Fifth, Neo-Humanists apply similar considerations to the evaluation of ethical principles and values. These grow out of human experience and can be examined critically. They are most effectively judged by appraising their consequences in practice. Indeed, there is a body of ethical wisdom that has been developed in human civilization, though old moral recipes may need to be reevaluated and new moral prescriptions adopted.

Sixth, Neo-Humanists are committed to key ethical principles and values that are vital in the lives of human beings. These are not deduced from theological absolutes, but evolve in the light of modern inquiry. Among these are the following:

- A key value is the realization of a life of *happiness and fulfillment* for each person. This is a basic criterion of humanistic ethics.
- This does not mean that "anything goes." Individuals should seek the *fullest actualization* of their best interests and capacities taking into account the interests of others.
- In the last analysis, however, it is *the individual person* who is the best judge of his or her chosen life stance, though there are a number of criteria that resonate with humanists, including the following:
- The creative development of a person's *interests* should be balanced with one's preexistent *talents and values.*
- The *rational life in harmony with emotion* is the most reliable source of satisfaction. This means that a person should be in cognitive touch with external reality, and his or her own innermost needs and wants—if the good life is to be attained.
- A person should strive to achieve the highest standards *of quality and excellence* that one can.

Seventh, Neo-Humanists recognize that no individual can live isolated from others, but should share values with others in the community.

148

- That is why *compassion* is an essential ingredient of the full life. This entails the capacity to love others and accept their love in return.
- This involves some mode of *sexual fulfillment and compatibility*, the willingness to overcome excessive repression, given the diversity of sexual proclivities.
- Women's needs should be considered equal to men's, and society should tolerate same-sex modes of expression.
- It also means that society should seek to cultivate *moral growth* in both children and adults.
- No person is complete unless he or she can *empathize* with the needs of others and have a genuine *altruistic concern* for their good.
- Such feelings are generated at first within the *family*, where children are made to feel wanted and loved.
- Children need to develop in time a sense of *responsibility* for their own well-being, but also for the well-being of others within the family and also for their friends and colleagues, and indeed for all persons within the community at large, and beyond to all of humankind.

Eighth, Neo-Humanists support the right to privacy as a central tenet in a democratic society. Individuals should be granted the right to make their own decisions and actualize their own values, so long as they do not impinge on the rights of others.

Ninth, Neo-Humanists support the democratic way of life and defend it against all enemies domestic or foreign. *The civic virtues of democracy* have taken a long time to develop, but are now well established; they provide for the principles of *tolerance, fairness, the negotiation of differences, and the willingness to compromise.*

Personal Morality/Good Will

Tenth, Neo-Humanists recognize the fundamental importance of good character in both personal life and the impact of a person on society. Historically, many non-believers, secularists, atheists, and agnostics have de-emphasized the topic of personal morality, for they were turned off by the language of sin, and the calls for repression by the virtue police. They preferred to deal with questions of social reform. But it is clear that this is a mistake and that it is foolhardy not to deal with the question of good character and the moral integrity of the individuals who make up society. We need to develop enlightened individuals who have achieved some measure of ethical maturity and moral virtue.

Accordingly, the moral education of children and young persons is of special concern to parents and society. This consideration also applies to adults, who may be married, have a job working with others, or participate in community affairs. Thus some guidelines would be useful, not enforced by legislation—unless a person harms others—but as parameters for evaluating behavior. Actually, there is wide consensus on many of these, and it is shared by members of the community. It cuts across religious or nonreligious lines.

- We wish to point out that to be a secularist is no guarantee of virtue and that many evil acts have been committed by both religious and nonreligious persons. Hence the relevance of the Humanist outlook can be evaluated in an important sense by whether it provides personal meaning and moral purpose for the individual.
- Unfortunately, people sometimes are nasty, uncaring, and insensitive to other people's needs. They have been overwhelmed by hatred, jealousy, greed, or lust—whether they are religious or not. The quest for power is often an inducement for corruption.

We submit that a good will to others is a basic moral principle that expresses a positive attitude toward life. How does this spell out in practice? A person of good will is kind, honest, thoughtful, helpful, beneficent, generous, caring, sympathetic, forgiving, fair-minded, and responsible. These are the *common moral decencies* that are essential for a peaceful and just society.

- The authoritarian personality, on the contrary, is often avaricious, suspicious, power-hungry, prejudiced, cunning, cruel, ruthless, mean-spirited, selfish, demeaning, resentful, inflexible, or vindictive.
- The person of good will needs to combine reason and compassion, the reflective mind and the caring heart. Therefore Neo-Humanism clearly has a list of desired and commendable personality traits by which we may evaluate the conduct of others: these are normative values and principles tested in civilizations by their authenticity. Those who violate the principles of decent behavior may be judged by the consequences of their conduct.

Progressive Humanism

Eleventh, Neo-Humanists accept responsibility for the well-being of the societies in which they live. Neo-Humanists support *the rule of law,* but also the application of the principles of *equality before the law* and *social justice.*

- This includes equal treatment of all persons in society no matter what their social status—class, ethnicity, gender, or racial, national, or religious background. Neo-Humanists support *Progressive Humanism;*

that is, the view that it is the obligation of society to guarantee, as far as it can, equal *opportunity* to all persons. These include the *right to education, universal health care,* the right, wherever possible, to be *gainfully employed* and to receive *adequate income* in order to lead lives in which their *basic needs may be satisfied.*

- Neo-Humanists generally support a *market economy* as the most productive mode for achieving and expanding the economic wealth of societies, one that optimizes entrepreneurial talent with a just distribution of economic benefits.
- They support a *fair taxation* system, and a *welfare concern* for those who, due to some incapacity, are unable to support themselves. This includes a social concern for people with disabilities, and a *just retirement system for the aged.*
- Neo-Humanists eschew utopian schemes. Along with a commitment to the principles of Progressive Humanism, there is a commitment to realism; for they recognize that progress is often slow and painful, achieved piecemeal. Nonetheless they are committed to the *melioristic* view that through persistent courage and intelligent action it is possible to create a better world. Accordingly, we are committed to the above set of noble goals.

Planetary Humanism

Twelfth, Neo-Humanists support a green economy wherever feasible. A growing concern today is *environmental degradation and pollution.* In the quest for new sources of clean energy, every person should consider her or himself as a guardian of nature and should help to limit overfishing of the seas, protect whenever possible the extinction of other species, and stop the pollution of the atmosphere. The planet Earth should be viewed as our common abode; each person has an obligation to preserve the environment, at least in his or her own domain. The callous destruction of rainforests and the acidification of river estuaries should be a concern to every person on the planet. Neo-Humanists advise humans to cultivate *affection* for this blue-green planet, Mother Earth, and a devotion to its renewal.

- Among the highest virtues that we can cultivate is some *reverence for nature,* and an appreciation of the bounty that it affords for the human and other species.
- It no longer is the right of anyone and everyone to plunder the richness of nature and to denude its resources.
- We have an obligation to future generations yet unborn, and a moral responsibility to *ecohumanism;* namely, a loving care and concern for our planet and life on it.

Thirteenth, Neo-Humanists recognize the urgent need for some form of population restraint. This includes guaranteeing women the right to autonomy in matters of pregnancy. We deplore the opposition, based on theological doctrine, of some powerful religious institutions to block effective policies to limit population growth. It is estimated that there were 200 million humans on the planet in the year 1; 310 million in the year 1000; 1.6 billion in 1900; 2.5 billion in 1950, and over 6 billion in the year 2000. If present trends continue, the Earth is projected to soar to 7.5 billion by 2020 and to over 9 billion by 2050. There is thus an urgent imperative to reduce the rate of population growth. With the improvement of medical science, public health, and sanitation, fortunately there has been a continuing decline in the death rate; but this means a surging population. In the past, humanists had always been in the forefront of those advocating rational population policies. These have been rejected by reactionary religious forces who have opposed voluntary contraception and/or abortion. That the green revolution will continue to provide abundant harvests is problematic. There is no guarantee that droughts will not devastate crops. Hence, the runaway growth of population is a gnawing problem that humankind needs to deal with forthrightly.

Related to this is the fact that the percentage of older persons in many societies is increasing. People over 60 now number one in ten in the developed world. This is expected to increase to two in nine by 2050. Whether the working population will be able to support those who are retired will become a critical issue in the future. The upshot of this is the need to constantly revise public policies in the light of altered social conditions. It is clear that economic-moral principles are crucial in guiding public policies in the light of changing economic realities.

Political Action

Fourteenth, Neo-Humanists recognize the need to participate actively in politics. Although humanist organizations generally have not endorsed candidates or political parties, a compelling argument can now be made that they should organize politically. The Christian Coalition and the Roman Catholic Church, Muslim, Hindu, and other religious denominations do so in democratic societies; why not secular humanists? We know that many humanists are active politically as individuals in political organizations; however, they have not as yet organized collectively with grassroots politics to meet challenges from the Religious Right and other politically organized groups, as well as to advance humanist social views.

One reason why they have resisted taking political positions is because of the nonprofit status in many countries of their organizations, which are precluded from doing so. This does not prevent Neo-Humanists quite independently organizing or joining political pressure groups, or entering into coalitions with other groups in society with whom they agree, or applying for a different tax status for a new affiliated organization that could engage in politics.

Another reason why they have eschewed taking political positions is that there has been a tendency to define secular humanism by its opposition to religion and many secular humanists have thought that as long as a person was an atheist or agnostic they shared a basic principle with others. Thus many right-wing libertarians were attracted to the antireligious stance of the secular humanists, though they rejected what they considered to be its too liberal economic agenda, which was labeled as "left wing."

We submit that the terms "left wing" or "right wing" are holdovers from earlier periods in history and have little meaning on the current scene. Very few object to the role of the Federal Reserve in the United States or similar government bodies in other countries from initiating programs of economic stimuli to jump-start faltering economies or to rescue financial institutions from bankruptcy. Nor is there any objection to supporting a strong defense budget, scientific research, space research, or institutes of health or education. Ideological symbols may generate rhetoric, but they do little to deal with concrete problems faced by nations.

Yet one can argue that the ethics of humanism is merely a set of abstract generalizations until it has some application to social problems. Relating Neo-Humanism to concrete issues of concern to society may very well attract a significant portion of the unaffiliated and discontented people in our society who may be looking to become involved with a Humanistic outlook that makes sense to them. Indeed, we can and do appraise economic policies in the light of humanist values and this has political implications. One of the purposes of humanism is to evaluate political and social organizations by their ability to *enhance* human life. Neo-Humanist organizations accordingly must be prepared to engage in political action.

Fifteenth, Neo-Humanists need to take progressive positions on economic issues. We offer the following moral guidelines:

- The overemphasis on price and profit in the past as the primary criteria of merit has led many to focus on "cash value." Many are wont to herald people of wealth as the paragons of social worth. This overlooks scientists, Nobel Prize winners, teachers, political leaders, artists, poets, or dedicated members of the helping professions, and the fact that many social activities are performed by nonprofit institutions or that government has a role to perform in society.
- There are several ethical principles that constrain the free market as the primary arbiter of social utility. One is expressed by Immanuel

Kant's *second categorical imperative,* namely *that we should treat persons as ends not as means.* This, according to Kant, is based upon reason, and it provides essential constraints on certain forms of economic behavior.

- There are other *imperatives* that place limits on unfettered free markets. We are referring here to a growing list of *human rights* that have developed in democratic societies. For example, we affirm our respect: for the right to life, liberty, and the pursuit of happiness, yes—but without discrimination rooted in gender, sexual orientation, race, ethnicity, or creed; the right to education of every child, and other rights as enumerated above.
- *Progressive tax policies* are essential in a just society. These policies have been adopted by virtually every democratic society in order to provide a level playing field so that equality of opportunity is made available to all individuals. In addition there are many social needs that cannot be fully implemented by the private sector alone and need the public sector: the common defense, roads and waterways, public health, science, and education, to mention only a few.
- *Extreme disparities in income and wealth* are characteristics of unjust societies, and progressive taxation is the fairest way to prevent these.
- A progressive humanist is aware of the powerful contributions that free markets make to the prosperity of nations. But the principles of social justice should also be part of our moral concern and the fruits of a free society should be made available to as many members of society as possible. Although the gross national product is an important criterion of economic progress, we also should seek to elevate the *gross national quality of life.* We should encourage people to achieve lives of satisfaction, excellence, and dignity; and to persuade them by means of education to develop their aesthetic, intellectual, and moral values, and thus enhance their quality of living.

New Transnational Institutions

Sixteenth, Neo-Humanists recognize that humanity needs to move beyond egocentric individualism or the perspective of chauvinistic nationalism. The planetary community needs to develop new transnational institutions. The new reality of the twenty-first century is the fact that no one on the planet can live in isolation, and every part of the world community is interdependent. This applies equally to nation-states, which are arbitrary jurisdictions based on historic contingent events of the past. The failure of the 192 nations meeting in Copenhagen in December 2009 to reach an accord that effectively controls global warming points to the urgent need to establish new international institutions.

- There is a need for a new transnational agency to monitor the violation of widely accepted environmental standards, to censure those nations that do, and to enforce such rules by the imposition of sanctions.
- The challenge facing humankind is to recognize the basic ethical principle of planetary civilization—that *every person on the planet has equal dignity and value as a person,* and this transcends the limits of national, ethnic, religious, racial, or linguistic boundaries or identities. We reiterate the ethical obligation of all members of the planetary community to transcend the arbitrary political boundaries of the past and help create new transnational institutions that are democratic in governance and will respect and defend human rights.
- To solve global conflicts, new transnational institutions need to maintain the peace and security of the citizens of the world and guard against violence and force. Eventually humankind will need an adequate multinational force subordinated to the established world authority to maintain peace and security. The United Nations peacekeepers serve as a model that needs to be strengthened.
- Transnational institutions will need to adopt a body of laws which will apply worldwide, a legislature to enact and revise these laws, a world court to interpret them, and an elected executive body to apply them. These institutions will allow a maximum of decentralized local and regional governance. They will foster the growth of multisecular societies in which individuals will be encouraged to participate in the democratic processes of governance and maximize voluntary choice. The cultural traditions of various areas will be respected, although an appreciation of the commonly shared ethical values of all peoples will be encouraged. Transnational institutions will deal with questions that overlap jurisdictions. They will encourage world commerce and trade, and will work with the governments of the world to maximize employment, education, and health care for the populations of the world.
- They will attempt to deal with environmental threats, such as global warming, and the pollution of the atmosphere and waterways, and to safeguard endangered species.
- They will seek to rid the world of disease and hunger, and endeavor to overcome the vast disparities in income and wealth.
- They will encourage cultural enrichment and an appreciation for the sciences and the arts.
- They will seek to facilitate the growth and availability of universal education for all age groups without discrimination. They will defend the rights of the child: Every child needs to have adequate nourishment and shelter; every child has a right to knowledge of the arts and the sciences and the history of the diverse cultures of the world.

- The transnational institutions will encourage open media, the free exchange of ideas and values. They will try to enrich human experience, by encouraging travel, leisure, and recreation. The purpose of these transnational institutions is to extend humanistic values and enable the good life to be experienced by all members of the human family. We now possess the scientific technology and knowhow to bring this about. For the first time in human history, we can rise above the national, ethnic, racial, religious, and cultural barriers of the past. The ethics of planetary humanism makes it clear that every person on the planet is precious and that we need to develop empathetic relationships and extend outreach and good will everywhere.

If humanity is to succeed in this noteworthy endeavor it will need to marshal confidence that at long last we can achieve the blessings of liberty, peace, prosperity, harmony, and creative enjoyment for all, not only for any national, ethnic, racial, or religious group, but for everyone. What a noble idea to strive for: the happiness of humanity as a whole, and for every person in the planetary community.

These are the vital principles and values that a secular, personal, progressive, and planetary humanism proposes for humanity. It is a Neo-Humanist Statement for our time.

Heretofore the great battles for emancipation, liberty, and equality were on the scale of nation-states. Today the campaign for equal rights and for a better life for everyone knows no boundaries. This is a common goal for the people of the world, worthy of our highest aspirations. Given the emergence of electronic media and the Internet, people can communicate across frontiers and barriers. Thus we are all citizens of a planetary village, where new ideas and values can spread instantaneously. If we set our minds to it, there is no reason why we cannot achieve these glorious ideals. We should resolve to work together to realize an ancient dream of the solidarity of human beings. We now are fully aware that we share a common abode, the planet Earth, and that the civilizations that have evolved have a responsibility to overcome any differences and to strive mightily to realize the ideal of a true planetary community.

We who endorse this Neo-Humanist Statement accept its main principles and values. We may not necessarily agree with every provision of it. We submit that the world needs to engage in continuing constructive dialogue emphasizing our common values. We invite other men and women representing different points of view to join with us in bringing about a better world in the new planetary civilization that is now emerging.

(*This statement was drafted by Paul Kurtz*)
(Copyright © 2010 Paul Kurtz.
Published here with the permission of Paul Kurtz.)

NOTES

PREFACE

1. Some of the information in this introduction is drawn from Anthony B. Pinn, "Atheists Gather in Burbank: A Humanist Response," *Religion Dispatches* (October 27, 2009), www.religiondispatches.org/archive/atheologies/1894/atheists_gather_in_ burbank%3A_a_humanist%E2%80%99s_response (accessed June 2012).
2. The Institute emerged in 2009, at a particularly propitious time for humanism. It does not replace other progressive efforts, but rather recognizes the need for creative collaborations and non-fundamentalist approaches to the development and application of creative agendas for human advancement. In doing this, the Institute draws from the best of the humanist tradition, offers correctives for its less productive postures and approaches, and forges new directions of thought and praxis. The idea is to encourage reflection on the benefits of humanism as well as critical attention to any barriers that prevent humanism from fulfilling its potential as an agent of human growth, human health, and advancement. In short, humanism might help forge more substantive frameworks of democratic living.

1. HUMANISM AS EXPERIENCE

1. In this chapter, I shall be dealing primarily with modern humanism in the US. It should be noted, however, that there are more than fifty nations around the globe with humanist member organizations and the number is growing. Needless to say, humanism in any given country is influenced by its history and culture. Nevertheless, humanism, wherever we find it, and whatever its particular organizational development, shares the core values I identify in the text that follows.
2. Douglas McDermid, "Pragmatism, A Method and A Maxim," *Internet Encyclopedia of Philosophy*, www.iep.utm.edu/pragmati/ (accessed June 2012).
3. Cited by Stow Persons, *Free Religion* (New Haven, CT: Yale University Press, 1947), 96.
4. From a sermon by John Dietrich, "The Folly Of Half-Way Liberalism," in *The Humanist Pulpit* 4 (Minneapolis, MN: The First Unitarian Society, c.1931).
5. Paul Kurtz, "A Secular Humanist Declaration," *Council for Democratic and Secular Humanism* (1980), www.secularhumanism.org/index.php?page=declaration&section =main (accessed July 2012). For copies, contact the Center for Inquiry International: www.centerforinquiry.net/

6. Paul Kurtz, 2010; see the Appendix.
7. While there is no formal census of humanist organizations in the US, my informal canvas of the various groups shows that the total membership of these organizations—the American Ethical Union (AEU), American Humanist Association (AHA), Unitarian Universalist Humanists (UUH), Society for Humanistic Judaism (SHJ)—would be about 30,000, with AHA being the largest and reporting about 20,000 "supporters." To be sure, many Unitarian Universalists, perhaps a majority of a claimed 250,000–300,000, identify themselves as humanists. Even if I have undercounted, this is surely minuscule when set against a national population of 310 million or the numbers affiliated with churches, synagogues, temples, and mosques. To put these numbers in context, in March 2009, the American Religious Identification Survey (ARIS) estimated that there were nearly four million "Nones" in the US, that is, those with no religious preference or identified as humanistic, ethical culture, atheist, and secular: see Barry A. Kosmin & Ariela Keysar with Ryan Cragun & Juhem Navarro-Rivera, *American Nones: The Profile of the No Religion Population* (Hartford, CT: Trinity College, 2009), available at http://commons.trincoll.edu/aris/publications/american-nones-the-profile-of-the-no-religion-population/ (accessed July 2012). The Pew Forum On Religion In Public Life found that the overall percentage of survey participants with no religious affiliation was 16.1 percent: "US Religious Landscape Survey," *The Pew Forum on Religion and Public Life* (2007), http://religions.pewforum.org/reports/ (accessed July 2012).
8. John Dewey, *Individualism, Old and New* (New York: Prometheus, 1999), 5.
9. For example see Karl Marx, *Economic and Philosophic Manuscripts, 1844* (Moscow: Foreign Languages Publishing House, 1959). In the section "Estranged Labour," Marx writes: "The worker becomes all the poorer the more wealth he produces, the more his production increases in power and size. The worker becomes an ever cheaper commodity the more commodities he creates. The *devaluation* of the world of men is in direct proportion to the *increasing value* of the world of things. Labor produces not only commodities; it produces itself and the worker as a *commodity*—and this at the same rate at which it produces commodities in general. This fact expresses merely that the object which labor produces—labor's product—confronts it as *something alien*, as a *power independent* of the producer. The product of labor is labor which has been embodied in an object, which has become material: it is the *objectification* of labor. Labor's realization is its objectification. Under these economic conditions this realization of labor appears as *loss of realization* for the workers; objectification as *loss of the object and bondage to it*; appropriation as *estrangement*, as *alienation*" (p. xliii).
10. "Humanist Manifesto III", a successor to the "Humanist Manifesto" of 1933; see the Appendix.
11. Dante's (1265–1321) *Divine Comedy* has three parts: "Inferno," "Purgatory," and "Paradise." In the first part, Dante is led by the Roman poet Virgil, a pagan, in the third part, by his beloved, Beatrice. The poem is in Italian, that is, the people's language. Many of the references, particularly in the "Inferno," are to the politics and politicians of Forence.

    A citation from Desiderius Erasmus's (1466–1536) *In Praise Of Folly* suggests his style and purpose: "all Christian religion seems to have a kind of alliance with folly ... consider first that boys, old men, women, and fools are more delighted with religious and sacred things than others, and to that purpose are ever next the altars; ... and in the next place ... that those first founders of it were plain, simple persons and most bitter enemies of learning. Lastly there are no more foolish collections of fools than ... these whom the zeal of Christian religion has once swallowed up; so that they waste their estates, neglect injuries, suffer themselves to be cheated, put no difference between friends and enemies, abhor pleasure, are crammed with poverty ...

tears, labors, reproaches, loathe life, and wish death above all things; in short, they seem senseless to common understanding, as if their minds lived elsewhere and not in their own bodies; which, what else is it than to be mad? For which reason you must not think it so strange if the apostles seemed to be drunk with new wine, and if Paul appeared to Festus to be mad" (*The Essential Erasmus*, J. P. Dolan [ed. and trans.] [New York: NAL, Penguin/Meridian 1983], 169).

Petrarch (1304–74) was an Italian scholar and poet ... often called the "father of humanism." In the sixteenth century, Pietro Bembo created the model for modern Italian based on Petrarch's works, as well as on those of Boccaccio and Dante. Petrarch's sonnets were admired and imitated throughout Europe during the Renaissance and became a model for lyrical poetry.

12. My references here are to Western cultures. There are, of course, humanist developments in the great civilizations of Asia, for example Confucius in China, Buddha in India. I am confident that African and South American cultures have their humanist history too. There are in fact modern humanist movements in Asia, Africa, and Latin America. But as a consequence of my illiteracy in these areas and as a practical matter in a short chapter, I need to stay with what I know best.

13. Humanism has a voice in more than fifty nations around the globe. The International Humanist and Ethical Union (IHEU), founded in Amsterdam in 1952 by humanist organizations from ten European countries, the US, and India, is growing. It has representation as a non-governmental organization (NGO) at the UN and at the Council of Europe. As of 2010, member organizations existed in twenty-five European countries, three in North America, and ten in Asia including both India and China. There are member organizations in six Sub-Saharan African nations, three in Latin America, one in Australia, and one in New Zealand.

14. David Grimm, "Is a Dolphin a Person?" in *Science* (February 21, 2010), published by the American Association for the Advancement of Science (AAAS), http://news.science-mag.org/sciencenow/2010/02/is-a-dolphin-a-person.html (accessed June 2012). For discussion of the ethical issues raised by research on non-human primates and other species, see Peter Singer, *Animal Liberation* (London: Pimlico, 1995) and *Practical Ethics* (Cambridge: Cambridge University Press, 1993).

15. In *Talks To Teachers* (1899), James wrote: "So far as we are thus mere bundles of habit, we are stereotyped creatures, imitators and copiers of our past selves. And since this, under any circumstances, is what we always tend to become, it follows first of all that the teacher's prime concern should be to ingrain into the pupil that assortment of habits that shall be most useful to him throughout life. Education is for behavior, and habits are the stuff of which behavior consists" (William James, "The Laws of Habit," in *Talks to Teachers*, 56–65 [London: W. W. Norton, 1959], 58).

In *Human Nature and Conduct* (1921), Dewey wrote: "When we think of habits in terms of walking, playing a musical instrument, typewriting, we are much given to thinking of habits ... We think of them as passive tools waiting to be called into action from without. A bad habit suggests an inherent tendency to action and also a hold, command over us. It makes us do things we are ashamed of, things which we tell ourselves we prefer not to do. It overrides our formal resolutions, our conscious decisions. When we are honest with ourselves we acknowledge that a habit has this power because it is so intimately a part of ourselves. It has a hold upon us because we are the habit" (John Dewey, "Habits and Will," in *Human Nature and Conduct*, 24–42 [New York: Henry Holt, 1922], 24).

16. The pre-Socratic metaphysics of Parmenides comes to mind: "The essence of what is conceivable is incapable of development, imperishable, immutable, unbounded, and indivisible. What is various and mutable, all development, is a delusive phantom.

Perception is thought directed to the pure essence of being; the phenomenal world is a delusion, and the opinions formed concerning it can only be improbable" ("Parmenides," *Internet Encyclopedia of Philosophy*, www.iep.utm.edu/parmenid/ [accessed June 2012]).

Zeno's paradoxes illustrate the reasons for Parmenides' thought. For example, Zeno imagines a race between Achilles and the tortoise: Achilles gives the tortoise a head start. Before he can overtake the tortoise, however, he must run to the place where the tortoise began. But the tortoise, of course, has moved on. From there, before Achilles can overtake the tortoise, he must run to the next place to which the tortoise has moved. But when he gets there, the tortoise has moved on again. Thus, Achilles can never pass the tortoise. Mathematically (before the calculus), he cannot win the race, but in fact he does! Either our logic or our world makes no sense.

17. For example, see Plato, *Timaeus*.

18. "The Cosmic Dance," *Einstein Online*, www.einstein-online.info/elementary/generalRT/GeomGravity (accessed July 2012).

19. For example, I think here of the theological naturalism of Henry Nelson Wieman and the "Chicago School" of theology. In "My Intellectual Autobiography" (in R. W. Bretall [ed.], *The Empirical Theology of Henry Nelson Wieman* [New York: Macmillan, 1963]), Wieman writes: "While at Harvard I became acquainted with the work of John Dewey and found him highly stimulating ... Dewey caused me to see something I have never forgotten; inquiry concerning what makes for the good and evil of human life must be directed to what actually and observably operates in human life. Otherwise, the inquiry will produce misleading illusions. The following statements indicate the impact of John Dewey upon my thinking.

"The transcendent, the supernatural, the ineffable, the infinite, the absolute being itself, and other such ideas inevitably lead inquiry astray unless they can be identified with something which observably operates in human life. What is observed is not necessarily identical with what enters immediately into sense experience. Rather, what we observe is what we infer from sense experience by predicting specific consequences and observing or failing to observe under required conditions what was predicted. Perception, including sense experience, can engage the total personality with all its resources of inquiry-intuition, inference, wonder, meditation, speculation, faith, love, aspiration. Perception always involves sense experience. But profound perception brings into action every means and every power by which knowledge is attained. It is a gross misunderstanding to say that sense experience can give us only knowledge of sense experience" (available at http://urantiabook.org/sources/wieman_autobiography.htm).

20. A reliable and accessible resource is the *Stanford Encyclopedia of Philosophy* (http://plato.stanford.edu). On the subject of philosophic idealism, see, for example, the articles on Hermann Cohen, Ernst Cassirer, Friedrich Albert Lange, Walter Benjamin, and Josiah Royce. Cohen and Lange were particularly influential in shaping Adler's thinking.

21. Ralph Waldo Emerson, "The Rhodora, On Being Asked, Whence is the Flower?" first published in *Poems* (Boston, MA: James Munro, 1847):

> In May, when sea-winds pierced our solitudes,
> I found the fresh Rhodora in the woods
> Spreading its leafless blooms in a damp nook,
> To please the desert and the sluggish brook.
> The purple petals, fallen in the pool,
> Made the black water with their beauty gay;
> Here might the red-bird come his plumes to cool,

And court the flower that cheapens his array.
Rhodora! if the sages ask thee why
This charm is wasted on the earth and sky,
Tell them, dear, that if eyes were made for seeing,
Then beauty is its own excuse for being:
Why thou wert there, o rival of the rose!
I never thought to ask, I never knew:
But, in my simple ignorance, suppose
The self-same power that brought me there brought you.

22. "Definition of a Tragedy and the Rules for its Construction," *The Poetics*, Ingram Bywater (trans), in *The Basic Works of Aristotle*, Richard Mckeon (ed.), 1455–87 (New York: Random House, 1941), 1466–7.

23. Typically, modern humanism relies on the work of the liberal academic world. It lacks the resources and perhaps the motivation for creating and sustaining an institutional setting where a humanist research community could do its work. Exceptions to this are the Humanist University in Utrecht, the Netherlands and the Center for Inquiry at Amherst, New York. The latter, however, is committed to a secularist mission and so does not embrace humanist pluralism and diversity.

24. See citations from Felix Adler and from John Dietrich in notes 3 and 4 above.

25. See Felix Adler's Inaugural Address to the newly founded New York Society for Ethical Culture, May 15, 1876, available in the archive of the American Ethical Union and the New York Society for Ethical Culture (contact details available at www.aeu.org).

26. Adler was consistent from the founding of the Working Man's School in 1878 (re-named the Ethical Culture School in 1895) to the Fieldston School in 1928. At the laying of the Fieldston cornerstone and the school's dedication in September 1927 he remarked, typically, "the ideal of the School is to develop individuals who will be competent to change their environment to greater conformity with moral ideals." See "The Fieldston Plan, A New Departure in Education" (1926), available in the archive of the American Ethical Union and the New York Society for Ethical Culture (contact details available at www.aeu.org).

27. For additional information on the Inaugural Address and the Fieldston Plan as well as for the reform efforts of Adler *et al.*, see my history of the Ethical Culture movement: Howard B. Radest, *Toward Common Ground* (New York: Ungar, 1969).

28. For a discussion of "paradigm shift" see Thomas Kuhn, *The Structure Of Scientific Revolutions* (Chicago, IL: University of Chicago Press, 1962).

29. For example, in an essay, "Speciesism and the Idea of Equality" (*Philosophy* 53[204] [April 1978], 247–56), the philosopher Bonnie Steinbock writes: "Most of us believe that we are entitled to treat members of other species in ways which would be considered wrong if inflicted on members of our own species. We kill them for food, keep them confined, use them in painful experiments. The moral philosopher has to ask what ... justifies this difference in treatment ... It has been suggested by Peter Singer that our current attitudes are 'speciesist,' a word intended to make one think of 'racist' or 'sexist' ... [Singer] agrees that nonhuman animals lack certain capacities that human animals possess, and that this may justify different treatment. But it does not justify giving less consideration to their needs and interests. Singer's real aim is to bring us to a new understanding of the idea of equality ... Equality is a moral ideal, not a simple assertion of fact" (p. 247).

30. "And God said, 'let us make man in our image, after our likeness: and let them have dominion over the fish of the sea, and over the fowl of the air, and over the cattle, and over all the earth, and over every creeping thing that creepeth upon the earth'" (Genesis 1:26).

31. *"Transhumanism* is a philosophy maintaining that humanity can, and should, strive to higher levels ... Physically, mentally and socially. It encourages research into such areas enhancements, life extentions, cryonics, nanotechnology, physical and mental enhancements, uploading human consciousness into computers and megascale engineering" (www.aleph.se/Trans/). For a brief history, see Andy Miah, "Posthumanism: A Critical History," in *Medical Enhancement and Posthumanity*, B. Gordijn & R. Chadwick (eds) (New York: Routledge, 2007).

32. "Neo-Humanist Statement of Secular Principles and Values: Personal, Progressive, and Planetary"; see the Appendix.

33. Friedrich Nietzsche, *Also Sprach Zarathustra, Ein Buch Für Alle Und Keinen* (Chemnitz: Verlag von Ernst Schmeitzner, 1883) [*Thus Spoke Zarathustra, A Book for All and None*, many translations].

34. Oli Stephano, "Earthly Amor Fati: On Overcoming and Affirmation," *Canon* (Spring 2011), http://canononline.org/archives/spring-2011/earthly-amor-fati-on-overcoming-and-affirmation/ (accessed July 2012).

35. As noted in the opening section of this chapter, the American Enlightenment made a very uneasy peace with slavery—see the US constitution, Jefferson on "Africans." The nineteenth century found a growing abolitionist movement that, among others, included Transcendentalists and liberal Unitarians, a new-born feminist movement, and toward the end of the century, a vigorous anti-imperialism movement as well. Views of *imago humani* continued to mature in the middle and end of the twentieth century. Its evolution, as I have indicated, continues today with gays and transgender people. Its future, as I have also indicated, remains unknown.

36. V. M Tarkunde (1909–2004) was inspired by M. N. Roy's humanism and played a crucial role in the Indian Humanist movement. Justice Tarkunde started his career by helping the so-called "untouchables" in India. He was a judge of the Mumbai High Court, a senior advocate before the Supreme Court and co-founder of Citizens for Democracy and of The People's Union for Civil Liberties and Democratic Rights. For many years, we served together on the IHEU board. At the 1978 London Congress, he received the International Humanist Award.

37. M. N. Roy (1887–1954) started as a Comintern Marxist, and became active in the Indian movement for independence. His undogmatic Marxism gradually became more individualistic and democratic. In 1947 he proclaimed his own interpretation of "new" or "radical" humanism in the form of a manifesto with twenty-two statements. He then transformed his Radical Democratic Party into a social movement, the Indian Renaissance Movement. Roy was elected IHEU vice-chairman at the founding congress in 1952. Sadly, he died before he could even begin to see the development of the international movement he had helped to start.

38. Ludwig Wittgenstein, *Tractatus Logico-Philosophicus*, C. K. Ogden (trans.) (London: Routledge & Kegan Paul, 1922).

39. "Any one who turns from the great writers of classical Athens, say Sophocles or Aristotle, to those of the Christian era must be conscious of a great difference in tone. There is a change in the whole relation of the writer to the world about him. The new quality is not specifically Christian: it is just as marked in the Gnostics and Mithras-worshippers as in the Gospels and the Apocalypse, in Julian and Plotinus as in Gregory and Jerome. It is hard to describe. It is a rise of asceticism, of mysticism, in a sense, of pessimism; a loss of self-confidence, of hope in this life and of faith in normal human effort; a despair of patient inquiry, a cry for infallible revelation; an indifference to the welfare of the state, a conversion of the soul to God. It is an atmosphere in which the aim of the good man is not so much to live justly, to help the society to which he belongs and enjoy the esteem of his fellow creatures; but rather,

by means of a burning faith, by contempt for the world and its standards, by ecstasy, suffering, and martyrdom, to be granted pardon for his unspeakable unworthiness, his immeasurable sins. There is an intensifying of certain spiritual emotions; an increase of sensitiveness, a failure of nerve" (Gilbert Murray, "The Failure of Nerve," in *Five Stages of Greek Religion*, 123–72 [Boston, MA: Beacon Press, 1951], 123).

40. William James referred to "temperament" in many of his works. Perhaps the most relevant here is a citation from *The Varieties Of Religious Experience* (New York: Macmillan, [1902] 1961): "Ought it, indeed, to be assumed that in all men the mixture of religion with other elements should be identical[?] ... I answer, 'no' emphatically. And my reason is that I do not see how it is possible that creatures in such different positions and with such different powers as human individuals are should have exactly the same functions and the same duties. No two of us have identical difficulties, nor should we be expected to work out identical solutions ... So a 'god of battles' must be allowed to be the god for one kind of person, a god of peace and heaven and home, the god for another ... If we are sick souls, we require a religion of deliverance; but why think so much of deliverance if we are healthy minded?" (pp. 378–9).

41. James Joyce, *Ulysses* (Paris: Sylvia Beach, 1922) (many editions available).

42. Isaac Asimov (1920–92) wrote more than 500 books and was best known for his works of science fiction and popular science. He served for a time as Honorary President of the American Humanist Association (1985–92).

43. Gene Roddenberry (1921–91), a television screenwriter and producer, was best known for creating the science fiction series *Star Trek*.

44. Martin Buber (1878–1965) was a Jewish philosopher best known for his distinction between the "I–thou" and the "I–it" relationship. A religious existentialist and mystic, Buber developed a challenging philosophy of dialogue.

45. Valerie Gribben, "Practicing Medicine Can Be Grimm Work," *New York Times* (July 1, 2011).

46. See Howard B. Radest, "The Politics of Sociability," in *Humanism With A Human Face: Intimacy and the Enlightenment*, 151–75 (Westport, CT: Praeger, 1995). In a related essay, I wrote: "The Humanist story then is already revealed in the universalism and cosmopolitanism of the Humanist tradition much as the setting for Dante's *Divine Comedy* is revealed in the church and politics of Renaissance Italy or the polis and the gods are announced by the chorus in a Greek tragedy. But, in its 18th Century incarnation, universalism and cosmopolitanism were likely to be introduced without apparent voice at all as in 'All men are created equal.' The narrative was objectified, even hid itself as narrative in the guise of social science or political pamphlet. Or else, the characters and plot were only two-dimensional vehicles for criticism. Thus, Voltaire's *Candide* is an inverted morality play. David Hume's *Dialogues Concerning Natural Religion*, follow the model of Plato's early dramatic dialogues but without the dialectic tenseness of the Socratic original. For all its 'optimism,' Enlightenment narrative carried its darker tones too. I listen to Mozart's *Don Giovanni* or *The Magic Flute* or *The Marriage of Figaro*. Betraying the seeming facility of the music and the seeming simplicity of the libretto are the themes of class and caste, of powerful and conflicted natural energies and of transcending human dreams. And that is why I return to Mozart over and over again. Of course, there are references of the moment too, e.g. to the free-masons in *The Magic Flute*. There are challenges to the conventionalities of the day. For example, *Don Giovanni* was not acceptable without an added moralist epilogue pointing out the sins and merited punishment of its lead figure. Typically, the minuet, the sculptured garden and the uncluttered column conveyed the line and structure of 18th Century classicism. Even at its most rational and Newtonian, the Enlightenment project had its aesthetic as well as its ideas, its passions as well as

its descriptions" ("Creating a Humanist Narrative", *Living as Humanists: Humanism Today* 10 [1996], 116).

47. Albert Camus (1913–60) was an author, journalist, and philosopher. He won the 1957 Nobel Prize for Literature. *The Myth Of Sisyphus*, a philosophical essay, was originally published in French by Hamish Hamilton (1942), translated into English by Justin O'Brien, and published in *The Myth of Sisyphus and Other Essays* (New York: Random House, 1955). Available at www.sccs.swarthmore.edu/users/00/pwillen1/lit/msysip. htm (accessed July 2012).

48. Andrew M. Greeley, "Because of The Stories," *New York Times Magazine* (July 10, 1994), 40.

49. Plato, *Republic*, book VII, 514a–520a.

50. A rich literature on institutional theory is available in specific fields of inquiry, such as sociology, economics, political science, business. I would suggest the following as a usable introduction to the subject: Geert Hofstede & Geert Jan Hofstede, *Cultures and Organizations: Software of the Mind* (New York: McGraw-Hill, 1991/2004); see also Seumas Miller, "Social Institutions," *Stanford Encyclopedia Of Philosophy*, http://plato. stanford.edu/archives/spr2011/entries/social-institutions/ (accessed June 2012).

51. Both Markovic (1927–2010) and Stojanovic (1931–2010) were fellow members of the IHEU Board of Trustees. I also served with Markovic and Piet Thoenes of the Netherlands as IHEU co-chairs from 1975 to 1980. Professors of Philosophy at the University of Belgrade, Markovic and Stojanovic, with six of their colleagues, were suspended from teaching in 1975. All were members of the Praxis Group, a Marxist study seminar developing an alternative to Leninism and to Marshal Tito's Marxism as well. They found Marx's manuscripts of 1844 (discovered in the 1950s, after the death of Stalin) more promising than the "class struggle" of the Communist Manifesto and the "economic determinism" of *Das Kapital*. See Mihaelo Markovic & Robert S. Cohen, *Yugoslavia: The Rise and Fall of Socialist Humanism. A History of the Praxis Group* (Nottingham: Spokesman Books, 1975).

    With a distinguished teaching career in Europe and the US, Stojanovic, whom I knew well and worked with, was also active in Serbian politics and helped in the overthrow of Yugoslav dictator, Milosevic. He was appointed to the Commission For Truth And Reconciliation by former Yugoslav President Kostunica and later became a member of the Council for Foreign Relations of the Ministry of Foreign Affairs of Serbia.

52. Apparently Marx and his ideas are still alive. Among recent articles that have appeared after a very long silence was Terry Eagleton, "In Praise of Marx," *Chronicle Review: Chronicle of Higher Education* (April 10, 2011).

53. Felix Adler, *An Ethical Philosophy of Life* (New York: Appleton-Century, 1918).

54. John Haynes Holmes, *I Speak for Myself* (New York: Harper, 1959), 259.

55. See Howard B. Radest, *Felix Adler: An Ethical Culture* (New York: Peter Lang, 1998).

56. In *Critique of Pure Reason*, Kant wrote, "Thoughts without content are empty, intuitions without concepts are blind" (*The Critique of Pure Reason* [editions 1781/1787], Werner Pluhar [ed.] [Indianapolis, IN: Hackett, 1996], 51/75).

2. HUMANISM AS GUIDE TO LIFE MEANING

1. My arguments here build and expand on my earlier writings on humanism and also frame some of my recent shifts in thinking. In this way, they provide a summary of some of the major points in *The End of God-Talk: An African American Humanist Theology* (New York: Oxford University Press, 2012). I alert readers to more substantial examples of this in corresponding footnotes.

2. Richard Wright, "The Man Who Lived Underground," in *Eight Men*, 19–85 (New York: Harper Perennial, 1996), 30.
3. See Alain Locke, "Introduction," in *The New Negro* (New York: Atheneum, 1968).
4. Richard Wright, *The Outsider* (New York: Harper Perennial, 1996).
5. Much of the above material on the history of humanism summarizes ideas presented in Anthony B. Pinn, "Anybody There? Reflections on African American Humanism," in *Religious Humanism* 31(3 & 4) (Summer/Fall 1997), 61–78; and Anthony Pinn, *Varieties of African American Religious Experience* (Minneapolis, MN: Fortress Press, 1998).
6. Barry A. Kosmin & Ariela Keysar with Ryan Cragun & Juhem Navarro-Rivera, *American Nones: The Profile of the No Religion Population: A Report Based on the American Religious Identification Survey 2008* (Trinity College, Hartford, CT), available at www.deism.com/NONES_08.pdf (accessed June 2012).
7. *Ibid.*
8. *Ibid.*
9. *Ibid.*, 14–15.
10. Corliss Lamont, *The Philosophy of Humanism* (New York: Ungar Publishing Company, 1949).
11. *Ibid.*
12. *Ibid.*
13. An earlier version of some of the above information regarding Corliss Lamont is found in Pinn, *Varieties of African American Religious Experience*, 154–60.
14. The American Humanist Association website contains links to Humanist Manifestos I–III: Manifesto I, www.americanhumanist.org/humanism/Humanist_Manifesto_I; Manifesto II, www.americanhumanist.org/humanism/Humanist_Manifesto_II; Manifesto III, www.americanhumanist.org/humanism/Humanist_Manifesto_III
15. Paul Tillich, *Dynamics of Faith* (New York: HarperOne, 2001).
16. Anthony B. Pinn, *Terror and Triumph: The Nature of Black Religion* (Maryknoll, NY: Orbis Books, 2004), chapters 7–8. Also see Anthony Pinn, *African American Humanist Principles: Living and Thinking Like the Children of Nimrod* (New York: Palgrave Macmillan, 2004).
17. William Ernest Henley, "Invictus," *Wikipedia*, http://en.wikipedia.org/wiki/Invictus (accessed June 2012).
18. This discussion of human nature summarizes ideas found in Pinn, *The End of God-Talk.*
19. This example is more fully developed in *ibid.*
20. A portion of material in this chapter related to the deconstruction of the idea of God is drawn from Anthony B. Pinn, "God of Restraint: An African American Humanist Interpretation of Nimrod and the Tower of Babel," in *African American Religious Life and the Story of Nimrod*, Anthony B. Pinn & Allen Callahan (eds), 27–34 (New York: Palgrave Macmillan, 2008).
21. This sense of community is more fully developed in Pinn, *The End of God-Talk.*
22. Richard Wright, *The Outsider*, 585.
23. *Ibid.*
24. This sense of community is developed more fully in Pinn, *The End of God-Talk.*
25. Pinn, *African American Humanist Principles*, 7.
26. This argument is developed more fully in Pinn, *The End of God-Talk.*
27. Henry D. Thoreau, *Walden* (Princeton, NJ: Princeton University Press, 1973).
28. This attention to Thoreau and being "good" is drawn from and more fully developed in Pinn, *The End of God-Talk.*
29. Walker received the American Humanist Association "Humanist of the Year" Award in 1996.

30. This list is drawn from "Living Li(f)e: African Americans, Humanism, and the Shape of Fulfillment," in *The Colors of Humanism*, Anthony Pinn (ed.), special issue of *Essays in the Philosophy of Humanism* 20(1) (2012): 23–30.

3. HUMANISM AS A MEANING FRAME

1. E. J. S. Hijmans, *Je moet er het beste van maken: Een empirisch onderzoek naar hedendaagse zingevingssystemen* (Nijmegen: Instituut voor Toegepaste Sociale Wetenschappen, 1994); T. Kuckmann, *The Invisible Religion: The Problem of Religion in Modern Society* (New York: Macmillan, 1967); R. Wuthnow, *The Consciousness Reformation* (Berkeley, CA: University of California Press, 1976); R. Wuthnow, *Meaning and Moral Order: Explorations in Cutural Analysis* (Berkeley, CA: University of California Press, 1989).
2. J. P. van Praag, *Grondslagen van humanisme: Inleiding tot een humanistische levens- en denkwereld* (Meppel/Amsterdam: Boom, 1978), 228; R. F. Baumeister & K. D. Vohs, "The Pursuit of Meaningfulness in Life," in *Handbook of Positive Psychology*, C. R. Snyder & S. J. Lopez (eds), 608–18 (New York: Oxford University Press, 2005).
3. R. F. Baumeister, *Meanings of Life* (New York: Guilford Press, 1991), 29–57.
4. A. Gewirth, *Self-fulfillment* (Princeton, NJ: Princeton University Press, 1998).
5. E. Hijmans & H. Hilhorst, "Hedendaagse vormen van zingeving: De 'onzichtbare' religie van de Nederlander," in *Religie in de Nederlandse samenleving: De vergeten factor*, O. Schreuder & L. van Snippenburg (eds), 137–64 (Baarn: Ambo, 1990); Hijmans, *Je moet er het beste van maken*.
6. Realism and self-acceptance are of great importance for a sound sense of self-worth. If you cannot realistically accept yourself as you are and can be (your weak spots included), it is very difficult to act productively in between powerlessness and omnipotence. And without that it is quite a task to acquire a positive self-image. See van Praag, *Grondslagen van humanisme*, 180–82, 206; and A. Smaling & H. Alma, "Zingeving en levensbeschouwing: Een conceptuele en thematische verkenning," in *Waarvoor je leeft: Studies naar humanistische bronnen van zin*, H. Alma & A. Smaling (eds), 18–23 (Amsterdam: SWP, Humanistics University Press, 2010).
7. D. Vaughan, *Uncoupling: Turning Points in Intimate Relationships* (New York: Oxford University Press, 1986).
8. Baumeister, *Meanings of Life*, 32.
9. A. Antonovsky, *Unraveling the Mystery of Health: How People Manage Stress and Stay Well* (San Francisco, CA: Jossey-Bass, 1987); J. H. Mooren, "Zingeving en cognitieve regulatie: Een conceptueel model ten behoeve van onderzoek naar zingeving en levensbeschouwing," in *Schering en inslag: Opstellen over religie in de hedendaagse cultuur*, J. Janssen, R. van Uden & H. van der Ven (eds), 193–206 (Nijmegen: Katholiek Studiecentrum voor Geestelijke Volksgezondheid, 1998).
10. So I do not agree with Terry Eagleton, who seems to think that finding meaning in life has nothing to do with comprehending life. See T. Eagleton, *The Meaning of Life* (Oxford: Oxford University Press, 2007), 64.
11. Baumeister & Vohs, "The Pursuit of Meaningfulness in Life," 609.
12. Smaling & Alma, "Zingeving en levensbeschouwing," 19.
13. H. J. M. Hermans & E. Hermans-Jansen, *Self-narratives: The Construction of Meaning in Psychotherapy* (New York: Guilford Press 1995), 235.
14. Smaling & Alma, "Zingeving en levensbeschouwing," 21. Translations from Dutch in this chapter are by the author of the chapter.
15. R. F. Baumeister & M. R. Leary, "The Need to Belong: Desire for Interpersonal

Attachments as a Fundamental Human Motivation," *Psychological Bulletin* 117(3) (1995), 497–529; and Baumeister, *Meanings of Life*, 14 and 146.

16. In *Meanings of Life* Baumeister sometimes writes about the need to belong (14, 15, 145–6, 185). However, it does not become clear to me how his four needs for meaning (29–57) relate to the need to believe and the need to belong (183–6), nor how needs for meaning exactly relate to sources of meaning.

17. Smaling & Alma, "Zingeving en levensbeschouwing," 21.

18. V. E. Frankl, *Man's Search for Meaning* (Boston, MA: Beacon Press, 2006).

19. F. de Lange, "Good Ageing: A Comprehensive Approach," in *Successful Ageing, Spirituality and Meaning: Multidisciplinary Perspectives*, J. Bouwer, H. Ross & W. Litjens (eds), 171–89 (Leuven: Peeters, 2010); A. Marcoen, "Zingeving en levensvervulling," in *Als de schaduwen langer worden: Psychologische perspectieven op ouder worden en oud zijn*, A. Marcoen, R. Grommen & N. Van Ranst (eds), 379–403 (Leuven: LannooCampus, 2006); G. T. Reker, "Theoretical perspective, dimensions, and measurement of existential meaning," in *Exploring Existential Meaning: Optimizing Human Development Across the Life Span*, G. T. Reker & K. Chamberlain (eds), 39–55 (Thousand Oaks, CA: Sage, 2000).

20. Quoted in H. Laceulle, "Laatmodern ouder worden: Een spiritueel perspectief," in *Goed ouder worden*, P. Derkx, A. Maas & A. Machielse (eds), 29–46 (Amsterdam: SWP, Humanistics University Press, 2011), 35.

21. de Lange, "Good Ageing: A Comprehensive Approach," 182.

22. See also the section "Subscale I: Transcendent Connection," in S. Bruyneel, A. Marcoen & B. Soenens, *Gerotranscendence: Components and Spiritual Roots in the Second Half of Life* (Leuven: Katholieke Universiteit, 2005), 21. Available at http://ssrn.com/abstract=870233 (accessed June 2012). Relevant items are: "I feel connected with the entire universe," "I feel that I am a part of everything alive," "My personality has both female and male components," and "I feel a strong connection with earlier generations."

23. H. A. Alma, *De parabel van de blinden: Psychologie en het verlangen naar zin* (Amsterdam: SWP, Humanistics University Press, 2005), 12, 18, 21. For "exciting life" as a construct underlying "existential meaning," see J. Morgan & T. Farsides, "Measuring Meaning in Life," in *Journal of Happiness Studies* 10(3) (2009), 197–214.

24. "Since Freud, a significant number of psychologists have put forth theories of human motivation that pit two general tendencies against each other. The first tendency appears to include the overlapping strivings for power, autonomy, independence, status, and experiences rich in the emotion of excitement. The second tendency subsumes the overlapping strivings for love, intimacy, interdependence, acceptance, and interpersonal experiences suffused with the emotion of joy. This motivational duality in human existence is probably best described by the psychologist David Bakan, who distinguishes between agency and communion" (D. P. McAdams, *The Stories we Live By: Personal Myths and the Making of the Self* [New York: Guilford Press, 1997], 71 and Appendix 1).

25. C. Anbeek, *Overlevingskunst: Leven met de dood van een dierbare* (Kampen: Ten Have, 2010), 27.

26. Baumeister, *Meanings of Life*, 78.

27. *Ibid.*, 77–115, 279.

28. The difference between Western and Asian culture has been investigated in this respect. In the self-concept dominant in the West independence and self-assertion are emphasized, in East Asia mutual dependence and self-criticism. See, for example, S. Kitayama & H. R. Markus, "The Pursuit of Happiness and the Realization of Sympathy: Cultural Patterns of Self, Social Relations, and Well-being," in *Culture and*

Subjective Well-being, E. Diener & E. M. Suh (eds), 113–61 (Cambridge, MA: MIT Press, 2000).

29. Baumeister, *Meanings of Life*, 30–32.
30. A recent survey of this kind of research is to be found in J. M. Twenge, W. K. Campbell & C. A. Foster, "Parenthood and Marital Satisfaction: A Meta-analytic Review," *Journal of Marriage and Family* 65 (2003), 574–83.
31. Baumeister, *Meanings of Life*, 166.
32. *Ibid.*, 214.
33. E. Diener, "The Evolving Concept of Subjective Well-being: The Multifaceted Nature of Happiness" [2004], in *Assessing Well-being: The Collected Works of Ed Diener*, E. Diener (ed.), 67–100 (Dordrecht: Springer, 2009).
34. C. D. Ryff & B. H. Singer, "Know Thyself and Become What You Are: A Eudaimonic Approach to Psychological Well-being," *Journal of Happiness Studies* 9(1) (2008), 13–39.
35. M. F. Steger, "Meaning in Life," in *Oxford Handbook of Positive Psychology*, C. R. Snyder & S. J. Lopez (eds) (Oxford: Oxford University Press, 2009), 679. See also N. Krause, "Meaning in Life and Mortality," *Journal of Gerontology: Social Sciences* 64B(4) (2009), 517–27.
36. S. de Beauvoir, *The Second Sex* [*La deuxième sexe*, 1949] (New York: Random House, Vintage, 2011).
37. These mutually related insights and values were already present in Renaissance humanism, as Stephen Toulmin, for one, enthusiastically emphasized. According to him they were lost in the seventeenth century, only to be rediscovered at the end of the twentieth century: S. Toulmin, *Cosmopolis: The Hidden Agenda of Modernity* (New York: Free Press, 1990). He ignores nineteenth-century thinkers such as Dilthey.
38. H. M. Kuitert, *Zonder geloof vaart niemand wel: Een plaatsbepaling van christendom en kerk*, 7th expanded edn (Baarn: Ten Have, 1989), 28.
39. See, for instance, J. Duyndam, "Inspiratie door voorbeeldfiguren: Een humanistische visie," in Alma & Smaling, *Waarvoor je leeft*, 107–19.
40. To be found near the end of the first section of his essay "The Ethics of Belief" (1877), *The Secular Web*, www.infidels.org/library/historical/w_k_clifford/ethics_of_belief.html (accessed July 2012).
41. L. Wittgenstein, *Über Gewissheit* (Frankfurt: Suhrkamp, 1970).
42. D. Hume, *Writings on Religion* (La Salle, IL: Open Court, 1992).
43. O. D. Duintjer, *Rondom metafysica: Over "transcendentie" en de dubbelzinnigheid van metafysica* (Meppel: Boom, 1988).
44. W. B. Drees, *Religion and Science in Context: A Guide to the Debates* (London: Routledge, 2010); N. Abu Zaid & E. R. Nelson, *Voice of an Exile: Reflections on Islam* (Westport, CT: Praeger, 2004).
45. R. Buitenweg, *Human Rights, Human Plights in a Global Village* (Atlanta, GA: Clarity Press, 2007).
46. B. Snell, *Die Entdeckung des Geistes: Studien zur Entstehung des europäischen Denkens bei den Griechen*, 5th revised edn (Göttingen: Vandenhoeck & Ruprecht, 1980); English translation in B. Snell, *The Discovery of the Mind in Greek Philosophy and Literature* (New York: Harper, 1960/New York: Dover, 1982).
47. T. Pogge, *World Poverty and Human Rights: Cosmopolitan Responsibilities and Reforms* (Cambridge: Polity, 2002), 44, 50–51.
48. T. Todorov, *Imperfect Garden: The Legacy of Humanism* (Princeton, NJ: Princeton University Press, 2002), 30.
49. *Ibid.*, 231–2. See also van Praag, *Grondslagen van humanisme*, 91–2.
50. Todorov, *Imperfect Garden*, 34.

51. For instance: "In everything that has been said in this book about the humanist conception of the good life, the concepts of freedom and autonomy have been central" (A. C. Grayling, *What is Good? The Search for the Best Way to Live* [London: Weidenfeld & Nicolson, 2003], 218); and van Praag, *Grondslagen van humanisme*, 92–4.

52. Gewirth, *Self-fulfillment*. See also: "Inseparably linked with humanism is the conviction that human beings can and should realize their own individual possibilities" (J. Vanheste, *Humanisme en het avondland: De Europese humanistische traditie* [Budel: Damon, 2007], 13, my translation).

53. R. Nozick, *The Examined Life: Philosophical Meditations* (New York: Simon & Schuster, 1989); M. C. Nussbaum, *Cultivating Humanity: A Classical Defense of Reform in Liberal Education* (Cambridge, MA: Harvard University Press, 1997), 15; J. Dohmen, *Brief aan een middelmatige man: Pleidooi voor een nieuwe publieke moral* (Amsterdam: Ambo, 2010), 130.

54. Both quoted passages, and also the one from Erasmus, are from S. Dresden, "Erasmus, een geleerdenleven," in *Erasmus: De actualiteit van zijn denken*, G. T. Jensma, W. P. Blockmans, J. Sperna Weiland *et al.* (eds), 93–111 (Zutphen: Walburg Pers, 1986), 110.

55. Dohmen, "Zorg voor zichzelf als actuele levensstijl" [Care for oneself as a topical lifestyle], in *Brief aan een middelmatige man*, 96–135.

56. Gewirth, *Self-fulfillment*, ix.

57. H. J. Pos, "Personalisme en humanism," in *Het Keerpunt: Internationaal Personalistisch Tijdschrift* 1(8) (September 1947), 472–83. See also P. Derkx, *H. J. Pos, 1898–1955: Objectief en partijdig. biografie van een filosoof en humanist* (Hilversum: Verloren, 1994), 338–46.

58. G. H. Mead, *Mind, Self, and Society from the Standpoint of a Social Behaviorist* (Chicago, IL: University of Chicago Press, [1934] 1974), 154.

59. Todorov, *Imperfect Garden*, 116.

60. *Ibid.*, 232.

61. *Ibid.*, 233–4.

62. J. Glover, *Humanity: A Moral History of the Twentieth Century* (London: Jonathan Cape, 1999); T. Todorov, *Hope and Memory: Lessons from the Twentieth Century* (London: Atlantic Books, 2003).

63. For more extensive treatment of this debate see: P. Derkx, "Engineering Substantially Prolonged Human Lifespans: Biotechnological Enhancement and Ethics," in *Valuing Older People: A Humanist Approach to Ageing*, R. Edmondson & H. von Kondratowitz (eds), 177–98 (Bristol: Policy Press, 2009); P. Derkx, *Humanisme, zinvol leven en nooit meer "ouder worden": Een levensbeschouwelijke visie op ingrijpende biomedisch-technologische levensverlenging* (Brussels: ASP, VUBPRESS, 2011).

64. M. Lerner, *The Left Hand of God: Taking Back our Country from the Religious Right* (San Francisco, CA: HarperSanFrancisco, 2006), 308–9.

65. J. Hughes, *Citizen Cyborg: Why Democratic Societies Must Respond to the Redesigned Human of the Future* (Boulder, CO: Westview Press, 2004), 29. See also G. Stock & D. Callahan, "Point-Counterpoint: Would Doubling the Human Life Span be a Net Positive or Negative for Us Either as Individuals or as a Society?," *Journal of Gerontology: Biological Science* 59(6) (June 2005), 554–9; and A. de Grey & M. Rae, *Ending Aging: The Rejuvenation Breakthroughs that Could Reverse Human Aging in Our Lifetime* (New York: St. Martin's Press, 2007).

66. Conversation with A. de Grey at the conference "Understanding Aging," University of California, Los Angeles (UCLA), June 28, 2008.

67. J. Baars, "Ouder worden: Leven in verschillende tijden," in *De kunst van het ouder worden: De grote filosofen over ouderdom*, J. Dohmen & J. Baars (eds), 415–17 (Amsterdam: Ambo, 2010).

68. C. Geertz, *The Interpretation of Cultures* (New York: Basic Books, 1973), quoted in T. R. Cole, "On the Possibilities of Spirituality and Religious Humanism in Gerontology or Reflections of One Aging American Cultural Historian," in *Cultural Gerontology*, L. Andersson (ed.), 25–45 (Westport, CT: Auburn House, 2002), 37.

69. M. Marmot, "Social Determinants of Longevity and Mortality," *Sage Crossroads* (August 24, 2005), http://sagecrossroads.com/webcast26 (accessed July 2012).

70. H. A. Alma, "Humanisme en christendom als bronnen van zin," in *Humanisme en religie: Controverses, bruggen, perspectieven*, J. Duyndam, M. Poorthuis & T. de Wit (eds), 339–54 (Delft: Eburon, 2005).

71. M. H. Wörner, "Untimely Meditations on Ageing, the Good Life and a Culture of Friendship," in *Health Promotion: New Discipline or Multi-discipline?*, R. Edmondson & C. Kelleher (eds), 205–18 (Dublin: Irish Academic Press, 2000).

72. R. Dworkin, "Playing God: Genes, Clones, and Luck," in *Sovereign Virtue: The Theory and Practice of Equality*, 427–52 (Cambridge, MA: Harvard University Press, 2000).

4. IF WAR IS NOT THE ANSWER

1. Jonathan Dean, "Some Reasons for Optimism," remarks delivered at the International Steering Committee Meeting of Global Action to Prevent War, January 26, 2005, Cuenca, Spain. Used with permission.

2. President Barack Obama, "Obama's Nobel Remarks," *New York Times* (December 10, 2009), www.nytimes.com/2009/12/11/world/europe/11prexy.text.html?_r=1& pagewanted=all (accessed December 11, 2009).

3. Some of the following material is drawn from Sharon D. Welch, "The Machiavellian Dilemma: Paradoxes and Perils of Democratic Governance," *Tikkun* (May/June 2010), 19.

4. Anna Peterson, "The Social Construction of Nature and Human Nature," in *Being Human: Ethics, Environment, and our Place in the World*, 51–76 (Berkeley, CA: University of California Press, 2001).

5. Fred Dallmayr, *Beyond Orientalism: Essays on Cross-Cultural Encounters* (Albany, NY: SUNY Press, 1996), 192.

6. Bartholomew Ryan, "Altermodern: A Conversation with Nicolas Bourriaud," *Art in America* (March 17, 2009), www.artinamericamagazine.com/news-opinion/conversations/2009-03-17/altermodern-a-conversation-with-nicolas-bourriaud/ (accessed July 2012); Nicolas Bourriaud, *The Radicant* (New York: Lucas & Sternberg, 2009), 17; Michael Hardt & Antonio Negri, *Commonwealth* (Cambridge, MA: Belknap Press of Harvard University Press, 2009), pt 2, "Modernity (and the Landscapes of Altermodernity)" and pt 3, "Capital (and the Struggles over Common Wealth)."

7. Claire Bishop, "Antagonism and Relational Aesthetics," *October* 110 (Autumn 2004), 51–79.

8. Nicolas Bourriaud, *Relational Aesthetics* (Dijon: Les Presses du reel, 2002), 52, emphasis added.

9. Hardt & Negri, *Commonwealth*, 104.

10. Bourriaud, *Relational Aesthetics*, 103.

11. Bourriaud, *The Radicant*, 40, 22.

12. *Ibid.*, 96. I explore the distinction between an ethic of control and an ethic of risk in Sharon D. Welch, *A Feminist Ethic of Risk* (Minneapolis, MN: Fortress Press, 2000).

13. "What is Humanism?" (brochure), Institute for Humanist Studies. May 2011.

14. For a fuller exploration of the amorality of creativity, power, and the religious, see Sharon D. Welch, "Return to Laughter," in *The Religious*, John Caputo (ed.), 301–17 (Oxford: Blackwell, 2002).

15. The remarks in this section are taken from Sharon D. Welch, "Spirituality Without God," *Tikkun* (May 1999), 69.
16. Mona El-Naggar, "The Legacy of 18 Days in Tahrir Square," *New York Times* (February 20, 2011), "Week in Review," 4.
17. Michael Slackman & Nadim Audi, "Police Attack in Bahrain, Keeping Protests in Disarray," *New York Times* (February 15, 2011), A12.
18. David D. Kirkpatrick, Steven Erlanger & Elisabeth Bumiller, "Allies Open Air Assault on Qaddafi's Forces," *New York Times* (March 20, 2011), www.nytimes.com/2011/03/20/world/africa/20libya.html?pagewanted=all (accessed July 2012).
19. Clifford Krauss, "Bahrain Rulers Tighten Their Grip on Battered Opposition," *New York Times* (April 7, 2011), www.nytimes.com/2011/04/07/world/middleeast/07bahrain.html?pagewanted=all (accessed July 2012).
20. David Kirkpatrick, "Revolt's Leaders Cite Failure to Uproot Powerful," *New York Times* (June 15, 2012), A1.
21. *Ibid.*
22. David Kirkpatrick, "At Qaddafi Compound, a Human Shield," *New York Times* (March 19, 2011), www.nytimes.com/2011/03/20/world/africa/20tripoli.html (accessed July 2012).
23. Obama, "Obama's Nobel Remarks."
24. Some of the following material on "The Responsibility to Protect" and the United Nations Emergency Peace Service is drawn from Sharon D. Welch, *Real Peace, Real Security: The Challenges of Global Citizenship* (Minneapolis, MN: Fortress Press, 2008), 21–40.
25. Thom Shanker, "Gates Warns Against Wars Like Iraq and Afghanistan," *New York Times* (February 26, 2011), A7.
26. Quoted in Michael R. Gordon, "Military Hones a New Strategy on Insurgency," *New York Times* (October 5, 2006), A1, A19.
27. United States, Dept. of the Army, *The US Army and Marine Corp Counterinsurgency Field Manual* (Chicago, IL: University of Chicago Press, 2007), 49–50.
28. Obama, "Obama's Nobel Remarks."
29. Mohandas K. Gandhi, "My Faith in Nonviolence" (1930), in *The Power of Nonviolence: Writings by Advocates of Peace*, Howard Zinn (ed.), 45–6 (Boston, MA: Beacon Press, 2002), 46.
30. Thomas Merton, "The Root of War Is Fear" (1962), in Zinn, *The Power of Nonviolence*, 96–104, esp. 97.
31. Sheryl Gay Stolberg, "Shy US Intellectual Created Playbook Used in a Revolution," *New York Times* (February 17, 2011), A1, A11.
32. Gene Sharp, *The Politics of Nonviolent Direct Action* (New York: Sargent, 1973).
33. Gene Sharp, *The Albert Einstein Institution* (Research, Publications and Consultations on Nonviolent Struggle), www.aeinstein.org (accessed July 2012).
34. Friends Committee on National Legislation, *Peaceful Prevention of Deadly Conflict: If War is Not the Answer, What is?* (Pamphlet) (Washington, DC: FCNL Education Fund, 2005).
35. President Barack Obama, "Obama's Remarks on Libya," *New York Times* (March 28, 2011), www.nytimes.com/2011/03/29/us/politics/29prexy-text.html?_r=1&ref=Africa (accessed July 2012).
36. William F. Schulz, "Peacemaking and Human Rights," foreword in Welch, *Real Peace, Real Security*, xi.
37. International Commission on Intervention and State Sovereignty, *The Responsibility to Protect: Report of the International Commission on Intervention and State Sovereignty* (Ottawa: International Development Research Centre, 2001).

38. *Ibid.*, 2.1.
39. H. Peter Langille, *Bridging the Commitment–Capacity Gap* (New York: Center for UN Reform Education, 2002).
40. Sir Brian Urquhart, "Preface," in *A United Nations Emergency Peace Service: To Prevent Genocide and Crimes Against Humanity*, Robert Johansen (ed.) (New York: Global Action to Prevent War, Nuclear Age Peace Foundation, and World Federalist Movement, 2006), 9.
41. "United Nations Emergency Peace Service Proposal," 9. Proposal examined at symposium entitled "To Prevent Genocide and Crimes against Humanity: Diverse Perspectives on a Standing, Rapid-Reaction UN Emergency Peace Service," sponsored by Global Action to Prevent War, the Rutgers Global Legal Studies Program, and the International Law Society, March 20, 2007, Rutgers School of Law, Newark, NJ. See also Johansen, *A United Nations Emergency Peace Service: To Prevent Genocide and Crimes Against Humanity*, 59–63.
42. International Commission on Intervention and State Sovereignty, *Responsibility to Protect*, 4.12.
43. *Ibid.*, 13:1.22.
44. David R. Gushee, "The Holocaust" and "European Gentiles," in *The Righteous Gentiles of the Holocaust: A Christian Interpretation*, 19–68 (Minneapolis, MN: Fortress Press, 1994).
45. Thomas G. Weiss & Don Hubert, *Responsibility to Protect: Research, Bibliography, Background. Supplementary Volume to the Report of the International Commission on Intervention and State Sovereignty* (Ottawa: International Development Research Centre, 2007), 146.
46. Dalai Lama, *Ethics for the New Millennium* (New York: Riverhead Press, 1999), 212–13.

5. HUMANIST OUTLAWS: THINKING RELIGION/LIVING HUMANISM

1. "For Atheists of Color, 'Coming Out' Can be Painful," *Religion News Service* (February 23, 2012), www.religionnews.com/ethics/race-and-ethnicity/for-atheists-of-color-coming-out-can-be-painful (accessed July 2012).
2. Here, I am referring to the recent academic and very public discussion and debate proffered by Eddie Glaude Jr.'s essay, "The Black Church is Dead," *Huffington Post* (February 24, 2010), www.huffingtonpost.com/eddie-glaude-jr-phd/the-Black-church-is-dead_b_473815.html (accessed April 2011).
3. See, for example, one such study: Byron R. Johnson, "The Role of African-American Churches in Reducing Crime Among Black Youth," CRRUS Report at the University of Pennsylvania (2008).
4. Monica Miller & Ezekiel Dixon-Román, "Habits of the Heart: Youth Religious Participation as Progress, Peril or Change?," *Annals of the American Academy of Political and Social Sciences* 637(1) (2011), 78–98.
5. Anthony B. Pinn, "Anybody There? Reflections on African American Humanism," *Huumanists*, www.huumanists.org/publications/journal/summer-fall-1997/anybody-there-reflections-on-african-american-humanism (accessed April 2011).
6. Here I invoke the paradigm "moral panics" as articulated by Stanley J Cohen. He argues that when a given society's reaction is "disproportionate to the actual seriousness" of the situation, the exaggerated "risk" often exceeds the actual conditions that are being signified on in a way that makes such claims both "irrational" and "unjustified." See Stanley Cohen, *Folk Devils and Moral Panics*, 3rd edn (New York: Routledge, [1972] 2002), xxvii.

7. Johnson, "The Role of African-American Churches," 8.
8. Christian Smith, "Theorizing Religious Effects Among American Adolescents," *Journal for the Scientific Study of Religion* 42(1) (2003), 18–19.
9. Miller & Dixon-Román, "Habits of the Heart," 94.
10. "Gay and Transgender Youth Homelessness by the Numbers," *Center for American Progress* (June 21, 2012), www.americanprogress.org/issues/2010/06/homelessness_numbers.html (accessed September 2011).
11. Susan Driver (ed.), *Queer Youth Cultures* (Albany, NY: SUNY Press, 2008).
12. "*IN THE LIFE* looks at the state of the gay ballroom scene, an urban phenomenon first revealed to the wider culture in the 1990 documentary, *Paris is Burning*. Ball culture continues to thrive in Newark, New Jersey, where community leader Bernie McAlister acts as father-figure to the queer youth who make up this vibrant community. His *House of Jourdon* expands its social role as an epicenter of ballroom culture to include AIDS awareness, safe-sex education, and positive role modeling—providing direction and hope for LGBT minority youth" (*Aids Connect* [February 13, 2009], http://aidsconnect.net/content/blog/life-documentary-stories-gay-experience-wttw-channel-11 [accessed September 2011]).
13. Cathy J. Cohen, "The Attitudes and Behavior of Young Black Americans: Research Summary," *Black Youth Project* (June 2007), 24, www.blackyouthproject.com/wp-content/uploads/BYP-Research-Summary.pdf (accessed July 2012).
14. Here, I refer to "making do" as explicated by Michel de Certeau in *The Practice of Everyday Life* (Los Angeles, CA: University of California Press, 1984).
15. de Certeau, *The Practice of Everyday Life*.
16. Dragon, *Rize* (Lions Gate Entertainment, 2005).
17. *Ibid.*
18. Lil' C, *Rize*.
19. Lil' C, interview with Charlie Rose (June 22, 2005), www.charlierose.com/view/interview/864 (accessed January 2010).
20. Lil' C, *Rize*.
21. Dragon, *Rize*.
22. Lil' C, *Rize*.
23. Dragon, *Rize*.
24. Lil' C, interview with Charlie Rose.
25. "50 Cent Robert Green Preview, *The 50th Law*," *YouTube* (September 3, 2009), www.youtube.com/watch?v=mBpGlWShkQI (accessed November 2009).
26. Robert Greene and 50 Cent, *The 50th Law* (New York: G-Unit Books, 2009), 15.
27. *Ibid.*, x.

6. BEYOND KUMBAYA: CULTURALLY RELEVANT HUMANISM IN AN AGE OF "POSTS"

1. O.g. is a slang term traditionally used in rap music and gangter culture that means "original."
2. See, for example, Sean Wilentz, "Confounding Fathers," *New Yorker* (October 18, 2010), www.newyorker.com/reporting/2010/10/18/101018fa_fact_wilentz?currentPage=all (accessed July 2012); and Robert Scheer, "Payback at the Polls," *Truthout* (November 3, 2010), www.truth-out.org/robert-scheer-payback-polls64788 (accessed July 2012).
3. "Old Alignments, Emerging Faults: Religion in the 2010 Election and Beyond," *Public Religion Research Institute* (November 17, 2010), www.publicreligion.org/research/?id=428 (accessed July 2012).
4. Maeve Reston, "Ex-Senator Warns Against Obama," *Los Angeles Times* (April 9,

2011), http://articles.latimes.com/2011/apr/09/nation/la-na-santorum-california-20110409 (accessed July 2012).

5. Michael I. Norton & Samuel Sommers, "Whites See Racism as a Zero-Sum Game Which They are Now Losing," *Perspectives on Psychological Science* 6(3) (May 18, 2011), 215–18.

6. As per Richard Nixon's widely touted 1960s "Southern Strategy," which was designed to court white Southern voters alienated by the Democratic Party's endorsement of civil rights legislation under the Johnson administration.

7. See, for example, Jervis Anderson, *A. Philip Randolph: A Biographical Portrait* (New York: Harcourt Brace Jovanovich, 1972). Anderson notes that "As a young man ... [Randolph] had attended Methodist and Baptist churches in Harlem ... even then, the reasons were more intellectual than religious, because he had already started having doubts about religion before leaving his father's house ... since then had only the most secular use for churches, mainly as platforms for his political opinions" (p. 25). Cynthia Taylor argues that Randolph publicly denied he was an atheist and that the "charge" atheist and communist were often yoked together to discredit progressive leaders; see Cynthia Taylor, *A. Philip Randolph: The Religious Journey of an African American Labor Leader* (New York: New York University Press, 2006), 80–82.

8. Nella Larsen, *Quicksand and Passing*, Deborah McDowell (ed.) (New Brunswick, NJ: Rutgers University Press, 1986), 133.

9. Cotton Mather, "The Negro Christianized: An Essay to Excite and Assist that Good Work: The Instruction of Negro Servants" (1706), http://digitalcommons.unl.edu/etas/28/ (accessed August 2012), 13 (original capitalization and emphasis altered).

10. Anderson, *A. Philip Randolph*, 41.

11. *Ibid.*, 114.

12. According to Cynthia Taylor, "When the magazine became the focus for the BSCP [Brotherhood of Sleeping Car Porters], Randolph openly denied he was an atheist for to be labeled an atheist in a predominantly religious culture would have automatically shut him out of the political debate" (*A. Philip Randolph*, 38).

13. During the 1920s and beyond, the racist exclusionary practices of the American Federation of Labor made many African Americans hostile to labor unionism. According to Anderson, "the majority of blacks held similar attitudes toward business and labor, due largely to their experience of racism in the major segments of the labor movement. Thus while few blacks were organized, the prevailing sentiment within their community at the time was that blacks should shun unions and that unions did not want them" (*A. Philip Randolph*, 90–91). See also Earl Ofari Hutchinson, *Blacks and Reds: Race and Class in Conflict 1919–1990* (Lansing, MI: Michigan State University Press, 1995), 9–11.

14. Taylor, *A. Philip Randolph*.

15. See Richard Wright, *The Outsider* (New York: Perennial, 1953); James Baldwin, *The Fire Next Time* (New York: First Vintage International, 1993); Zora Neale Hurston, "Religion," in *Dust Tracks on a Road* (New York: HarperCollins, 1996), 215–26.

16. Newt Gingrich, *To Save America: Stopping Obama's Secular Socialist Machine* (New York: Regnery Books, 2010).

17. Marlow Stern, "Left Behind Author Tim LaHaye on the Rapture," *Daily Beast* (May 19, 2011), www.thedailybeast.com/blogs-and-stories/2011-05-19/rapture-isnt-may-21-says-tim-lahaye-the-author-of-left-behind/4/ (accessed July 2012).

18. It is important to note that the US is alone among so-called First World nations both in its anti-abortion, anti-choice, religious-right-driven legislative agenda as well as in acts of domestic terrorism committed by anti-abortionists.

19. Toni Morrison, *Playing in the Dark: Whiteness and the Literary Imagination* (New York: Vintage, 1992), 38.

20. Alice Walker, *In Love and Trouble* (New York: Harcourt Books, 2001), 119–20.

21. Michele Alexander, *The New Jim Crow: Mass Incarceration in the Age of Colorblindness* (New York: New Press, 2010).

22. Baldwin, *The Fire Next Time*, 58.

23. Kevin Powell, "Men Speak Out About Sexist Coverage of Rape: A Call to Action," *KevinPowell.net* (April 2011), www.kevinpowell.net/blog/2011/04/men-speak-out-about-sexist-coverage-of-rape-a-call-to-action (accessed July 2012). Powell was one of several signatories to this statement.

24. See, for example, Mark Anthony Neal, *New Black Man: Rethinking Black Masculinity* (New York: Routledge, 2006). Neal calls for anti-sexist, anti-patriarchal models of masculinity based on parity among genders, loving male–female relationships, male caregiving, respect for differences across sexuality and gender identity, and non-violence in black communities and families.

25. Jefferson opined in his *Notes on the State of Virginia* that "this difference of color, and, perhaps, of faculty, is a powerful obstacle to the emancipation of these people ..." Questioning the wisdom of incorporating black slaves into Anglo-American society, Jefferson said, "To these objections which are political might be added others which are physical and moral," partly due to the fact that the differences between whites and blacks were "fixed in nature" (*Notes on the State of Virginia* [New York: Penguin 1999], 235). Black physical inferiority was exemplified by the primitive beauty standards of Africans in contrast to those of Europeans (*ibid.*, 230–40).

26. Harriet Washington, *Medical Apartheid: The Dark History of Medical Experimentation on Black Americans from the Colonial Times to the Present* (New York: Random House, 2006), 59–60.

27. Paulo Freire, *Pedagogy of the Oppressed* (New York: Continuum, 2000).

28. "Study: White and Black Children Biased Toward Lighter Skin," *CNN.com* (May 13, 2010), http://articles.cnn.com/2010-05-13/us/doll.study_1_black-children-pilot-study-white-doll?_s=PM:US (accessed July 2012). This study was based on the original study by Kenneth Clark and Mamie Clark, "Emotional Factors in Racial Identification and Preference in Negro Children," in *Readings in Social Psychology*, G. E. Swanson *et al.* (eds), 551–60 (New York: Henry Holt, 1952).

29. Po Bronson & Ashley Merryman, *Nurture Shock: New Thinking About Children* (New York: Hachette, 2009), 28–50; "See Baby Discriminate," *Newsweek* (September 9, 2004), www.newsweek.com/2009/09/04/see-baby-discriminate.html (accessed July 2012).

30. Louise Derman-Sparks, Carol Tanaga Higa & Bill Sparks, "Children, Race, and Racism: How Race Awareness Develops," *Interracial Books for Children Bulletin* 11(3 & 4) (1980), 3–9.

7. HUMANISM AND THE BIG PROBLEM

1. Jennifer Michael Hecht, *Doubt: A History* (New York: HarperOne, 2003), xii.

2. Michel de Montaigne, *Essays*, William Hazlitt (ed.) (Boston, MA: Houghton, Osgood and Co., 1879), 37.

3. *Ibid.*

4. Lewis Thomas, *Lives of a Cell* (New York: Penguin, 1978), 50.

5. Melvin Konner, *The Tangled Wing* (New York: Macmillan, 2003), 369.

6. Richard Dawkins, *Unweaving the Rainbow* (New York: Mariner Books, 2000), 1.

8. GROWING HUMANISM IN A FAITH-DOMINATED SOCIETY

1. "US Religious Landscape Survey," *The Pew Forum on Religion and Public Life* (2007), http://religions.pewforum.org/reports/ (accessed July 2012).
2. *Ibid.*
3. *Ibid.*
4. American Humanist Association, "About Humanism," www.americanhumanist.org/Who_We_Are/About_Humanism (accessed July 2012).
5. Greg Epstein, *Good Without God: What a Billion Nonreligious People Do Believe* (New York: HarperCollins, 2009), xii.
6. American Humanist Association, "Humanist Manifesto III," www.americanhumanist.org/who_we_are/about_humanism/Humanist_Manifesto_III (accessed July 2012).
7. Susan Jacoby, *Freethinkers: A History of American Secularism* (New York: Metropolitan, 2004), 4.
8. Pat Roberston, *The New World Order* (Nashville, TS: Thomas Nelson, 1992), 218.
9. "Black President More Likely than Mormon or Atheist," *Outside the Beltway* (February 20, 2007), www.outsidethebeltway.com/black_president_more_likely_than_mormon_or_atheist_/ (accessed July 2012).
10. Sam Harris, *The End of Faith* (New York: W. W. Norton, 2005).
11. Daniel Dennett, *Breaking the Spell: Religion as a Natural Phenomenon* (New York: Penguin, 2007).
12. Richard Dawkins, *The God Delusion* (New York: Mariner, 2008).
13. Christopher Hitchens, *God is Not Great: How Religion Poisons Everything* (New York: Twelve Publishers, 2009).
14. Harris, *The End of Faith*, 3.
15. Jacoby, *Freethinkers*.
16. American Humanist Association, "Humanists Launch 'Naughty' Awareness Campaign" (November 21, 2011), www.americanhumanist.org/news/details/2011-11-american-humanist-association-naughty-atheist-awaren (accessed July 2012). Used by permission of the American Humanist Association.
17. Nathan Black, "N.C. Atheists Declare 'One Nation Indivisible' Without God," *Christian Post* (June 24, 2012), www.christianpost.com/news/nc-atheists-declare-one-nation-indivisible-without-god-45662/ (accessed July 2012); Dan Harris, "Billboard Battle in Bible Belt: One Nation 'Under God' or Not?," *ABC World News with Diane Sawyer* (July 19, 2010), http://abcnews.go.com/WN/evangelicals-respond-nation-billboards-nc/story?id=11197974 (accessed July 2012); David Waters, "Defacing the Pledge of Allegiance (again?), *Washington Post* (June 29, 2012), http://newsweek.washingtonpost.com/onfaith/undergod/2010/06/defacing_the_pledge_of_allegiance_again.html (accessed July 2012).
18. Harris, "Billboard Battle in Bible Belt."
19. Rob Kendt, "Questioning Religious Faith And Yet Finding Inspiration," *New York Times* (October 24, 2006), http://theater.nytimes.com/2006/10/24/theater/reviews/24ars.html?pagewanted=print (accessed July 2012).
20. Lexington, "Glad to be Godless," *The Economist* (July 16, 2009), www.economist.com/node/14031492 (accessed July 2012).
21. Jake P. Tapper, "Atheist Group Heralds 'First Time in History' Policy Briefing with White House Officials," *ABC News* (February 26, 2010).
22. Liptak, "Justices Rule Against Group that Excludes Gay Students," *New York Times* (June 28, 2010).
23. Barack Obama, *Dreams from My Father: A Story of Race and Inheritance* (New York: Broadway Publishing, 2004), 50.

24. "President Obama's Inaugural Address," *The White House* (January 20, 2009), www.whitehouse.gov/blog/inaugural-address/ (accessed July 2012).

25. "In (Blank) We Trust," *The Economist* (October 12, 1996): 48, http://kunklet.people.cofc.edu/herb.html (accessed July 2012).

26. Herb Silverman, "How to Win Friends and Influence People," *Washington Post: On Faith* (March 1, 2010).

27. Leslie Miller, "'No God? No Problem!' Say Humanist Group's New Holiday Ads," *USA Today* (November 23, 2009).

28. Bill O'Reilly, "The O'Reilly Factor," *Fox News* (December 3, 2009), www.youtube.com/watch?v=sX_URHACJPw.

29. Philip Paulson, "I Was an Atheist in a Foxhole," *The Humanist* (September/October 1989), 29–30.

30. Associated Press, "Pagan Student Settles Case Against Tennessee District," *First Amendment Center* (November 8, 2004), www.firstamendmentcenter.org/pagan-student-settles-case-against-tennessee-district (accessed July 2012).

31. Lauri Lebo, "Student Says He's Ostracized for Objecting to Graduation Prayer," *Religion Dispatches* (May 20, 2011), www.religiondispatches.org/dispatches/laurilebo/4631/student_says_he%E2%80%99s_ostracized_for_objecting_to_graduation_prayer/ (accessed July 2012).

32. Paul Davis, "Prayer Sparks Atheist's Fight," *Providence Journal* (October 11, 2011).

33. John Stossel, Sylvia Johnson & Lynn Redmond, "The Black Sheep of Hardesty," *ABC 20/20* (May 11, 2007).

34. Associated Press, "'No God' Comment Adds Up to No Job for Fired Math Teacher," *USA Today* (June 1, 2010), www.usatoday.com/news/religion/2010-05-29-fired28_ST_N.htm (accessed July 2012).

35. Randi Kaye, "Atheist Soldier Sues Army for 'Unconstitutional' Discrimination," *CNN.com* (July 9, 2008), www.cnn.com/2008/US/07/08/atheist.soldier/index.html (accessed July 2012).

36. Rachel Tabachnick, "The 'Christian' Dogma Pushed by Religious Schools that are Supported by Your Tax Dollars," *AlterNet* (May 23, 2011), www.alternet.org/tea-party/151046/the_'christian'_dogma_pushed_by_religious_schools_that_are_supported_by_your_tax_dollars (accessed July 2012).

37. Brad Buck, "Town Prayer Debate Heats Up," *Daily Commercial* (April 2, 2011), www.dailycommercial.com/040211Llprayer (accessed July 2012).

38. "History of 'In God We Trust,'" *US Department of the Treasury* (March 8, 2011), www.treasury.gov/about/education/Pages/in-god-we-trust.aspx (accessed July 2012).

39. Tom Curry, "Atheist Pleads with Justices to Stop Recitation of the Pledge," *MSNBC.com* (March 24, 2003), www.msnbc.msn.com/id/4594537/ns/politics-tom_curry/t/atheist-pleads-justices-stop-recitation-pledge/ (accessed July 2012).

40. Marci Hamilton, "The Healthcare Bill and its Troubling 'Religious Conscience' Exception," *FindLaw* (August 6, 2009), http://writ.news.findlaw.com/hamilton/20090806.html (accessed July 2012).

41. Associated Press, "Parents Claim Religion to Avoid Vaccines for Kids," *MSNBC.com* (October 17, 2007), www.msnbc.msn.com/id/21347434/ns/health-childrens_health/t/parents-claim-religion-avoid-vaccines-kids/#.TsHKAsNCqU8 (accessed July 2012).

42. Randy Shilts, *The Mayor of Castro Street: The Life and Times of Harvey Milk* (New York: St. Martin's Griffin, 2008), 224–5.

43. *New York City Atheists*: http://nyc-atheists.org/ (accessed July 2012).

SELECT BIBLIOGRAPHY

This bibliography contains some of the materials referenced in the various chapters of this book. It does not pretend to offer a full depiction of humanism's nature and meaning in that it does not constitute a review of the available literature. For additional materials, readers should consider the bibliographies of the books below as well as the suggestions offered by the American Humanist Association and other organizations.

Abu Zaid, N. & E. Nelson. *Voice of an Exile: Reflections on Islam.* Westport, CT: Praeger, 2004.

Adler, F. *An Ethical Philosophy of Life.* New York: D. Appleton-Century, 1918, reprinted 1987.

Adler, F. *The Reconstruction of the Spiritual Ideal.* New York: D. Appleton, 1924.

Andersson, L. (ed.) *Cultural Gerontology.* Westport, CT: Auburn House, 2002.

Baumeister, R. F. *Meanings of Life.* New York: Guilford Press, 1991.

Baumeister, R. F. & M. R. Leary. "The Need to Belong: Desire for Interpersonal Attachments as a Fundamental Human Motivation." *Psychological Bulletin* 117(3) (1995): 497–529.

Bishop, C. "Antagonism and Relational Aesthetics." *October* 110 (Autumn 2004): 51–79.

Black, A. D. *Without Burnt Offerings.* New York: Viking, 1974.

Blackham, H. J. *Humanism.* Harmondsworth: Penguin, 1968.

Bourriaud, N. *The Radicant.* New York: Lucas & Sternberg, 2009.

Bouwer, J. (ed.) *Successful Ageing, Spirituality and Meaning: Multidisciplinary Perspectives.* Leuven: Peeters, 2010.

Buitenweg, R. *Human Rights, Human Plights in a Global Village.* Atlanta, GA: Clarity Press, 2007.

Bullock, A. *The Humanist Tradition in the West.* New York: W. W. Norton, 1985.

Caputo, J. (ed.) *The Religious.* Oxford: Blackwell, 2002.

Cohen, C. J. *Democracy Remixed: Black Youth and the Future of American Politics.* New York: Oxford University Press, 2010.

Cohen, S. *Folk Devils and Moral Panics,* 3rd edition. New York: Routledge, 2002, first published 1972.

Dalai Lama. *Ethics for the New Millennium.* New York: Riverhead Press, 1999.

Dallmary, F. *Beyond Orientalism: Essays on Crosscultural Encounters.* Albany, NY: SUNY Press, 1996.

Das, S. *Dedication To Freedom: M.N. Roy—The Man And His Ideas.* Delhi: Ajanta, 1987.

Dawkins, R. *Unweaving the Rainbow.* New York: Mariner Books, 2000.

de Beauvoir, S. *The Second Sex* [*La deuxième sexe,* 1949]. New York: Random House, 2011.

de Certeu, M. *The Practice of Everyday Life*. Los Angeles, CA: University of California Press, 1984.

de Grey, A. & M. Rae. *Ending Aging: The Rejuvenation Breakthroughs that Could Reverse Human Aging in Our Lifetime*. New York: St. Martin's Press, 2007.

Dennett, D. *Breaking the Spell: Religion as a Natural Phenomenon*. New York: Penguin, 2007.

Dewey, J. *A Common Faith*. New Haven, CT: Yale University Press, 1934.

Diener, E. & E. M. Suh (eds). *Culture and Subjective Well-being*. Cambridge, MA: MIT Press, 2000.

Diener, E. *Assessing Well-being: The Collected Works of Ed Diener*. Dordrecht: Springer, 2009.

Drees, W. B. *Religion and Science in Context: A Guide to the Debate*. London: Routledge, 2010.

Dworkin, R. *Sovereign Virtue: The Theory and Practice of Equality*. Cambridge, MA: Harvard University Press, 2000.

Eagleton, T. *The Meaning of Life*. Oxford: Oxford University Press, 2007.

Edmondson, R. & C. Kelleher (eds). *Health Promotion: New Discipline or Multi-discipline?* Dublin: Irish Academic Press, 2000.

Edmondson, R. & H.-J. von Kondratowitz (eds). *Valuing Older People: A Humanist Approach to Aging*. Bristol: Policy Press, 2009.

Epstein, G. *Good Without God: What a Billion Nonreligious People Do Believe*. New York: HarperCollins, 2009.

Ericson, E. L. *The Humanist Way*. New York: Continuum, 1988.

Frankl, V. E. *Man's Search for Meaning*. Boston, MA: Beacon Press, 2006.

Gewirth, A. *Self-fulfillment*. Princeton, NJ: Princeton University Press, 1998.

Glover, J. *Humanity: A Moral History of the Twentieth Century*. London: Jonathan Cape, 1999.

Grayling, A. C. *What is Good?: The Search for the Best Way to Live*. London: Weidenfeld & Nicolson, 2003.

Greene, R. & 50 Cent. *The 50th Law*. New York: G-Unit Books, 2009.

Gushee, D. R. *The Righteous Gentiles of the Holocaust: A Christian Interpretation*. Minneapolis, MN: Fortress Press, 1994.

Harris, S. *The End of Faith*. New York: W. W. Norton, 2005.

Hecht, J. M. *Doubt: A History*. New York: HarperOne, 2003.

Hermans, H. J. M. & E. Hermans-Jansen. *Self-Narratives: The Construction of Meaning in Psychotherapy*. New York: Guilford Press, 2005.

Hitchens, C. *God is Not Great: How Religion Poisons Everything*. New York: Twelve Publishers, 2009.

Hughes, J. *Citizen Cyborg: Why Democratic Societies Must Respond to the Redesigned Human of the Future*. Boulder, CO: Westview Press, 2004.

Hume, D. *Writings on Religion*. La Salle, IL: Open Court, 1992.

Huxley, J. *Religion Without Revelation*. New York: Mentor, 1957.

Huxley, J. *Essays of a Humanist*. New York: Harper & Row, 1964.

Jacoby, S. *Freethinkers: A History of American Secularism*. New York: Henry Holt, 2004.

James, W. *The Varieties Of Religious Experience*. New York: Macmillan, 1902, reprinted 1961.

Konner, M. *The Tangled Wing*. New York: Macmillan, 2003.

Krause, N. "Meaning in Life and Mortality." *Journal of Gerontology: Social Sciences* 64B(4) (2009): 517–27.

Krikorian, Y. H. (ed.) *Naturalism and the Human Spirit*. New York: Columbia University Press, 1944.

Kurtz, P. (ed.) *The Humanist Alternative*. Buffalo, NY: Prometheus, 1973.

Kurtz, P. *Eupraxophy: Living Without Religion*. Buffalo, NY: Prometheus, 1989.

Lamont, C. *The Philosophy of Humanism*. New York: Ungar, 1982.

Langille, H. P. *Bridging the Commitment–Capacity Gap*. New York: Center for UN Reform Education, 2002.

Lerner, M. *The Left Hand of God: Taking Back Our Country from the Religious Right*. San Francisco, CA: HarperSanFrancisco, 2006.

Lewis, T. *Lives of a Cell*. New York: Penguin Books, 1978.

Locke, A. (ed.) *The New Negro*. New York: Atheneum, 1968.

Luckmann, T. *The Invisible Religion: The Problem of Religion in Modern Society*. New York: Macmillan, 1967.

Lyttle, C. H. *Freedom Moves West: A History of the Western Unitarian Conference, 1852–1952*. Boston, MA: Beacon, 1952.

McAdams, D. P. *The Stories We Live By: Personal Myths and the Making of the Self*. New York: Guilford Press, 1997.

Mead, G. H. *Mind, Self, and Society from the Standpoint of a Social Behaviorist*. Chicago, IL: University of Chicago Press, 1974, first published 1934.

Miller, M. & E. Dixon-Román. "Habits of the Heart: Youth Religious Participation as Progress, Peril or Change?" *Annals of the American Academy of Political and Social Sciences* 637(1) (2011): 78–98.

Mondale, L. *The New Man Of Religious Humanism*. Peterhead: Volturna, 1973.

Montaigne, M. de. *Essays*. Palo Alto, CA: Stanford University Press, 1958.

Morgan, J. & T. Farsides. "Measuring Meaning in Life." *Journal of Happiness Studies* 10(3) (2009): 197–214.

Negri, A. & M. Hardt. *Commonwealth*. Cambridge, MA: Belknap Press of Harvard University Press, 2009.

Nozick, R. *The Examined Life: Philosophical Meditations*. New York: Simon & Schuster, 1989.

Nussbaum, M. C. *Creating Capabilities: The Human Development Approach*. Cambridge, MA: Belknap Press of Harvard University Press, 2011.

Nussbaum, M. C. *Cultivating Humanity: A Classical Defense of Reform in Liberal Education*. Cambridge, MA: Harvard University Press, 1997.

Olds, M. *Religious Humanism In America*. Washington, DC: Georgetown University Press, 1978.

Persons, S. *Free Religion*. New Haven, CT: Yale University Press, 1947.

Peterson, A. *Being Human: Ethics, Environment, and Our Place in the World*. Berkeley, CA: University of California Press, 2001.

Pinn, A. B. *Varieties of African American Religious Experience*. Minneapolis, MN: Fortress Press, 1998.

Pinn, A. B. *By These Hands: A Documentary History of African American Humanism*. New York: New York University Press, 2001.

Pinn, A. B. *African American Humanist Principles: Living and Thinking Like the Children of Nimrod*. New York: Palgrave Macmillan, 2004.

Pinn, A. B. *Terror and Triumph: The Nature of Black Religion*. Maryknoll, NY: Orbis Books, 2004.

Pinn, A. B. *The End of God-Talk: An African American Humanist Theology*. New York: Oxford University Press, 2012.

Pinn, A. B. & A. Callahan (eds) *African American Religious Life and the Story of Nimrod*. New York: Palgrave Macmillan, 2008.

Pogge, T. W. *World Poverty and Human Rights: Cosmopolitan Responsibilities and Reforms*. Cambridge: Polity, 2002.

Radest, H. B. *Toward Common Ground*. New York: Ungar, 1969, reprinted 1987.

Radest, H. B. *The Devil and Secular Humanism*. New York: Praeger, 1990.

Radest, H. B. *Humanism with a Human Face*. New York: Praeger, 1996.

Reker, G. T. & K. Chamberlain (eds) *Exploring Existential Meaning: Optimizing Human Development Across the Life Span.* Thousand Oaks, CA: Sage, 2000.

Richardson, J. *Handbook of Theory and Research for the Sociology of Education.* New York: Greenwood, 1986.

Ryff, C. D. & B. H. Singer. "Know Thyself and Become What You Are: A Eudaimonic Approach to Psychological Well-being." *Journal of Happiness Studies* 9(1) (2008): 13–39.

Sharp, G. *The Politics of Nonviolent Direct Action.* New York: Sargent, 1973.

Sher, G. S. (ed. and trans.). *Marxist Humanism and Praxis.* Buffalo, NY: Prometheus, 1978.

Shilts, R. *The Mayor of Castro Street: The Life and Times of Harvey Milk.* New York: St. Martin's Griffin, 2008.

Snell, B. *The Discovery of the Mind in Greek Philosophy and Literature.* New York: Harper, 1960; New York: Dover, 1982.

Snyder, C. R. & Shane J. Lopez (eds) *Handbook of Positive Psychology.* New York: Oxford University Press, 2005.

Stock, G. & D. Callahan. "Point-Counterpoint: Would Doubling the Human Life Span be a Net Positive or Negative for Us Either as Individuals or as a Society?" *Journal of Gerontology: Biological Sciences* 59 (June 6, 2004): 554–9.

Storer, M. B. (ed.) *Humanist Ethics.* Buffalo, NY: Prometheus, 1980.

Tapp, R. *Religion Among the Unitarian Universalists: Converts in the Stepfather's House.* New York: Academic Press, 1973.

Tarkunde, V. M. *Radical Humanism.* Delhi: Ajanta, 1983.

Thoreau, H. D. *Walden.* Princeton, NJ: Princeton University Press, 1973.

Todorov, T. *Hope and Memory: Lessons from the Twentieth Century.* London: Atlantic Books, 2003.

Todorov, T. *Imperfect Garden: The Legacy of Humanism.* Princeton, NJ: Princeton University Press, 2002.

Toulmin, S. *Cosmopolis: The Hidden Agenda of Modernity.* New York: Free Press, 1990.

Turner, J. *Without God, Without Creed: The Origins of Unbelief in America.* Baltimore, MD: Johns Hopkins University Press, 1985.

Twenge, J. M., W. K. Campbell & C.A. Foster. "Parenthood and Marital Satisfaction: A Meta-analytic Review." *Journal of Marriage and Family* 65 (2003): 574–83.

Vaughan, D. *Uncoupling: Turning Points in Intimate Relationships.* New York: Oxford University Press, 1986.

Weiss, T. G. and D. Hubert. *Responsibility to Protect: Research, Bibliography, Background. Supplementary Volume to the Report of the International Commission on Intervention and State Sovereignty.* Ottawa: International Development Research Centre, 2007.

Welch, S. D. *A Feminist Ethic of Risk.* Minneapolis, MN: Fortress Press, 2000.

Welch, S. D. *Real Peace, Real Security: The Challenges of Global Citizenship.* Minneapolis, MN: Fortress Press. 2008.

Wine, S. T. *Humanistic Judaism.* Buffalo, NY: Prometheus, 1978.

Wright, R. *Eight Men.* New York: HarperPerennial, 1996.

Wright, R. *The Outsider.* New York: HarperPerennial, 1996.

Wuthnow, R. *The Consciousness Reformation.* Berkeley, CA: University of California Press, 1976.

Wuthnow, R. *Meaning and Moral Order: Explorations in Cultural Analysis.* Berkeley, CA: University of California Press, 1989.

Zinn, H. (ed.) *The Power of Nonviolence: Writings by Advocates of Peace.* Boston, MA: Beacon Press, 2002.

CONTRIBUTORS

Maggie Ardiente is the Director of Development and Communications at the American Humanist Association (AHA) and editor of the AHA's weekly e-zine, *Humanist Network News*. She is a former board member of the Secular Student Alliance and a graduate (Class 15) and board member of The Humanist Institute.

Peter Derkx is Professor of Humanism and Worldviews at the University of Humanistics (Utrecht, Netherlands). His main fields of interest are the theory of humanism as a world-view, and science, technology, and meanings of life. Derkx is a senior fellow at the Institute for Humanist Studies. His publications include *Goed Ouder Worden* (2011).

Sikivu Hutchinson is editor of blackfemlens.org. She is a leading figure in African American humanism, a popular blogger and speaker, and a commentator for KPFK 90.7 FM. Hutchinson is a senior fellow at the Institute for Humanist Studies. Her publications include *Moral Combat: Black Atheists, Gender Politics, and the Values Wars* (2011).

Dale McGowan is co-author of *Raising Freethinkers* (2009), the first comprehensive resource for nonreligious parents. He writes the secular parenting blog *The Meming of Life* and presents seminars for non-theistic parents across the United States. In 2008 he was named Harvard Humanist of the Year by the Humanist Chaplaincy at Harvard University. Dale's past non-profit work includes service as US Communications Coordinator for Nonviolent Peaceforce, a global civilian peacekeeping organization based in Brussels.

Monica R. Miller is a Mellon Postdoctoral Fellow in Religion and Popular/Material Culture in the Department of Religious Studies at Lewis & Clark College. Dr. Miller's work involves attention to cultural studies and theories of social interaction. Miller is a senior fellow at the Institute for Humanist Studies. Her publications include *Religion and Hip Hop* (2012).

Anthony B. Pinn is Agnes Cullen Arnold Professor of Humanities and Professor of Religious Studies at Rice University. He is also Director of Research for the Institute for Humanist Studies. His publications include *The End of God-Talk: An African American Humanist Theology* (2012).

Howard B. Radest is Chair of the Biomedical Ethics Committee of Hilton Head Regional Medical Center, and consultant to the Ethics Committee of the South Carolina Medical Association. Radest is a senior fellow at the Institute for Humanist Studies. His publications include *Humanism with a Human Face: Intimacy and the Enlightenment* (1996).

Roy Speckhardt is Executive Director of the American Humanist Association. He has appeared on CNN Headline News, Fox News, and numerous national radio shows, and has spoken to dozens of local humanist groups across the country. He also serves as a board member of the Institute for Humanist Studies and the United Coalition of Reason, and as an advisory board member of the Secular Student Alliance.

Sharon D. Welch is an internationally known scholar with award-winning work related to issues of social ethics and culture. She is currently Provost and Professor of Religion and Society at Meadville Lombard Theological School. Welch is a senior fellow at the Institute for Humanist Studies. Her publications include *After Empire* (2004).

184

INDEX

185